HOW A MAN AGES

HOW A MAN AGES

CURTIS PESMEN
and the Editors of ESQUIRE

A Ballantine/Esquire Press Book
Ballantine Books • New York

Contents

Acknowledgments

Curtis Pesmen and the editors of *Esquire* would like to acknowledge the work of John Tierney, who wrote "The Aging Body" for the May, 1982, issue of *Esquire*. In addition, we would like to thank the more than 100 medical professionals who gave generously of their time and knowledge in the preparation of this book. In particular, we wish to thank: Nathan W. Shock, Ph.D., Jan S. Ehrman, Dan Rogers, and others of the staff of the Gerontology Research Center of the National Institute on Aging, Baltimore; the information office of the National Institute on Aging, Bethesda, Md.; the American Heart Association, Dallas; the American Society of Plastic and Reconstructive Surgery, Chicago; the American Academy of Dermatology, Evanston, Ill.; the American Academy of Periodontology, Chicago; Dr. Theodore Rebich of the Bureau of Dental Health, State of New York Department of Health, Albany, N.Y.; the College of Optometry, State University of New York, New York City; Dr. Robert Swezey of the Arthritis and Back Pain Center, Santa Monica, Calif.; Dr. Robert Rosenzweig, orthopedic specialist, Highland Park, Ill.; the Metropolitan Life Insurance Company corporate communications staff, New York City; the American Lung Association, New York City; the National Kidney Foundation, New York City; Dr. Michael Pollock, Division of Cardiac Rehabilitation, Mount Sinai Medical Center, Milwaukee; Dr. Robert Morin of the American Longevity Association, Torrance, Calif.; the Fund for Integrative Biomedical Research (FIBER), Washington, D.C.; the Gerontological Society of America, Washington, D.C. Vincent J. Cristofalo, Ph.D., director of the Center for the Study of Aging at the University of Pennsylvania, was kind enough to read the manuscript and offer suggestions for clarity and accuracy.

Preface

The physical changes that accompany the passing years seem to appear suddenly, with stunning clarity. One morning a man has a full head of hair; the next, it seems, his hairline has receded an inch or more. One day he takes a favorite jacket from the closet, pulls it on, and discovers that it no longer fits. One afternoon after his usual tennis game, he senses a distinctly unusual heaviness in his legs. One night, in bed with a familiar and loving partner, he notices that it takes longer than usual for him to become aroused.

Such signals of maturing manhood can cause a good bit of anxiety. Luckily, however, there is much that a man can learn and much that he can do to adjust to these changes. He has many options. Especially nowadays. Today, this country is in the midst of a fitness boom. We have discovered the value of exercise and good nutrition, and we are learning more each day about the ways that our bodies respond to training. The health-conscious man today can thus benefit from the wealth of new information coming out of scientific and medical circles. Biological research, the new field of sports medicine, and new studies of the aging are all contributing to our understanding of the body over time.

As he learns what is likely to happen to his body as he grows older, a man also discovers that age-related changes do not mean the end of prowess. He can meet change with change. He can make adjustments, both large and small, in every area of his life. If his diet has been heavy in steak and eggs since his college-football days, he can cut down on protein and increase his carbohydrate intake. If he's been jogging exclusively for exercise, he can benefit from expanding his routine with weight-training, or yoga, or swimming. If he senses his mind running on automatic, he can seek new stimulation—the kind that comes from broadening his interests, developing an avocation, or simply learning a new skill. As for his sex life, he'll discover it can go in interesting new directions, once he understands that growing older does not mean a loss of sexual feelings or capabilities.

We take the position that none of the marks of age that occur in a healthy man are *bad*—only thinking, or neglect, can make them so. The whole man is body *and* psyche. A commitment to fitness can make an enormous difference to a man's mental health, just as a positive attitude toward physical change can have an effect on how the body works. In these pages, we focus on the physical aspects of aging, because we believe that the habits of fitness established in a man's younger years will greatly enhance his total sense of well-being as time goes on.

For too many years Americans have worshipped youth. Today, as our demographic makeup is changing, and the baby boom moves into middle age, we are looking anew at the aging process, trying to see it with clear eyes, without prejudice.

All over this country, there are vital men and women who are helping to revise our expectations of growing older. Many of these people might once have been considered "past their prime," but they are proving in large numbers that vitality is not synonymous with youth. Valuing their health and strength, they are taking aggressive steps to ensure their continuing fitness. Well past the age of 50, they maintain excellent cardiovascular fitness. They work to keep strong bones and well-toned muscles—not so they can compete with 20-year-olds, but because they believe that a strong body feels good and looks good at any age. They finish marathons. They go on Outward Bound trips. They demonstrate with their lives how a sense of well-being is fostered by reaching out to new people, new interests, new physical experiences. They are our pioneers in the aging game. Those in the next generation, men and women in their 20s and 30s, will reap the benefits of their shining examples.

In *How a Man Ages,* you will find much scientific and medical evidence for a more hopeful view of aging. You will also learn about the predictable changes that accompany a man down the road from the age of 30, and what can be done to stave off or ameliorate age-related disorders. You will learn to recognize the "symptoms" of aging for what they are, and you will find, we hope, reassurance in the fact that much of what once seemed inevitable about aging is indeed open to change.

We believe that when a man commits himself to pursuing his physical potential, he will find all sorts of benefits. His concentration improves. He is more productive. He has a greater desire, it seems, to develop the interests and relationships that really matter to him. He is fuller, more alive. He stretches himself toward new goals, discovers new insights, opens up to new experiences. And each passing year can be better than the one before.

—the Editors of *Esquire*

Introduction

When we are young or even middle-aged, it is difficult to project ourselves into our own future as older people. It is easy to avoid thinking about aging, even to deny its inevitability. Therefore, it is important whenever a significant book, television documentary, radio discussion, or film helps us to understand better the future we all face. I especially welcome this useful volume, *How a Man Ages,* because it presents carefully researched information on growing older in a most engaging and lively style. It offers a positive, yet realistic, account of the changes associated with age and the research into the many clinically significant manifestations of aging.

Over the past several decades, we have seen the emergence of gerontology—the study of aging from biological, psychological, and social perspectives. The flowering of this fascinating discipline accelerated with the creation of the National Institute on Aging at the National Institutes of Health by Congress in 1975. This remarkable institution, which I directed from its inception to 1982, is dedicated to the conduct, support, and promotion of research on aging, both within its own laboratories as well as in biomedical centers throughout the country. It continues to demonstrate that an understanding of the fundamental biological mechanisms of aging can contribute significantly to knowledge about the cause and treatment of the many afflictions associated with age. The events of cell replication and senescence are now being studied through new biological techniques, such as recombinant DNA. Through this work, we are learning more and more about the changes in the great integrative systems of the body—the central nervous system, the endrocrine system, and the immune systems.

We have made strides, too, in revising the many unfortunate stereotypes related to aging, which I have characterized as "ageism." While discrimination on the basis of age remains, we are discovering that it has little basis in fact. Much of the so-called deterioration associated with age occurs later than was originally thought and is also less profound. What used to be viewed as the consequence of age is often the function of disease. This is a very important distinction, since it suggests various possible prophylactic and therapeutic interventions.

We've also come to realize that aging is not simply a downhill course. We do continue to grow and develop throughout life. Judgment, experience, and creativity do further unfold with time.

Such changes in the perceptions of aging have meant a great deal to me. I was originally attracted to gerontology because of my childhood experiences and important relationships that I enjoyed with my grandparents. Soon this personal motivation was reinforced by excitement over the opportunities for research in the field. Since 1955 I have made aging my life work, and since then I have seen the picture of age change from one of steadily declining abilities to one that emphasizes a positive, interventionist approach. We understand that, as the physician-historian Gerald Gruman has said, "it is now possible to enjoy significant extension of human life by human action."

It has not been easy to persuade policy-makers that health promotion and disease prevention are not just for the young but for the middle-aged and the old as well. However, we now know, for example, that cessation of smoking, even after years of heavy tobacco intake, can lead to substantial recovery of pulmonary function. We know also that aerobic and muscular-skeletal conditioning can lead to, and help maintain, a vigorous old age.

In the late 1960s, I became increasingly aware of the importance of prevention. Like others, I took up jogging, and, also like others, I've had my ups and downs in maintaining a rigorous schedule of physical activity. But I believe that each of us is capable of furthering our own health and increasing both the length and quality of our lives. Is it worth the discipline that moderation and health habits require? I think so.

The list of important preventive measures includes eating food low in saturated fats and cholesterol, stopping smoking, reducing if you're overweight, exercising moderately and regularly, controlling high blood pressure, obtaining a periodic medical checkup, moderating alcohol intake, and only using medications when necessary. And one more thing: Moderate the stress under which you function. This is an easy piece of advice to give, but difficult to follow.

I would also urge that we move beyond the area of physical fitness and be attentive to the need for mental, emotional, and social fitness as well. It is important to have a social network of good friends and acquaintances who can sustain us in times of crisis, especially in times of loss and grief. We must also have a sense of purpose beyond our occupation—a passion, something that guides us—be it love of baseball, a grandchild, books, or civic activity. It is wise, too, to have a balanced portfolio of interests: If one loves music, but becomes deaf, it helps to have something else to turn to.

It is an obvious fact that many people look and feel younger or older than they are chronologically. As scientists unravel the fundamental mechanisms of aging, one of the most important goals will be to understand better this important discrepancy between chronological age and functional status. And as research continues to locate the physiological markers of aging, we may even look forward to measures that markedly slow the process.

How I wish I could enjoy an evening's conversation with Benjamin Franklin! I wish I could tell him what has happened since 1780, when he wrote: "The rapid progress true science now makes occasions my regretting sometimes that I was born so soon. It is impossible to imagine the height to which it may be carried in a thousand years, the power of man over matter. . . . All diseases may by sure means be prevented or cured, not excepting even that of old age."

We may be close to realizing Franklin's vision. In America, since 1900, we have experienced a rise in life expectancy of nearly 30 years. As we face a watershed change in the makeup of our population, we need to see the link between our present and future selves. Books such as *How a Man Ages,* which increase medical and social literacy, can help greatly.

No longer can we afford to view older people as aliens, strange interlopers from a strange land. We are likely to enter that land ourselves, and we would do well to prepare for it.

Robert N. Butler, M.D.
Chairman, Department of Geriatrics
and Adult Development

Mount Sinai Medical Center
New York City

1

The New Look of Aging

At first glance, the scene in the White House Rose Garden seemed like nothing but good news for anyone interested in aging. The day was a clear, fine Friday morning in April, 1982. President Ronald Reagan, age 71, was about to sign a proclamation making May "Older Americans' Month" and endorse the elimination of mandatory retirement based on age—both of which he did promptly. The bad news, though, if you could call it that, was not lost on the reporters present. Arriving at the ceremony with characteristic aplomb and a smile, the President, the oldest in our nation's history, strode right past the podium and a bank of microphones set up directly in front of television cameras and went straight to a nearby table to read a prepared statement. "I goofed," said Reagan when informed of his gaffe. "I usually never walk by a microphone." He then agreed to repeat the ceremony at the podium, where he told the administrators on aging in attendance that he was "making the world safer for people like us."[1] The cameras in attendance clicked and whirred.

Earlier that week in Hollywood, millions of Americans had witnessed a glorious turning point for aging in general. Katharine Hepburn and Henry Fonda had both won top Academy Awards for their portrayal of a scrappy aging couple coming to terms with retirement and death in the movie *On Golden Pond*. Based on the play by Ernest Thompson that had received lukewarm reviews on Broadway in 1979, the film tugged at the hearts of the Academy members voting for the 54th annual Academy Awards. Rather suddenly, it seemed, aging and the aged were "in."

It's a curious phenomenon, aging. Count all the people in the world and you will have the number of all those who are aging. It is not a disease that strikes us down at any particular time. It is instead a biological process that can be said to begin the moment we emerge from the womb. We think "youth" when we see children scampering around the swings in the park playground. And we think "old age" when we see gray-haired, frail retirees relaxing on wooden benches in that same park. But we don't usually think of what the swingers and the sitters have in common.

It's hard to say when youth ends and adulthood begins. We have the childhood years, the teen years, young adulthood—and then one is grown-up. Likewise it's hard to say when middle age begins, although anyone in his late 30s, 40s, or 50s certainly *feels* middle-aged from time to time. And it is equally difficult to say when old age begins, although thanks to the Prussian bureaucracy and its retirement policies in the late 1800s, we tend to focus on the 65th year of life.[2]

More than ten years ago, sociologist Bernice Neugarten of Northwestern University tackled the terminology of aging and came up with a solution that seems to have stuck. She calls those in their 60s and early 70s the "young-old" and those in their late 70s, and beyond, the "old-old." A distinction originally made for research studies, it is one that is now widely used to discuss aging in general. Because the proportion of elderly in the U.S. keeps rising each year, eventually millions of young-old and old-old will be part of a gray boom the likes of which have never before been seen. Just over 15 years ago, those of the baby boom who were in their teens and early 20s grabbed the spotlight in demographer's charts at the same time they massed in the streets and grabbed headlines as activists for social change. Today, some of them have teen-age children of their own. Before too long, the older members of the baby boom will hit their 60s. Like everything else that has happened to this generation, their aging is likely to have profound effects on American society as a whole.

The steadily increasing aging population is one factor motivating the rapidly developing research into aging today. Another major push has come from exciting developments in molecular biology. Since the discovery of the precise structure of DNA in the late 1950s, research in genetics has progressed to a point where unlocking the genetic codes that govern life has become a reality. And with this intense interest in exactly how cells grow and differentiate have come new insights into the reasons why cells break down and die. It may soon be possible, scientifically, to answer one of man's oldest questions: Why do we die? What are the mechanisms that govern our aging? And what can be done to prolong life?

"Biology now is advancing at a rapid rate," says Dr. Roy Walford, an immunologist and professor of pathology at the University of California's Los Angeles medical school, as well as a well-known authority on aging. "This is the era not only of the information revolution but also of the biology revolution."[3] And since the revolution Walford cites is only in its infancy, we can expect it will enormously increase our understanding of the aging process in the future. As a result, this means that those in their 20s, 30s, and 40s should benefit from the fruits of this research. We are already benefiting from increasingly sophisticated medical technology of replacement parts for the body. Transplantation of major organs—considered only a pipe dream a generation ago—has become almost routine.

Today, gerontology (the study of the aging process) and geriatrics (the study of the care of the elderly) are becoming known as "hot sciences." A wide cross-section of researchers in many specialties recently have uncovered many mysteries about the passage of our bodies through time. Throughout this book, the reader will make stops along various pathways in the gerontological field in order to learn which areas offer the most hope toward delaying the aging process. What might not yet be appreciated is that many physical aspects of aging are indeed modifiable and not the inevitable result of growing older.

For example, dermatologists and plastic surgeons are now offering detailed information on how to keep the skin looking younger longer—information men are not disregarding in cavalier fashion anymore. In the area of dental and mouth care, experts seem to have caught wind of the coming aging boom as they have shifted research studies away from the youth-oriented problems of cavities. Instead, dentists and periodontists are fixing their fluorescent lamps on the plight of young-adult and middle-aged teeth and gums, as debates about the best gum care and periodontal disease treatment continue.

Probing deeper inside the body, exercise physiologists and cardiologists have turned up surprising evidence on just how effective rigorous workouts can be over, say, ten years or more. They can now point, for the first time, to charts and graphs that show how hearts and lungs stay stronger longer with regular, regulated aerobic exercise. It is something that has long been suspected but is finally working its way into the medical literature. Plenty of evidence also exists in the field of nutrition that can help health-conscious adults put off or bypass completely the age-related troubles of vitamin deficiencies, constipation, or excess cholesterol counts. In fact, stringent dietary manipulation may hold more clues to aging than any layman ever thought plausible.

In terms of brain function in later life, what we find is that senility isn't a normal or predictable aspect of aging. Neurologists have identified and are working on more refined diagnoses of Alzheimer's disease and other related disorders that are now known to cause impairment in hundreds of thousands of elderly today. Some of these can be treated, and while the cause of Alzheimer's disease remains elusive, when one considers how little was known about senile dementia just 15 years ago, there is ample room for optimism even here. Combining these clues with scores of others mentioned in this guide to aging, readers will be able to appreciate why researchers no longer feel that the mysteries of aging will remain elusive forever.

The aim here is not to glorify aging, nor to deny the very real anguish of older people who are suffering from disease, neglect, or poverty. It is to inform the reader of a whole new way of looking at the aging process so that he may better understand the changes that will occur in his own body and the disorders that are more prevalent among the middle-aged and elderly. There is a great deal that a man in his 20s, 30s, 40s, 50s, 60s, or 70s can do to mitigate or even stave off the waning of his physical capacities. He may never see 20 again, but he can dedicate himself to a level of physical and mental fitness that will not only enhance the quality of his life, it may indeed allow him to live longer.

AGING AND THE RECTANGULAR CURVE

Research into aging is going forward on many fronts. Like the "cure" for cancer, the "cure" for aging—or at least the aids that will arrest the process —is likely to come from a combination of basic research in many areas. Gerontologists are concerned that funds be directed for basic laboratory work into all kinds of biological processes, and they worry that such basic work may not be perceived by the public as "sexy."

What is "sexy"—both to those inside and outside the scientific community—is the possibility of extending human life, perhaps by as much as ten or 20 years. Astounding rates of life extension have been achieved in scores of laboratory experiments with animals, but scientists like Roy Walford have only just begun the attempt to get such results in humans (see chapters 13 and 14). To appreciate fully how far we may someday be able to travel along the life-extension highway, it helps to check the rearview mirror to see how far we've come.

Strolling through the agora in ancient Athens, one would not have seen many gray heads. The average life expectancy in the fifth century B.C. was only 22 years. More than 2,000 years later, it was only about twice that. An American born in 1800 could look forward to an average life expectancy of 48. By 1920, the life expectancy for American males just born was 53.6 years. And today, a newborn male baby should probably stop his wailing. He can expect to live 74.5 years. In 1983, a panel of the American Association for the Advancement of Science predicted that life expectancy will continue to increase into the twenty-first century, eventually reaching 95 years.[4] (These figures are not the same as man's *life-span,* which at about 115 years represents the outside limit of human life that only a very few persons realize, and that hasn't changed for centuries.)

The main reason for the rise in life expectancy of Americans at birth is the steady decline in infant mortality. For every 1,000 babies born in 1940,

47 could be expected to die as infants. The mortality rate fell to 29.2 per 1,000 in 1950, to 26 in 1960, to 20 in 1970, and down to 11.7 in the latest available figures from the National Center for Health Statistics. Put another way, an average of more than 988 of every 1,000 babies now born in the U.S. not only leave the hospital diapered and healthy, they will survive their infancy.

In the study of aging, one inevitably runs into something statisticians call the "rectangular curve," which for all its dots, plots, and axes is a simple tool for perceiving how well a society is doing in terms of survival. The shape of the graph line shows what percentage of a population has survived, and for how many years. A look at the line for 1970 reveals a curve that has a squared, rectangular shape. Compared with the line for 1910, which has a downward slope, the rectangular curve indicates that for every age less than 100, a higher percentage of the U.S. population had survived in 1970 than in 1910. It is not surprising perhaps, but it is important, for the rectangular curve is the map of our future travels toward extending life.

Many things have contributed to the shape of this curve, in addition to improved infant survival; yet they are commonly overlooked. In the mid-1800s, for example, tuberculosis was the leading cause of death in the United States and in most of the world. In 1920 the death rate from the disease in this country was 154 per 100,000 people each year. By 1930 the death rate had been cut in half; by 1940 it had been cut nearly in half again; by 1950 in half again; likewise for 1955, 1960, and 1970. In short, mortality from what used to be called "consumption" or "white plague" declined in the 1900s by 99 percent![5] Similarly, due to a combination of better health, better nutrition, and drugs, we have watched the death rates from diseases such as smallpox, diptheria, tetanus, typhoid, and whooping cough plummet to almost zero. All these changes together have helped us reach the rectangular curve. Today, Americans simply take for granted that they will live through the ages of 30 to 55, which could not be said with any certainty only 80 years ago.

In the meantime, partly because people are living longer and partly because of environmental factors, death rates from cardiovascular diseases and cancer have steadily risen. Medicine has yet to get a firm handle on these killer diseases, although changes toward a healthier life-style seem to be reducing the incidence of heart disease. Another major factor affecting survival curves is the still persistent threat of accidents. "Accidental and violent deaths constitute three-quarters of all deaths between the ages of 15 and 25 and over half of all deaths occurring prior to age 45," say Drs. James Fries and Lawrence Crapo in their 1981 book, *Vitality and Aging*. "This is a far more important 'epidemic' than any cancer.... Violent death is the only

The Rectangular Curve

One way of plotting survival data is to show what percentage of a population survives from birth to a fixed maximum life-span of 100. The survival curves for 1910 and 1970 below are calculated from age-specific mortality rates (number of deaths per year per 1,000 individuals entering each age), starting with 100,000 live births. The curve for 1970 takes its distinctive shape from the lower infant mortality rates and increased survival at older ages. This phenomenon is known among statisticians and gerontologists as "rectangularization of the survival curve," and it promises to be the shape of the future in longevity.

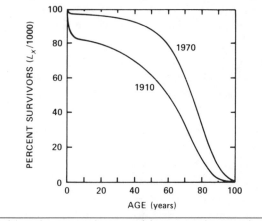

Chart from *Vitality and Aging: Implications of the Rectangular Curve* by James F. Fries and Lawrence M. Crapo. W. H. Freeman and Company. Copyright © 1981.

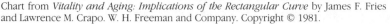

numerically important cause of death in the United States at the present time that is not a disease."[6]

In terms of survival, if a man reaches age 70, the odds are that he'll live to see 80. Diseases wreak far more havoc than normal aging. In fact, geriatricians like to point out that a healthy 70-year-old has more in common with a healthy 30-year-old than he does with an ill man of his own age. Although 70.7 is the average life expectancy for an adult American male today (while for American women it is 78.3), this is so only because accidents and disorders kill so many men before then.[7] A man who survives until his 70th birthday, according to the actuarial tables, will live 11 more years.

AGING IN THE SPOTLIGHT

Observing a convention of the Gerontological Society of America, one is immediately struck by how many people from a number of disciplines are focusing their attention on aging. At the Society's 35th Annual Scientific Meeting, held in November, 1982, at the Sheraton-Boston Hotel, thousands of professionals from the biological, clinical, behavioral, and social sciences convened in hundreds of sessions over five days. One of the best-attended meetings, early one Saturday morning, was called "Changing Images: The Impact of Today's Social Trends on the Future of Aging," and it featured Betty Friedan as one of the panelists.

Peering ahead toward the millennium, the members of the panel tried to discern what life would hold for the millions of Americans who will then constitute the graying boom. Speakers raised the possibility that there might be even more multiple marriages that we are seeing today, based on current trends in family life. Some spoke of a more sexually liberated generation being more accepting of lesbianism among the numbers of aging women who will be left without male partners. Others speculated on the reasons for the longer life expectancy of females and whether this discrepancy between the sexes would continue. Friedan, who since writing *The Second Stage* has taken up the study of aging, postulated that the integration of so-called masculine and feminine traits might be the elusive key to the concept of "vital aging." It is possible that men who have taken on more of the nurturing and supportive roles, traditionally assigned to the female, will be better able to withstand the stresses of aging and retirement.

Yet, after all is said and done, no one really knows, not even the experts, what life will be like for the coming generation of gray boomers—except that it will be different. Such a large group of elderly citizens with enormous potential political power will be a new phenomenon for our society. One thing is for sure: There will be too many elderly to ignore. The future of Social Security is just one of the problems we have already glimpsed. Another is the growing need for support for the elderly from the so-called caring professions. As Dr. Lionell Corbett, an internationally known geriatric psychiatrist at Rush-Presbyterian St. Luke's Medical Center in Chicago, put it: "We don't yet have a solid developmental psychiatric program for people sixty-five to eighty-five years old. Only nowadays are we starting to see so many of them. We really have a need for this."

Experts in advertising and consumer marketing don't view the coming gray boom as a health or societal problem as much as a sticky problem of markets and sales. According to Edith Gilson, senior vice-president for J. Walter Thompson/USA, the demographic shift to an older society portends a possible overall trend away from market expansion to compression. "The postwar baby boom created strains on maternity wards while catapulting Gerber Foods into a major corporation," observed Gilson, who was quoted recently in a glossy trade magazine. "Single-family homes sprang up like weeds in the suburbs. Supermarket chains and fast-food restaurants prolif-erated. Candy and gum sales soared. Soft-drink manufacturers toasted the boom generation, who boosted their sales to undreamed-of levels. The re-cording industry rocked and rolled up numerous million-selling albums."[8] But the baby boomers who fueled that market expansion have already left their teens, and the markets that grew with them have already had to adjust to their shifting interests.

Underscoring Gilson's point, in the summer of 1983, Mick Jagger of the Rolling Stones turned 40. Facing flashbulbs and roving reporters, he was asked: "What are you going to do now, Mick?" He didn't answer that tiiii-iiii-iiiime was on his side. In 2008, Jagger will turn 65. Even in 1983, more than 1,000 Americans each day celebrated their 65th birthday.

While Jagger was dodging media types en route to a Vermont retreat, Dr. Roy Walford was making the rounds of TV talk shows. Early in 1983, his book, *Maximum Life Span,* hit the bookstores and received much favorable attention. Prior to writing this guide to life extension for the general public, Walford had spent some 30 years in laboratories at UCLA and elsewhere studying diseases and how the body might be made tougher to last longer. But in those days he wasn't invited on too many talk shows. His scholarly writings, such as *The Immunologic Theory of Aging, The Isoantigenic Systems of Human Leukocytes: Medical and Biological Significance,* and papers with titles like "The Influence of Controlled Dietary Restriction on Immunologic Function and Aging" were intended for an audience of his peers.

Now, however, he found his face and bald head being patted with makeup in preparation for a chat with Merv Griffin. With Merv and some huge fraction of the television-viewing audience, he then shared his knowl-edge of theories for prolonging life, such as dietary restriction and antioxi-dant vitamin therapy. As a spokesperson for life extension, Walford often faces a bewildered and skeptical public. But he persists. "If we expect the public to give us large amounts of research money for its tax dollar, we need to give them feedback [through the media]," he says.

Walford, who has won armfuls of aging-research awards and sits as a member of the National Academy of Sciences Committee on Aging, not only feels we are on the brink of extending the average life expectancy, but that we can already increase the maximum life-span using knowledge gleaned from animal experiments. "In my own laboratory at the UCLA Medical Center, we have extended the maximum life-span of fish by 300 percent. It's high time. Not only for fish, but for us."[9] He talks a lot about "retarding" the rate of aging, and points out the importance of maintaining vigor in order to stave off disease. "If you can *delay* the onset of diseases such as cancer for ten to twenty years," he said in an interview for this book, "it is equivalent to a cure for the earlier age group."

CAN YOUTH SPRING ETERNAL?

Many theories now exist as to what exactly causes aging. There are dietary theories, biological time-clock theories, genetic and error theories, and the "free-radical" theory based on oxygen-waste breakdown in cells. Walford and other gerontologists think all of these may contribute to the process.

The more pressing and pragmatic question, as Walford asks, is, Can aging be slowed? As one might expect, there are at least two schools of thought about that. Those scientists who believe that an inner clock automatically shuts down each cell at a predetermined time suggest it is nearly impossible to lengthen the life-span. Less fatalistically minded clinicians think a cell ages because of gradual processes that take their toll, and therefore man probably has the capacity to slow the decline somehow. They just haven't yet proven with humans how this can be done.

Likewise, there are both conservative and radical schools when it comes to methods of extending one's life. When asked for any great secrets that he had gleaned from all the studies on the aging process, Dr. Jordan Tobin of the National Institute on Aging's Gerontology Research Center in Baltimore appears to belong to the first school. "I guess the best general rule is to practice moderation in the way you live," he says. "Well, it's probably a good idea not to get yourself extremely overweight. Don't drink and drive. And wear seat belts." Walford and other leaders in gerontology are taking a more radical approach, yet one based on solid scientific data. By subjecting themselves to regimens of diet, exercise, and other guidelines explained in the following chapters, they could very well be the pioneers who will push aging into the more distant future. Even without a dramatic increase in life extension, the prospects of prolonging youthful vitality are—at the very least—encouraging.

The Skin Matures

By anybody's standards, it was compelling footage. There on the screen was Paul Newman, vintage 1973, looking good and looking tough as Henry Gondoroff in *The Sting,* taking a lungs-full deep breath and plunging his face into a sink full of ice water—seemingly just for the hell of it. But there was more to it than that. The idea was to demonstrate to filmgoers part of this rugged man's character—how he simply couldn't start the day *without* dunking his face in an icy sink. The device was a familiar one for Newman: As a private eye in *Harper* in 1966, he had used his face as a swizzlestick in a similar ice-filled basin to good effect. And nearly two decades later in late 1982, when Newman's 57-year-old face appeared on the cover of *Time,* there was scarcely a crow's foot or wrinkle to be found.

"In person now, without makeup, he might be a man in his mid-40s," reported *Time,* adding that Newman occasionally soaked his face off-camera. Since then, millions of middle-aged men may have been plunging their jowls into ice water every day. Will it do any good? Probably not, except as a character builder. Youthful-looking skin has more to do with heredity, climate, diet, and protection from the sun than with any cosmetic routine. Mr. Newman would probably be the first to agree that the aging male face is better cared for by tapping scientific knowledge rather than by following cinematic example.

The largest organ of the body is not the stomach, heart, lungs, or intestines but the skin. If by some odd circumstance it were separated from the rest of the body, the body's largest organ would cover nearly 20 square feet and weigh in at about six or seven pounds. The skin could also boast of its extreme versatility and efficiency. It protects the vital internal organs from outside elements and bacteria; it prevents the body from becoming dehydrated; it regulates body temperature and helps dispose of bodily wastes. And unlike the stomach, heart, or lungs, the skin regenerates itself. Once every 28 days, worn-out dead cells on the skin's outer layer are replaced with fresher ones, woven together in a tight, protective coat. In an average lifetime, a man will shed up to 40 pounds of dead skin.[1]

However, despite its admirable regenerative qualities, it cannot by itself conceal the years. Chances are, upon seeing specimens in a medical laboratory, most people, including trained physicians, would not be able to differentiate readily a 53-year-old heart or stomach from a 33-year-old one. However, the face of a 53-year-old man is certainly distinguishable from that of a man 20 years younger. The reasons are at least two layers deep.

The epidermis, or outermost layer of skin, is the part that replaces itself automatically. Composed of millions of cells that constantly work their way upward and outward, the epidermis consists of some 15 to 20 connected sublayers that act as the skin's true coat. Beneath the epidermis, hidden from view, is the dermis, a layer of living tissue rich in blood vessels, glands, and nerve endings. It is the protected layer of skin as opposed to the protective, and it contains the connective tissue that gives a young person's skin its ability to spring back and retain its shape. From a dermatologist's view, this connective tissue, consisting of elastic fibers and collagen fibers, is what breaks down with age—ice water baths notwithstanding. For once the elastic and collagen fibers begin to stiffen, the face starts to wrinkle and sag, taking on a lax appearance. These fibers start to wane in youth, and they become scarcer in middle age as the fatty layer and muscle layer beneath the dermis also show signs of weakening. Accordingly, the skin loses elasticity even though it is healthy and continues to perform its body-regulating chores.

If there were one prescription for prolonging young-looking skin on which dermatologists, plastic surgeons, and cosmetologists would agree, it might be, oddly, to spend a few hours a day in a closet. Then and only then could skin experts be certain that their prospective patients were protecting themselves from ultraviolet rays. For, without question, the root of so much evil in the saga of aging skin is the sun.

SUN VERSUS SKIN

Long before manufacturers of tanning lotions and the Food and Drug Administration devised sun protection ratings for the various tanning products, science writer and author Isaac Asimov ruminated on the effect of sun on man's skin. Comparing it with various animals' pelts, skins, and feathers, he wrote:

> Man is unusual in that his dry naked skin is exposed to the sun with only the relatively thin layer of epidermis as protection. To the ultraviolet rays of the sun, the epidermis of those men with fair skin is transparent and might as well not be there.[2]

Man is also unusual in that, of all mammals, he is the only one who periodically picks up the telephone, calls a travel agent, and orders airplane tickets to the self-proclaimed sun capitals of the world, in order to strip off clothing and bathe in rays of piercing ultraviolet light. While tanning is said to promote health of the mind, it certainly promotes aging of the skin, most notably that of the face. Because unprotected skin exposed to the sun quickly becomes sunburned skin, our bodies produce a dark pigment known as melanin to absorb harmful rays. The darker a person's skin, the more melanin that is available for protection. But people with darker bodies and a lot of melanin, while their skin may not burn, are not immune to the dangers of too much sun.

Climate has noticeable long-term effects. In the 1970s, during the filming for *Cinderella Liberty* at the Harborview Medical Center in Seattle, Hollywood makeup artists noticed something different about the natives. "They kept commenting on how our skin looked so good compared with the people they were used to seeing in California," one Harborview staff member recalls. Dr. Loren Engrave, who is associate professor of surgery at the University of Washington and chief of plastic surgery at Harborview, says it is not Seattle's moist air but its relative lack of sun that makes the difference. "The incidence of skin cancer and other changes associated with the sun is far less here," he notes. The cloud-filled skies are quite clearly a positive factor in the way the faces of Seattlites age over time.

That having been said, the question remains as to what should be done once the plane lands in the Virgin Islands or Palm Springs or Key West and the beach beckons. The professional answer would be something like: Sit under an umbrella and wear a floppy hat and loose, shielding clothes. A more realistic solution: Use a good sunscreen liberally. Basically, there are three types of sunscreen lotions and oils: those that absorb the sun's rays to prevent damage, those that reflect incoming rays, and those that both absorb and reflect sunlight. Of those that absorb sunlight as it reaches the skin, sunscreens with para-aminobenzoic acid (or PABA), a vitamin, are among the most effective because they absorb the ultraviolet rays in the sunburning part of the spectrum.[3] The reflective sunscreens are probably safer to use, as they contain a combination of chemicals that more completely block out sun exposure. In recent years, cosmetic companies have combined reflective and absorbing ingredients and refined their suntan products to meet a standard called the Sun Protective Factor, or SPF, as computed by the FDA. It is based on how long a sunscreen allows an individual to stay out in the sun without burning. As an example, if your skin normally starts to turn red after 12 minutes in the Florida sun and a sunscreen allows you to stay in the sun 120 minutes before your skin starts to turn color, the SPF would be 120 minutes divided by 12 minutes, or ten. Those who wish more protection can find sunscreens with SPF ratings of up to 15, which dermatologists typically recommend as a precaution. Not only can the sun's ultraviolet light cause a prematurely aging face, it can damage the skin's DNA and is the leading detectable cause of skin cancer in man. Which is why some skin experts are pushing for the use of products with SPF ratings of 25 or higher.

THE LOOK OF OLDER SKIN

From a man's teens until his mid-30s, his oil glands and sweat glands are most active. His sex life probably is too. This is not the time to worry about sagging facial skin or drooping eyelids, but it is a good time to become more aware of the skin's needs. One of the sad truths about skin is that the oil glands that caused so much trouble during the teen-age years finally quit—and the skin becomes drier.

This shift is inevitable, and signals other age-related skin changes. During his late 20s and early 30s, a man's forehead lines become evident. Bags under the eyes begin to form and stubbornly remain. Over time, simple mechanical forces such as gravity and muscle action working on the skin have a lot to do with facial wrinkling. Dr. Norman Orentreich, a prominent dermatologist and inventor of the hair transplant, says that squints, furrows, frowns, grimaces, and smiles all contort the face to produce the major skin folds or wrinkles. Overall, the skin is thinning as it loses elasticity. The tight, protective coat mentioned earlier slackens. A full fold of skin can be pinched beneath the jaw between the thumb and index finger. "With age there is excess skin around the eyes and a sagging in the jowl area," says Dr. James R. Reardon, director of the Cosmetic Surgery Center of New York and plastic surgeon at Brooklyn Hospital. "One of the dead giveaways [of age] is the neck."

For a man in his 30s, though, it is not yet time to fret. Unlike a woman, who may be aware of increasing wrinkles in her 30s, a man will not really notice his aging skin until about ten years later. Because his skin has more oil (in the sebaceous glands) to begin with, it is slower to dry out than his mate's. "A man has thick skin to start off with, which is a natural advantage," says Dr. Randall E. McNally, a leading plastic surgeon in Chicago. And shaving seems to have a renewing effect on the skin by removing dead skin cells along with a sprouting beard.

"Today," continues McNally, "there is a greater understanding of the aging face, how cheek muscles and neck muscles interact with the skin." Procedures for male plastic surgery have been updated in the past five years to incorporate some of this new information. Also, the demand for plastic surgery has increased with an aging population that is more concerned with a youthful appearance. Plastic surgeons all over the United States have re-

The Face of Wisdom

A man's skin becomes thinner and less elastic with age. And, because of the cartilage that begins to accumulate after age 30, by the time he is 70 his nose has grown wider and longer, his earlobes have fattened, and his ears themselves have grown a quarter inch longer.

A middle-aged man makes his own wrinkles: The lines on his face are drawn from repeated facial expressions. But, as he gets older, the wrinkling happens automatically—the inside of his skin loses water, and nearby molecules bind to one another, making for a stiffer structure. Meanwhile, the skin itself thins and spreads out, and gravity pulls it downward.

Age 30: Lines in forehead are present.

Age 40: Lines from other facial expressions show up, especially crow's feet (from squinting) and arcs linking the nostrils to the sides of the mouth (from smiling).

Age 50: Lines are more pronounced; skin begins to loosen and sag in the middle of the cheek.

Age 60: Excess skin and fat deposits etch bags under the eyes.

Age 70: Face wrinkles everywhere; skin is rougher and has lost its uniform color.

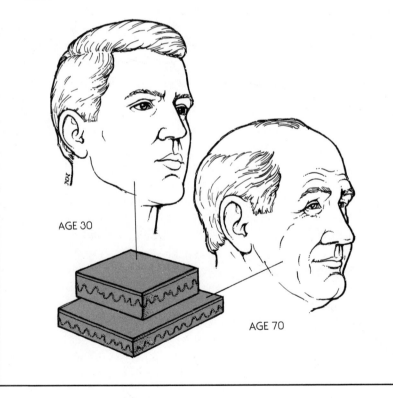

AGE 30

AGE 70

cently seen more men walking into their offices for consultations; eventually many of these men choose some form of plastic surgery.

"The trends you might see in New York or California are slowly involving me," says McNally in his Chicago office. "I believe that ten years ago maybe one of every twenty patients I had was a man. Now, it is probably one of every ten."

Not surprisingly, James Reardon, who wrote a book in 1981 called *Plastic Surgery for Men,* has also seen his male patients increase. Pondering that shift in his well-appointed Park Avenue office and outpatient clinic, Reardon hefts a gold-colored silicone breast implant and places it to one side of his desk where three other breast implants are at rest. "I would say approximately forty percent of my patients are now male," he says. In contrast, Dr. Loren Engrave of Seattle's Harborview Medical Center guesses that about 10 percent of the cosmetic surgery patients in his practice are men. But he hastens to point out that because he is affiliated with a university hospital, he tends to see a higher proportion of reconstructive cases (for congenital defects, disease, and injury) than purely cosmetic ones. Dr. Sheldon Sevinor of Boston reports that, of all the eyelid surgery he performs, 40 percent of the caseload is male. Estimates from other doctors in the Boston area float around 33 percent, higher perhaps than even the top plastic surgeons would have predicted five years ago.

When the American Society of Plastic and Reconstructive Surgeons (ASPRS), a 2,000-member group based in Chicago, celebrated its 50th birthday in 1981, it surveyed its members on their practices and confirmed that the face of plastic surgery had changed noticeably. The study showed that some 2,000 board-certified plastic surgeons performed more than one million procedures annually, of which 40 percent were aesthetic and 60 percent reconstructive. *U.S. News & World Report* has reported that, with a swelling demand for cosmetic surgery, the frequency of cosmetic operations has more than doubled in the past decade. Concurrently, dermatologists and ear-nose-and-throat specialists trained in plastic surgery are receiving many more requests for age-related corrective procedures. On the evening news, viewers are told about new requests for youthful faces and what that could mean to them—and to the companies that make cosmetics. All of which eventually may make a face-lift as acceptable for middle-aged men as a fitness regimen. There should be far fewer cases like the one recently recalled by Sheila McNally-Hoy, a registered nurse at Chicago's Rush-Presbyterian St. Luke's Medical Center: "We had one guy who was getting his face lifted and didn't know anyone at the hospital—but still he wanted us to bandage his whole head (including his face) as we wheeled him to and from the operating room." Thus concealed, the patient kept his cover, literally, until he was released from the recovery room.

Still, while it is becoming more acceptable, a man would do well to ask himself some hard questions before he goes in for extensive cosmetic surgery. What, exactly, does he want to change about himself? Take the celebrated case of John Z. DeLorean, the automobile maverick executive who gladly traded in his aging face, among other things, for a newer model. In 1976, six years before he was to be arrested for alleged involvement in a cocaine-financing scheme, Gail Sheehy wrote in her book, *Passages:*

> As the mid-life crisis closed in, DeLorean grew more frenzied about making external changes. He tightened the pressure on dealers and drove up sales, hoisted heavier weights, raced more motorcycles, divested himself of a wife his own age, lifted his face, dyed his hair, turned up in discotheques with bosomy film stars, turned around the failing Chevrolet division in a virtuoso performance, and took a wife younger than most GM officers' daughters. Having retooled the whole package, he adopted a son, his first child. . . . Today . . . he banishes all physical reminders of his advancing age: the fat, the same-aged wife, his own sagging face and graying hair.[4]

FACING PLASTIC SURGERY

Dr. Randall McNally, president of the Chicago Society of Plastic Surgery, has had a hand in perhaps 10,000 operations or procedures since 1957, when he began his surgical residency in Chicago. Included in his résumé is a 15-year stint with the Chicago Blackhawks hockey team as Mr. Fixit for the often gory injuries sustained on the ice at Chicago Stadium. McNally is also a noted specialist in the injury and burn field of plastic surgery; his hands have been praised by unlucky factory workers as well as more fortunate socialites who come to him for facial improvement. His temperament is cool and self-assured at first meeting, his wit not initially apparent. It resides deeper, at least as deep as the level of dermis. A compact man in his 50s, with dark hair and a wry smile, McNally admits that all that glitters in his profession these days is not gold—or even golden silicone.

With all the emphasis on youth and fitness, especially in the past decade, McNally has seen many unwelcome developments in his office, especially related to men in mid-life. "The desire to have plastic surgery should come from within and without," he says. "It is already a disaster if a man has been driven to come here because his wife is telling him to get the bags out of his eyes." It should come as no surprise to most educated men that surgery is available to fix most physical defects, McNally says, but the *hard* part is getting those men to appraise their faces realistically, so that they come to his office with the proper self-motivation. He thinks that a prospective patient should have at least two, and sometimes three, consultations before an appointment for surgery is made. (Other plastic surgeons typically offer one or two consultations prior to plastic surgery, at $35 to $75 for sessions lasting from 15 minutes to one hour.) As part of the consultation, the doctor interviews the client and offers a mirror for pointing out specific facial details. "This way the process is more to the fore," says McNally. "It is in the arena of informed consent, where sometimes after seeing someone several times you may pick up on something that might not have come out in the first couple of meetings. Psychologists and psychiatrists, if you were to ask them about this, would bring up the mid-life crisis as a factor in many of these interviews."

In some of the interviews for popular procedures, McNally has the prospective patient lie down to get a better look at himself. Due to gravity, a person's face looks different photographed while he is lying down, and most plastic surgeons will say that photographs are critical to proper prescreening procedures, both to give reassurance and to provide honest assessments before and after surgery. Although plastic surgery can dramatically improve a person's appearance, it should be noted that any surgery involves some serious risk, and the surgical results certainly will not last a lifetime. Plastic surgeons generally speak of face-lifts lasting on the order of five to ten years, depending on the person's age at the time of the surgery and the condition of the skin. Repeated face-lifts on the same individual are not uncommon.

THE EYE-LIFT

Sometimes as early as age 25, or as late as age 70, a man's skin will droop off the eyebrow, and puffy bulges will appear under the lower eyelid. Depending on the amount of excess skin, an eye-lift, or blepharoplasty, may be considered. This operation is relatively simple surgery, usually performed with local anesthesia, and costing, generally, from $1,000 to $1,500. Though the surgical technique is not complicated, extreme precision is critical, as the skin of the eyelid is only .55 millimeters thick and ultrasensitive. Blepharoplasty can be performed by itself or in tandem with a total face-lift, and in 1981, 56,500 eye-lift procedures were recorded (for men and women combined) by the American Society of Plastic and Reconstructive Surgeons. In a typical eye-lift, incisions are made in the upper and lower eyelid, and smallish fat pads are excised from the lids. The upper eyelid has one of these pads, while the lower lids have three distinct fat pads, often a source of visible bulging in an aging man's face. With the removal of extra skin and fat from the eyelids, years appear to vanish—and all within an hour, in most cases. Once complete, the last phase of an eye-lift involves applying cold compresses or eyepatch dressings to the eyes for a few hours. There will be bruising and swelling following the procedure, but it will fade by the tenth day after surgery. Stitches usually are removed four or five days after the operation. "Today it is a perfectly acceptable thing," says Dr. Reardon. "I did my lawyer's eyes a few years ago, and he was featured in *Newsday*."

THE FACE-LIFT

If, in a plastic surgeon's estimation, an eye-lift procedure will fall short of providing the desired look, a total face-lift, or rhytidectomy, can be considered. Most often performed on men and women in their 40s and 50s, the operation seeks to remove the most visible signs of aging in a drastic yet compact procedure. The operation usually costs between $2,000 and $5,000 (more in some large cities), not including hospitalization expenses. Some 39,000 rhytidectomies were performed by ASPRS members in 1980–81. Sometimes, an aging man or woman will seek a face-lift after a sudden, significant weight loss. It can be unusually depressing to complete a rigorous fitness program over many months, only to find after shedding 25 pounds that the 48-year-old skin no longer fits the underlying bone structure, which itself has been changing.

In a standard face-lift, incisions first are made at the hairline and then around the ear, through which the skin is "elevated" and separated from the muscles and bones of the face underneath. After the skin is pulled upward and backward, excess skin is cut away so the altered skin line can be reattached to the incisions about the ear and hairline. The procedure typically takes two to four hours, depending on the patient's characteristics and the surgeon's technique and staff.

Although a drain is inserted to collect any blood that might accumulate under the skin, postoperative swelling, bruising, and some pain will follow a face-lift. Dressings are kept intact for at least 24 to 48 hours until the surgeon inspects them. Some sutures are removed in the first week following surgery, while others remain for up to ten days. Before one can attend social or business functions after a face-lift, Dr. McNally recommends two weeks of recovery. After that, doctors often prescribe longer sideburns and longer hairstyles to shroud the signs of incision. Nevertheless, slight swelling may remain for several weeks after the procedure.

Standard face-lifts are fast being complemented by face-and-neck-lifts, which seem to offer promise for better, longer-lasting results. One procedure involves tightening the skin supported by the broad, thin platysma muscle on each side of the neck, to take care of what often has been called the "turkey waddle." Those who do the procedure talk of achieving better "angles" of jaw and neck delineation, but it is a more complicated operation and therefore is riskier than the conventional face-lift. Only time will tell if it is longer lasting. "It is true that more attention is being paid to the facial [neck] muscles underneath than there used to be," says Harborview's Dr. Engrave, "but although it is relatively new knowledge and a new technique, whether it is going to hold up better over time—I don't know." In judging the various options, it helps to think about the original goal: to look re-freshed, not 25 years younger.

Dr. Reardon recalls, "I had one patient, an insurance executive, who was a superb tennis player, who was fit, but the problem was that his face went. He said, 'I'm fifty-six but I feel twenty-five! My face is tired,' " says Reardon. "Sometimes a man will be forty-three, sometimes in his fifties, when one day he looks in the mirror while shaving and says, 'I can't take it anymore!' " When that day comes, the man may find himself calling a plastic surgeon for an appointment. Or, instead, he may learn to live with his looser, excess skin. After all, no matter how baggy the cheeks or jowls may appear, there is nothing inherently unhealthy about them. As McNally advises, the healthy request for plastic surgery ought to come from *within*.

THE LASER LIFT

In the name of youth, science, and fresher looking faces, some physicians, chiropractors, and health-care practitioners have butted heads recently with plastic surgeons in a struggle over the dubious properties of the so-called laser beam face-lift, or "laser lift."

The controversy rages over the question, Can a device using a low-power laser beam help smoothe out wrinkling, aging faces? Or have the properties of the device been grossly overstated? In the past few years, advertisements have cropped up in local newspapers and health-care-ori-ented publications proclaiming: "Look Years Younger with Laser Therapy—Nonsurgical Face-lift . . ." or "New, Nonsurgical Face-Lift Produces Amazing Results," or some similar gleeful exclamation.

In answer to these claims, Dr. John C. Munna replies: "The laser lift is a fraudulent technique. Basically, it is nothing more than hip marketing that takes advantage of the high-technology sound of the laser and preys upon the vulnerability of those who want to look younger." Munna, an Atlanta plastic surgeon, chairs the False and Deceptive Advertising Practices Com-mittee of the ASPRS. Understandably, he is not at all pleased with the claims being made for the laser acupuncture devices, as they are also called. In fact, Munna enrolled in a laser lift course in 1982 to learn not only how the devices were being used, but also to learn how the manufacturers' representatives were pitching them to prospective practitioners. The Food and Drug Administration classifies laser acupuncture machines as "Class III medical devices," which means that patients must be told that their use is considered "investigational."

In defense of the laser lift, cosmeticians and chiropractors, among others, claim the helium-neon laser devices actually remove wrinkles in a series of brief, safe, nearly painless, and relatively inexpensive procedures. Unlike plastic surgery, they point out, a scalpel is not used. Approximately 1,500 lasers have been used for laser lifts to date, as consumers have spent an estimated $5 million on the treatments since 1980.[5] Jacqueline Tousley, a licensed cosmetologist who runs two Face Toners Limited salons in southern California, told the *Los Angeles Herald Examiner:* "It's another option in the twentieth century for those who want to look youthful, and it's not as scary as facial surgery."[6] According to Munna, a regular series of 12 to 14 treatments costs in the range of $1,400, with one or two "tonification" treatments to follow, at additional cost.

Adding a touch of mystique to the laser procedure is the equipment itself. The device has two "wands"—one resembling a penlight, the other a small hammer. A grounding wire is also used, as the two wands are directed to a certain wrinkle or series of wrinkles in the face. An electrical current then passes through the skin, producing a temporary swelling that appears to remove wrinkles. The question remains, for how long?

Munna took the course and had treatments, and says the wrinkling diminishes only for "three to four hours." After petitioning the FTC and FDA, both of whom are looking into the laser device, ASPRS, through Munna, consistently has beamed its own message to consumers: The laser lifts cannot be advertised as "safe and effective." At least not yet.

THE ATTRACTIVE FACE

Back in the private office of Dr. James Reardon, a recently discarded fibrous surgical mask rests neatly in a plastic-lined wastebasket. Reardon, 42, leans back in a padded leather desk chair, twirls a paperclip he has just unbent, and weighs the positive and negative aspects of cosmetic surgery. He prefers, of course, to accent the positive, and doesn't mind prognosticating, "Of course," he says, "as people live longer and longer, they want to look better.

There is something about being vigorous and yet, at the same time, seeing skin hanging off of your face."

Accordingly, it would be dishonest to write that an aging face is a prime stimulant when considering relationships between the sexes in mid-life and beyond. But it would not be incorrect to say that women often admire and seek "mature" faces when choosing partners and mates. And the reasons go beyond the cosmetic.

Masters and Johnson long ago concluded that greater sexual interest and activity are often displayed among postmenopausal women and their partners. It is not the less elastic facial skin of the mate that piques the female's desires, but more likely a rekindling of the sexual spirit after the fear of pregnancy is gone. Then, too, the famed sex researchers found that oftentimes after women had completed years of raising a family, they sought "new directions" as outlets for unexpended physical energy. If this still holds true today, then aging men have little to fear. There are a lot of energetic women out there looking for able-bodied, experienced, mature men—and they'll take them, wrinkles and all.

MAINTENANCE: THE SKIN

A man's skin, because it's oilier and thicker than a woman's, does not age as quickly. But eventually the glands produce less oil and the connective tissues break down; the skin loses its elasticity and its ability to retain moisture, and wrinkles result. Aside from plastic surgery, there's no "cure." But what you can do is be aware of the skin's increased sensitivity and susceptibility to dryness and treat it accordingly. Avoid dry skin at all costs, whatever your age. Dry skin doesn't cause wrinkles, but it does tend to make the skin look older than it is. Some tips for men of all ages:

- Clean your face gently. Use a soap that rids the skin of dirt and grease without completely stripping it of natural oils. Select a soap that's appropriate for your skin type. Those with dry skin should use a superfatted soap; oily skin can be cleansed with most of the unadulterated soaps on the market. In general, the fewer ingredients the soap contains, the less likely your skin will come in contact with an irritant. If you have sensitive skin, never wash your face with one of the deodorant soaps; they're too harsh.

- Wash only as frequently as you feel you need to without letting the skin get dried out. And don't scrub your face; the skin is too delicate. You won't solve an oily skin problem by overwashing because the skin will just react and produce more oil.

- When washing the face or body, avoid water of extreme temperature. Hot water dehydrates the skin, and cold water, despite the myth, has no miraculous pore-closing properties.

- If your skin is dry, stay away from astringents, most of which contain alcohol. Likewise, use an after-shave moisturizer instead of an alcohol-based after-shave lotion. But if you have oily skin, use an astringent for a midday refresher.

- Unless you have oily skin, use a moisturizing lotion or cream regularly. Both face and body will benefit.

- Adjust your skin care to the seasons. In the winter, for instance, the skin is battered by both the cold and the dry indoor heat. To combat dryness, use a humidifier to replace the air's moisture.

- Limit exposure to the sun. The sun's ultraviolet rays damage the skin permanently, leading to premature aging and sometimes to cancer, especially in fair-skinned individuals. If you must get a tan, do it gradually. Try to avoid the sun during the peak hours of 11 a.m. to 3 p.m. when you're more likely to burn. And when you're out, always wear a sunscreen. Look for the ingredient PABA (para-aminobenzoic acid), which absorbs the ultraviolet rays. Dermatologists typically recommend those sunscreens with a Sun Protective Factor of 15. But no matter what the number, your skin is still being exposed to the sun's ultraviolet rays, so beware.

- Although isometric exercises will not prevent wrinkles or sags, any vigorous exercise gets the blood flowing and makes the skin look healthier.

- Eat a balanced diet with plenty of fruits and vegetables. Drink a lot of water and avoid excessive caffeine and alcohol.

The Story of Man's Hair

When Dr. Norman Orentreich contemplates the head of Ronald Reagan, he tends quizzically to scratch his own. "It's a hairline you normally see only on a child or a eunuch," says the inventor of the hair transplant, who has studied men's scalps for three decades and still has a hard time accounting for Reagan's hefty hairline. Men typically lose hair around their temples as they age. It's an effect of testosterone, a hormone produced in the testicles beginning in puberty, and it seems to happen to all men, even those who otherwise keep a thick head of hair all their lives. Then there is Ronald Reagan, in his 70s, with a straight line of hair above his forehead. "He's not wearing a hairpiece," Orentreich says, "and he hasn't been castrated, so I'd have to assume that he happens to have some sort of rare hereditary variation."

It is good that the doctor mentions variation, because, in a sense, that is one of the only constants in the study of aging hair and balding. Both men and women lose hair every day for a variety of reasons, the primary one being the simple hair growth cycle. At the same time a healthy scalp is losing hairs, it is also growing hairs—thousands, in fact, each day. Studies show that an average 30-year-old man with a full head of hair will normally have about 100,000 hairs, with slightly fewer for redheads but slightly more for blonds. The hairs will grow approximately 1/72 of an inch each day,[1] which means it will take nearly two and one-half months for the hairs to grow one inch. In their respective growth cycles, these hairs tend to grow anywhere from two to six years and then rest for three months. The hair that ends up in your brush or comb after a shower or shampoo, at any age, is hair that happens to be in the resting phase. On any random day, about 10 percent of one's hair is in the resting or "nongrowth phase," while 90 percent remains in what dermatologists call the "active growth phase."[2] It is perfectly normal for a full head of hair to lose some 20 to 60 hairs in a day.

The stray strands of hair in the brush aren't troublesome for a man until they coincide with graying or baldness. Then the normal hair loss may become associated with the uninvited marks of age; it may seem that every hair lost is a sign of lost youth. Balding can be particularly disturbing: While graying tends to happen to men and women equally, women lose much less hair through the years largely because they have higher levels of estrogen and fewer androgens in their bodies.

Bald Progress

Men actually do get hairier with age, but, alas, not where it does them any good. Hair grows in the ears, in the nostrils, and sometimes on the back. Eyebrow hairs tend to get longer and more noticeable. As for the top of the head, there are different hormones at work. Men bald at different rates, of course, and some never bald at all. But according to *The AMA Book of Skin and Hair Care,* over time, male-pattern baldness becomes noticeable in approximately

12% of men aged 25
37% of men aged 35
45% of men aged 45
65% of men aged 65.

Men with male-pattern baldness first notice a receding hairline, then hair loss on the "monk's spot." Finally, receding hairline meets monk's spot and the scalp is bared.

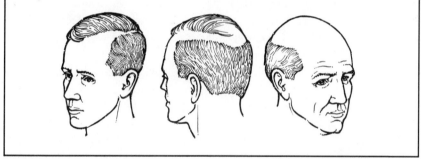

MALE-PATTERN BALDNESS

There can be many causes of a man's baldness, such as disease or reactions to certain drugs, but the discussion here will focus primarily on male-pattern baldness, or as Orentreich calls it, "androgenetic alopecia."[3] Contrary to popular belief, the genes for this type of baldness are inherited equally from both the father's and mother's sides of a man's family. Baldness in previous generations, however, does not aid a man in predicting exactly when he might become bald. Variation rules.

All hair consists of a protein called keratin and grows beneath the surface of the skin in follicles. What you see, touch, and brush is actually dead tissue. There are basically two types of hair on our bodies: vellus, which is fine, barely pigmented, and nearly invisible, and terminal, which is relatively thick and usually pigmented. Male-pattern baldness is caused by the gradual conversion of terminal to vellus hairs; it happens only in follicles that are genetically predisposed to react in a certain way to the stimulation of testosterone.

Exactly how testosterone affects these follicles is not understood, but the result is a shortening of the hair's normal growth phase (usually a two-to-six-cycle). After a man begins balding, the hair roots still repeat the growth and rest phases, but eventually only short, fuzzy hairs appear. Finally, some 20 years after the baldness begins, the affected roots vanish. In an odd way, baldness is part of the price paid for masculinity. For without testosterone, the genetic potential for hair loss would remain dormant.

Baldness usually begins at the temples, producing a widow's peak. One comforting fact to keep in mind is that a 25-year-old man will often show signs of a widow's peak even though he may never suffer severe baldness. But for men with male-pattern baldness, the widow's peak continues to recede as they get older. The next vulnerable portion of the scalp is the monk's spot, the circle on the back of the head from which unruly hairs so often awkwardly protrude during childhood. If a man is marked for extensive baldness, the monk's spot eventually will grow to a point where it meets the receding widow's peak, leaving the top of the head nearly bare.

The all-too-frequent occurrence of male-pattern baldness has led to a variety of "miracle cures" over the years. Just a few years ago, a former factory foreman from Bekescsaba, Hungary, named Andras Banfi claimed he had invented a hair restoration formula after being inspired, he said, by Egyptian manuscripts. It was called Mr. Banfi's Lotion, a suitable name but probably not inspired by ancient Egyptian manuscripts. Hungarians, however, were inspired enough to purchase the stuff en masse, resulting in such unruly lines of balding customers that the police had to be called in to keep order in the shops. The lotion contained alcohol, orange oil, and jelly from bees, smelled like garlic, was said to take six months to work, and required five bottles' worth of application. Apparently, its turbid, brownish composition, foul odor, and $3 price tag didn't deter those who feared the increasing transformation of their hairs from terminal to vellus. According to *The New York Times,* at least one dermatological clinic said Mr. Banfi's Lotion might work, prompting smugglers reportedly to peddle the glop at highly inflated prices in Vienna's black market.

It has been stated many times, but probably not enough, that products that claim to restore lost hair by "stimulating," "rejuvenating," or "nourishing" bald areas are worthless because baldness is not caused by poor blood flow or undernourished hair. Three known factors cause baldness: (1) a genetic predisposition to the condition; (2) the age of the man; and (3) the activity of the male sex hormones. At this writing, no known topically applied substance is available for purchase that effectively counteracts these causes. Usually, the onset of baldness is a gradual process, whereby the hair-producing follicles begin to function less and less deep down in the dermis. Skin experts estimate that as many as 80 percent of all men will have some hair loss during their lifetime, Mr. Reagan notwithstanding.

THINNING AND GRAYING

Whether the top of the head remains well covered or not as one ages, there does seem to be a consistent pattern in the way individual hairs thin. A man's hairs are thickest at about age 20, measuring about 101 microns, or mil-

Thinner, Lighter Hair

Although there are marked differences among men in the rate at which hair falls out or turns gray, there does seem to be a consistent pattern in the way individual hairs thin. A man's hairs are thickest at about the age of 20; after that each hair shrinks, and by 70 his hairs are as fine as they were when he was a baby. According to information supplied by the Orentreich Institute for the Advancement of Science, the diameter of a single hair, measured in microns (millionths of a meter), changes like this:

Age 20: 101 microns
Age 30: 98 microns
Age 40: 96 microns
Age 50: 94 microns
Age 60: 86 microns
Age 70: 80 microns

AGE 20   AGE 70

lionths of a meter, in diameter. After that each hair shaft shrinks until by age 70 or so the hairs are as fine as when he was an infant, about 80 microns in diameter.

As with other changes of the aging body, it is not easy to predict if or when a man will see his hair turn gray "before its time." The strange thing about graying hair is that it is not actually gray. With age, the production of pigment in the hair follicles slows down and sometimes ceases, leaving the individual hairs colorless. The difference between a man's graying hair at 50 and at 75, typically, is that the 50-year-old still has pigment in his hair follicles while the 75-year-old's hairs are nearly colorless or completely white. This process is a normal part of aging and most people develop noticeable "gray" hairs by their middle 40s. With luck, one might make it to the early 50s without considerable graying, and there have been instances where the color change has been postponed into the middle 50s and beyond. Although a stubborn strand of gray might pop out of the widow's peak in one's early 20s, hair generally begins to gray at the temples and eventually works its way from there throughout the scalp.

Most graying is due to genetics and age, and thus is not reversible (without hair coloring, that is). In rare instances, premature graying can be caused by a reversible condition such as a vitamin B-12 deficiency, or a hereditary disposition toward diseases such as anemia. In such cases, researchers have reported somewhat positive results in reversing the graying process by giving experimental subjects doses of para-aminobenzoic acid, or PABA, a B vitamin.[4] The research has not been substantiated on a large-enough scale, however, to generate much excitement among dermatologists or gerontologists.

REPLACING LOST HAIR

There comes a time in every man's life when he stares into the mirror and fails to see what he'd like to see—namely, a younger-looking reflection. The inexorable expansion of the forehead is in most cases troubling, and in some cases traumatic. To most men bald is not a handsome look, but a constant reminder of their advancing age. One simple solution, of course, would be to combat the male hormones associated with balding by injecting estrogen into the body. The catch is, this would cause your voice to change, your sex life to shrivel, your breasts to enlarge. Not a prudent remedy.

In the shadow of the Empire State Building, smack in the center of New York City, sits the carpeted salon of Joseph Paris, designer of hairpieces for men.

It is called Joseph Paris Naturally. The sign that greets customers upon entrance is a large, green, backlit number with white script lettering that reads: "If your hair concerns you . . . it concerns us." To the right and above this lettering is a color photograph of Joseph Paris, comb in hand, tending to the head, and implicitly the Paris hairpiece, of Frank Sinatra, sometime not long ago, backstage, maybe in Las Vegas or Atlantic City. Apparently it is there to show prospective customers that the clientele is first-rate. On the main desk counter in the salon lobby, a letter of thanks from Bernard Meltzer of WOR radio, a popular New York talk show host, stands prominently on display. It praises the work of Joseph Paris for the toupee he recently had made, using words such as "golden hands" and "extremely pleased." (One can't help but wonder whether he would have written the same letter had he been a television emcee.) For $690 to $1,000, men can have their heads fitted here for toupees made with synthetic hair. The $1,000 pieces have hairs sewn into them individually. Why synthetic hair rather than natural fiber? "It lasts longer," an associate of Joseph Paris says. "It's a fiber made in the Orient. Instead of one year, synthetic hairpieces can last two or three years if they are made well."

There are other differences between the $690 toupee and the $1,000 one—measurement and fitting, for instance. At the Paris salon and at many others around the country, getting fitted for a hairpiece involves first taking an impression of the head. For a relatively inexpensive piece, a proprietor normally will fit a piece of plastic wrapping about the customer's head, using tape to make certain the mold is absolutely snug. When a more expensive hairpiece is ordered, a plaster of Paris mold is made using materials much like those used in casts to help mend fractured bones. Hence, a better fit. The expensive toupee also has a sheer, netted fabric that bares the scalp underneath "naturally" when the wind blows. Once the proper measurement is made, the balding customer is offered a series of color charts to choose from. The charts look oddly reminiscent of samples one might see in a carpet showroom, except that these are countless swatches of *hair* of all shades, textures, and colors. At the Paris salon, the selection and fitting take place in a secure, private booth with barber chair, large mirror, and another backlit display of Paris touching up Sinatra, replete with the salon slogan in script.

When the hairpiece is completed (usually about one month after ordering), the customer should allow two to three weeks to get used to his toupee —a period of adjustment both to the look and the feel of the hairpiece. "Men shouldn't wait to do it until they are into their fifties," says Carl, a Paris associate clad in a forest green and navy smoking jacket. "It ought to be earlier so they can enjoy it more. I don't care how old he is—every man who has lost his hair, or most of it, has a complex about it." For the squeamish, consultations at places such as Joseph Paris are predictably "private and confidential."

Around the corner from Sinatra's hairpiece place, the proprietors of the Hair Club for Men are at work, shuffling from room to secluded room, switching on slide shows and videotaped television presentations, explaining to prospective customers just exactly what their nonsurgical hair replacement technique is all about. "We're very creative," is overheard from one of the private consultation booths. "It beats being bald," comes the reply.

At the first meeting between the stylist and prospective customer, furtive glances to the tops of each other's head accompany the initial handshakes. The technique isn't advertised as hair weaving, and it is quite different from what is done at a hairpiece salon. Usually, the procedure takes about two hours to complete, once preparations, measurements, and particular style have been made and selected. First, a nylon filament is interwoven into the existing hairline, which at this point more often than not is horseshoe-shaped. Then, carefully matched human hairs are attached to thin nylon filaments that have been connected to the man's hairline and balding-area "anchor." This is not quite a toupee, not quite a hair weave, but is supposed to offer the benefits of both, at a price that exceeds both. Depending on the work required and the particular scalp involved, it costs $2,000 to $4,000 for starters. But because the hair replacement is anchored to an existing human hair, it must be refitted and restyled every couple of months, or an average of five to six times a year at $50 a visit. These visits can take place in Boston, Beverly Hills, New York, or other cities where there are stylists who have been appropriately trained in the method. The $50 update visits include a shampoo and "precision geometric cut." One advantage of this type of hair replacement, its proponents say, is that it is totally reversible. Should a customer cringe at the resulting look, the entire process can be undone in five to ten minutes, the weaves and strands removed, the head returned to its presalon state. Surgical hair replacement techniques, by their nature, are more permanent propositions.

REFLECTING ON HAIR TRANSPLANTS

In October, 1982, in the shadow of some of Hawaii's impressive mountains, attendees at the 51st annual convention of the American Society of Plastic and Reconstructive Surgeons, the Plastic Surgery Educational Foundation, and the American Society of Maxillofacial Surgeons convened one mid-week afternoon to view a videotape on "Scalp Reductions with the Shaw Hemostatic Scalpel." Presiding over the session were Dr. John W. Devine of Miami and Dr. Steven Kay, his associate. Devine is a plastic surgeon who specializes in techniques of hair replacement. He has an especially perceptive eye toward future medical techniques, and, in a field that occasionally is accused of preoccupying itself with the petty, Devine, 73, conveys a refreshing air of honesty and levity. At age 60, after practicing general surgery for 30 years in Lynchburg, Va., at just about the time he might have considered retiring, he applied to several medical-school residency programs in plastic surgery to broaden his career. Numerous rejections later, Devine was welcomed, along with an eager band of recent interns in their mid-20s, by Dr. Ralph Millard, head of the plastic-surgery department at the University of Miami. Now Devine is sought after as a top-of-the-head pioneer. He spends his supposed vacation time on the medical-conference circuit, giving talks on new hair-transplant and scalp-reduction procedures.

Says Devine with a trace of a Southern accent. "I tell my patients two things: one, they could have had better parents; and two, they could be castrated [to stop the balding]. There is not a greal deal of demand for that."

However, there does seem to be a pretty steady demand these days for one form or another of surgical hair replacement. "I think more and more males are seeking hair transplants because of their jobs and careers," says Devine. "They have learned that we can transplant and grow hair like trees." Ever since Dr. Orentreich first reported his use of hair plugs to correct certain cases of male-pattern baldness in 1959, the hair transplant has made its way into the mainstream of dermatology's and plastic surgery's battery of procedures. The basic scientific reasoning behind hair transplants is that hair follicles from various parts of the scalp have what is known as "predetermined hereditary persistence potential," which remains even after hair is transplanted to a new location on the scalp.[5]

In its earliest form (one still widely used today), the hair transplant involved removing hair plugs containing 15 to 20 hairs each from the sides and back of the head and then inserting them into the prepared balding area. Sports fans might recall one day in 1971 when the "Golden Jet" of hockey, Bobby Hull, appeared on the ice before a game (and before helmets were prevalent) sporting scores of blond hair plugs on top of his formerly bald head. These were not the sort of scars fans were used to seeing on the pros of the National Hockey League, yet the hair plugs and scars eventually helped Hull restore lost confidence about his looks, and it didn't hurt his promotional appearance and endorsement income either. What did hurt, if only slightly, was the procedure itself. Although a hair transplant doesn't require general anesthesia, mild sedation and novocaine injections are used to numb the pain.

In the case of Hull, as with most common hair transplants, a hair punch or other motor-driven coring device was used to remove some of his golden hair for eventual replacement. Because hair does not normally grow straight out of the scalp but instead at an angle, the hair punch is tilted at an angle when taking a plug, to maximize the number of follicles that can be taken with each punch. Once the plugs are taken and stored in a sterile solution, and the site has been prepared for transplant, hair plugs then are placed in corresponding sites in the balding area and held in place with pressure. Sometimes stitches are used to help close the resulting wounds in the donor areas, but not always. Though stitches make the procedure more complex, they can help reduce resultant excess bleeding and scarring. Nowadays, to reduce possible excess bleeding, doctors often use an inflatable band, or scalp hemostat, capable of applying great pressure equally about the head. During a normal procedure, as few as 25 punches can be taken at a time or as many as 100, depending on the patient's preference or degree of baldness. The cost can range from about $2,500 to well over $6,000, depending on the number of hair plugs ultimately taken, usually at $12 to $15 each.

"A lot depends on the type of hair you're working with," says Devine. "Latin hair is the best—it's like crabgrass. It just keeps coming at you." If several hundred hair plugs are deemed necessary to restore a good-looking head of hair, the sessions will be spaced about six weeks apart to minimize pain and general discomfort. Following the transplant, the plugs of hair will be in a state of semishock during which the transplanted hair will shed and wait three to four months before regrowing. Unfortunately, the new hairs will grow back more slowly, so that it could take eight to 12 months for the transplanted hair to reach its original length prior to the procedure. When it comes to transplants, patience is the byword.

"I'll turn down three out of four [prospective] patients that come to me," says Devine, who devised the use of square grafts for transplants, "because they are either uncertain about the potential results or unsure of how they will cope with the waiting. It's not like a face-lift, where you do it and it is over with. You will be dealing with this for six months to a year."

Besides developing a square graft procedure for hair transplants, Devine has been on the cutting edge of the increasingly popular scalp reduction and scalp-flap techniques. Devine likes to refer to the scalp-flap procedure as "instant hair." Often these two techniques are used together with hair plug transplants. There is another type of transplanting called the strip graft, whereby a five-inch crescent-shaped strip of skin and hair is taken from the back of the head where hair is full and placed in the balding frontal, or anterior, portion of the scalp.[6] The strip serves as the new hairline, with hair plugs usually inserted behind it. This combined technique is said to leave a more natural hairline in place than one reconstructed solely with hair plugs.

In the scalp-reduction videotape viewed at the Hawaiian conference of plastic surgeons, Devine and Kay showed how reducing the bald area of the head can now be done more safely and efficiently than before, in a fashion roughly analogous to a face-lift procedure. Before removing parts of the balding scalp to highlight more hair cover, doctors were shown making elliptical incisions three to four centimeters in diameter on both sides of the head. In simple terms, the bald area is reduced and the remaining hair rearranged to give a fuller effect. According to the two doctors, "This has become one of the most useful surgical techniques available in the treatment of male-pattern baldness.

The scalp-flap technique, in contrast, is more elaborate and involves a bit of excision and a bit of skillful rotation. Flaps of hair still growing thickly above the ears and around the back of the head, about one inch by five inches, are excised, but not completely. Above each of the ears, the rectangular flaps are left attached to the blood supply; then they are each carefully repositioned from the back to the front to form two strips of a new hairline that meet in the middle of the forehead. The biggest advantage to this method, proponents claim, is that it doesn't result in massive hair fallout and a tedious regrowth at the hairline. Even so, hair plugs normally are used to fill in the balding area behind the new hairline.

There does tend to be more scarring with this technique where hair has been removed, although these scars are covered by the strong growth of hair on each side of the head just above the ear. It also should be explained, Devine adds, that with the repositioning of the scalp flaps, the "new" hair along the hairline will grow in the "wrong" direction. In essence, as the flaps have been rotated nearly 180 degrees, the individual hairs will continue to grow out of the skin at the same angle they have always grown, which may not look quite natural to the discerning eye. "I tell them that no matter how good I am, and no matter how good they look, this may bother them," says Devine. "With the incisions with this and other techniques, there is no way it can be done without scars. They will show up after a dip in a swimming pool."

Contemplating such drawbacks, a balding man might well agree with the positive thinking of New York writer Guy Martin. Martin, who began to lose his hair in his early 20s, offered this advice in the October, 1982, issue of *Esquire:*

> Stop thinking of tunnel grafts, plugs, scalp flaps, weaves, et al. as action within the realm of possibility. These postures not only are intrinsically degrading; their true danger lies in the implication of a cure, or the hope for one. There is no cure, because—this is crucial—*there is no disease.*

He concluded:

> Since balding in real life is infinitely more difficult than balding on paper, I include a few points of balding etiquette, suggestions, really, to help you get over some of the rough spots. . . .
> —Learn balding history so that you may speak with authority at cocktails. Y. A. Tittle, Ken Kesey, and Marcel Duchamp are balding history. Henry Miller, Henry Adams, and Haile Selassie are balding history. Philip Roth and Terry Bradshaw don't deserve it. Menachem Begin doesn't either.
> —Appear in a tuxedo as often as possible.
> —Take a vacation in Japan to coincide with the annual Bright Head Contest, the beauty pageant for bald men.
> —Have one round, shiny, expensive object in a prominent place in your house.
> —Bring a baby to your next social engagement.

CONQUERING BALDNESS?

It is a rare man who never has wondered if or when he will become bald. Rarer still seems to be scientific hope for a realistic solution to the persistent condition. One of the current possibilities lurking in the research community involves applying female hormones to the scalp to inhibit the activity of male hormones responsible for male-pattern baldness. This is said to prevent further fallout, but usually doesn't result in hair regrowth. Then there was the substance devised by a major pharmaceutical company in recent years that still brings a chuckle from Devine: "They got something that grows hair all right, but the problem was that it was growing hair all over—it was even growing on the nose!" In the meantime, scientists at the Orentreich Institute and other laboratories are testing various drugs that stimulate hair growth or retard baldness. Minoxidil (in lotion form) and spironolactone (a diuretic) are two substances that have so far been cited in medical and lay literature as having had positive effects. Every so often scalp experts seem to surmount a stumbling block, only to run into another unexpected side effect or mystery. The application of research and chemicals goes on.

"Orentreich has been saying that he is just around the corner from a solution," says Devine, who at 73 has not quite the head of hair of Ronald

Reagan, "but he has been saying that for twenty years. I'm not looking around the corner too much these days, waiting."

As for all the lotions, potions, and secret formulas on the market, government agencies aren't, for the most part, having any of it. Back in November, 1980, the Food and Drug Administration proposed a ban on the sale of products that are supposed to grow hair where it isn't growing or has already fallen out. After reviewing scores of ingredients of hair growth concoctions —such as olive oil, lanolin, wheat germ oil, and various vitamins—an FDA panel asserted that no products offered at the time were effective in doing what their makers claimed they should be doing to balding heads.[7] Once a hair shaft emerges from the scalp, said the panel, nothing done to it will influence its growth. To prove that a product restores hair, the manufacturer must prove to the FDA that the active ingredient actually stimulates hair growth by getting into the hair root or by some means heretofore not proposed to the agency.

In a further note, the FDA noted that baldness may have an underlying medical cause. Iron deficiencies, crash diets, unusual stress, hormonal imbalance, or exposure to radiation can all cause hair loss and should be ruled out before a man resigns himself to the most common type—male-pattern baldness.

MAINTENANCE: THE HAIR AND SCALP

Since the predisposition to go bald or gray is an inherited trait, there's nothing much you can do to combat it. What you can do is to keep your hair and scalp clean and healthy-looking, so that what hair you do have looks good.

- Wash your hair regularly. Lather the shampoo in your palms and massage it into your scalp with the fingertips. Work the shampoo out to the ends of the hair and rinse thoroughly with lukewarm—not hot—water.

- Select a shampoo that's right for your hair and for the number of times per week you wash your hair. For instance, if you have oily hair and wash your hair daily, an oily-hair shampoo might be too harsh. A good shampoo should leave no soapy residue and should make your hair feel clean, but not dry. Some experts recommend diluting shampoo by half with water. It works into a lather more easily and saves rinsing time.

- Alternate brands of shampoo. Hair, over time, can become resistant to the benefits of one shampoo.

- Wash as many times a week as you like. Normal hair can usually go a couple of days, but if you have especially oily hair or if your hair is regularly subjected to dust or smog, wash more frequently.

- Conditioners can be used after shampooing to make the hair softer and more manageable. They don't alter the hair's structure, but they do coat the hair shaft and help keep moisture in.

- Dandruff is the result of excessive dryness of the scalp. As a man ages, his scalp, like his skin in general, tends to be drier. To combat flakes, use an antibacterial dandruff shampoo. As with regular shampoos, rotate brands so that your hair gets the most out of the active ingredients. If the condition does not improve, consult a dermatologist.

- Hair dryers, while convenient and useful for styling, can dry out the scalp. Hold the hair dryer at arm's length from your head. Better yet: Towel dry your hair, comb with a wide-toothed comb, and, as your hair continues to dry, use your fingers to lift hair from the scalp for a fuller look.

- Sun and chlorinated pools also have a drying effect on the hair and scalp. Help replenish lost moisture by using a conditioner. Or take a dab of hair cream, rub it on your hands, and then run your fingers lightly through your hair.

A Clear View
of the Eyes

The eyes are often described as our "windows to the world." Certainly they allow us to see the outside world, but, just as important, they allow us to interact with that world by sending signals to our brains every waking moment of the day. Perhaps more properly, the eyes could be described as information processors, considering that they bring in 80 to 90 percent of the input we use each day. They speedily seek and sort constant flows of visual *information,* using properties of depth perception, acuity, binocular fusion, contrast sensitivity, night vision, color vision, peripheral vision, and more. In man, vision is overwhelmingly the dominant sense. During most of our lives, the eyes are unheralded heroes, feeding us millions of visual clues and images each year until at some point, unannounced, they start to ask for assistance. This request might take the form of a squint at a dinner menu in a dimly lit restaurant, or perhaps a couple of errors are found in the monthly checkbook reckoning. In any case, some loss of vision is a fairly predictable occurrence in middle age.

One mildly comforting fact to keep in mind comes from the National Health Survey of 1971–1972, which showed that males at each stage of life tend to have somewhat better visual acuity than females. Subjects between the ages of four and 74 were tested "with usual correction"—meaning that those who usually wore glasses or contact lenses wore them during testing. The proportion of males who tested at least 20/20 was 75.2 percent, compared with 70.5 percent among females. At the same time, the proportion of those with defective distance vision of 20/50 or worse was 2.9 percent for males and 3.6 percent for females.[1] (A person with 20/50 vision would need to be 20 feet away to see clearly what a person with healthy, more perfect eyes could see at a distance of 50 feet.)

Clear vision is a physiological feat to behold. In brief, light reflecting off of objects first passes through the cornea, then through the pupil, lens, and vitreous of the eyeball to the retina, where visual cues and images are received. These cues, in turn, work as food for the brain. But even before the eyes can send signals through the optic nerves to process information (to tell the brain what is going on), the eyes must perform athletic feats of their own. As the clear cornea admits light to the eyeball, the iris filters the light by controlling the size of the pupil. The pupil grows and shrinks in diameter, much like the aperture on a 35-millimeter single-lens reflex camera. Except, of course, that the camera has but a single "eye." Behind the iris, the lens

---

Diminishing Vision

The lens of the eye steadily hardens throughout life and begins to cause problems for a man in his early 40s. By then the lens is too big for the eye muscles to focus properly on close objects. Eventually this can cause cataracts, but the odds are that the man will die before that happens. The amount of light reaching the retina steadily declines with age (perhaps because the pupil shrinks),. which means that the man will have trouble seeing in the dark; he will need especially bright light to read.

Age 30: 20/20 vision; reads without glasses.

Age 50: 20/20 for distance vision, but needs glasses to read; a less elastic eye lens makes him more sensitive to glare; his depth perception is beginning to get worse.

Age 60: 20/25 vision; a less elastic, yellower lens filters out some shorter wavelengths of light, making it harder for him to distinguish between blues and greens.

Age 70: 20/30 vision; peripheral vision is diminished; night vision is worse, and his eyes take longer to adjust to the dark

---

focuses the speeding light on the tissue-thin retina that forms the back of the eyeball. It is the retina's job, through its more than 100 million sensory receptors, to register the patterns of light that eventually call forth the appropriate action from the brain. If the eye is pictured as a camera, the retina would be the ultrasensitive film. It's a complicated process, to be sure, and much can go wrong along the way. Just ask a 46-year-old squinting diner in a dark restaurant, a tennis player who has just pinged a backhand, or an investment counselor who is having trouble with the stock-price reports in the business pages. Inevitably, the eyes' timing and flexibility begin to slow down with age.

One of the reasons this slowdown occurs has to do with the six major muscles of the eye, which move the eyeballs in much the same way a video game joystick sends a Pac-Man creature scurrying around a tight corner. While tracking objects and aiding perception, the medial rectus and lateral rectus muscles control side-to-side movement of the eyeball; the superior rectus and inferior rectus allow movement up and down; and the superior oblique and inferior oblique muscles move the eyeball torsionally. Normally, they are far more powerful than people need them to be; they don't need to be stretched, relaxed, or massaged to produce clear vision. But, with age, these muscles lose elasticity. Partly because of muscle deterioration, partly because the lens begins to cloud and stiffen, and partly because the brain takes longer to react, a man's visual skills are often not as sharp, not as perfectly synchronized, as they may have been in the 20s and 30s.

The major vision problems of mid-life and beyond—myopia (nearsightedness), presbyopia (a type of farsightedness caused by the hardening of the eye lens), glaucoma, and cataracts—stubbornly are still with us. Fortunately though, recent technology has improved detection methods markedly. Devices now exist that can instantly size up an eye's ability. Other machines can photograph the eye and its insides in cases where serious eye problems are suspected. Still other devices make it possible to measure the eye's pressure, at a touch, without pain or lack of precision. This has been a boon to glaucoma care.

The brighter side of the inevitable decline of sight is that it can be reversed in part or sometimes completely with the aid of glasses or contact lenses and by the principles of relatively new eye care specialties—orthoptics and behavioral optometry. Happily, the choices of remedies for eye problems today are far more varied than ever before. The advent of extended-wear contact lenses, bifocal contact lenses, improved diagnostic devices, painless laser beam treatments, and refined surgical procedures and medicines have all contributed to the worthy goal of better future sight.

The eyes of a man with no visual defects are working at their peak around age 20. Most commonly, men will notice a falloff in visual acuity around age 40. "Up to ages forty to fifty, little change in acuity has been noted, but after this time there is marked decline. By age seventy, without correction, poor vision is the rule rather than the exception," says Jack Botwinick, director of the Aging and Development Program at Washington University in St. Louis.[2] Usually in mid-life the first visit to an eye doctor for blurry vision will result in a diagnosis of myopia or presbyopia, often called "the normal aging process of the eye." Digby Diehl, a California writer and editor, viewed the onset of middle age in a March, 1981, piece for *Esquire*. He told of a friend who "settled down on the eve of his fortieth to read *Passages,* a book he had been told would offer insight into his problems. He opened the paperback version only to discover to his horror that the page was a blur. He spent his birthday at the ophthalmologist being fitted for reading glasses."

PRESBYOPIA

Most likely, Diehl's friend was noticing the effects of presbyopia (from the Greek *presby,* meaning "old," and *opia,* meaning "eye"). In both presbyopia and myopia, objects are no longer being brought into proper focus through

The Presbyopia Effect

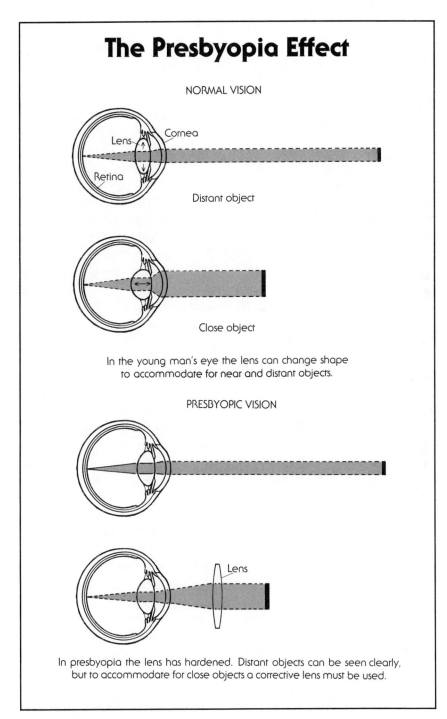

NORMAL VISION

Lens Cornea

Retina

Distant object

Close object

In the young man's eye the lens can change shape
to accommodate for near and distant objects.

PRESBYOPIC VISION

Lens

In presbyopia the lens has hardened. Distant objects can be seen clearly,
but to accommodate for close objects a corrective lens must be used.

the lens and eyeball onto the retina, which results in what are known as refractive errors. In presbyopia, this is because, after decades of loyal service, the natural crystalline eye lens has begun to harden. Dr. Martin Kreshon, a Charlotte, N.C., ophthalmologist, explains it as "a condition in which the eyes' own lenses begin to lose some of the elasticity that allows them to adjust to seeing at reading distance." This happens to all of us gradually to some degree, until one day blurred images become bothersome. No matter how hard we try to see images clearly, or how hard the brain tries to resolve the blur, an overwhelming majority of people with presbyopia will need corrective lenses to offset farsightedness.

The problem of presbyopia is not difficult to understand. The eye lenses grow throughout life, as new fibers affix themselves to the periphery, making the lenses flatter. The consistency of the lens changes over time. It can be described as like pliable plastic at birth, while by age 50 it is stiffer, nearly glasslike. Accordingly, the lens is less able to change shape in response to changes in light patterns. Then the refractive errors appear, time and again, squint after squint. The visual skill known as accommodation becomes more difficult, until as one ophthalmologist puts it, "By and large, after fifty, most people require some sort of reading help."

Hank Greenberg is one reason why the ophthalmologist says *most* people. A member of the Baseball Hall of Fame, Greenberg hit a lofty .313 with the Detroit Tigers and Pittsburgh Pirates before bowing out of the major leagues in 1947. He also stroked 331 homeruns in the span of 13 seasons, a feat that is at least partially attributed to his fine eyesight. In 1980, at the age of 69, Greenberg took part in a baseball vision screening program in Sarasota, Fla., and astounded attending optometrists. According to Donald Teig, O.D., a Ridgefield, Conn., vision specialist who conducted the players' screening, Greenberg still had excellent vision. Dr. Teig reported not only that Greenberg was seeing better than 20/20, but that from a vision point of view, he was "still capable of putting the ball out of the park." It ought to be noted, just for the record book, that the Hall of Famer does wear glasses for reading.

Another encouraging fact: there are a few people with presbyopia who have improved their vision without the aid of glasses. They have learned to correct the errors whereby images for close objects are improperly focused *behind* the retina. New York optometrist Richard Kavner tells of one patient, about 50, who worked in television and did not want to wear glasses or contact lenses. She knew, though, that her vision was failing. After reading an article about behavioral optometry and vision training, she approached a skeptical Kavner with the unlikely goal of correcting her vision without corrective lenses. Three months later, her acuity had jumped from 20/300 to

20/30 in good light. The trick here, as Kavner and coauthor Lorraine Dusky described it in their book, *Total Vision,* was a combination of determination, luck, and fine-print, low-light visual exercises. Unfortunately, success in such cases is rare. The problem is partly one of motivation. As Kavner and Dusky wrote of Kavner's patient: "To maintain her improved vision—and to keep away from using her dreaded glasses—she needs remedial therapy every eighteen months or so, for eight to ten weeks. Therapy seems to arrest the deteriorating condition for a while, but then the old wheel of time keeps revolving. A key factor in her success appears to be her high motivation, which is crucial to all aspects of vision therapy, but especially when treating presbyopia. It's just like going on a diet. Losing weight and improving visual skills are not done *to* you—you have to make the decision that they are worth the time and trouble and then proceed."[3] Visual exercises, it seems, can be thought of as health food for the eyes. However, it must be remembered that no matter how "hungry" one is to conquer presbyopia without glasses, most patients need to rely on corrective lenses.

MYOPIA

Nearsightedness, or myopia, is the most common problem of aging eyes. Nearly 3 million persons who sought an eye doctor's help in 1976 to correct a visual defect turned out to be nearsighted, according to a study conducted by the National Society to Prevent Blindness. More than one million of these people were between the ages of 25 and 44, but after age 45, the study added, there were three times as many diagnoses of presbyopia as there were of myopia.[4]

In short, nearsightedness results when visual images came to a focus in front of the retina, a type of refractive error. Defective vision typically follows, and a visit to a mirrored, gleaming optician's office is too often in order. And yet, while it is true that nearsightedness is common, it may not be "natural"; it is quite possible that we "learn" myopia. By living in a society that stresses and prizes near-point work, and by repeatedly focusing on near objects throughout life, we in the United States (and in other literate cultures) have trained our eyes and brains to consider faraway objects less important.[5] This disturbs doctors such as Kavner who see myopia as an unnecessary handicap. Synthesizing years of research, Kavner and Dusky reported: "At the U.S. Naval Academy the first-year plebes arrive with good acuity, since it is a requirement for admission. By graduation, a high percentage have become myopic. In one class more than half ended up nearsighted. . . . A study at Dartmouth found that those with the most severe eye defects were the best achievers. At

Checkups: When and Where

When it comes to eye care, the first guideline to remember is that there are no exact guidelines as to how often a person with good vision ought to have his eyes examined. Eye specialists have long recommended annual examinations for those aged six to 20, exams every two years between the ages of 20 and 45, and again annually each year thereafter. But it is by no means a consensus. Prognostications vary widely. One estimate that holds firm, however, is that at age 40 we become more vulnerable to common eye disorders. It would not be a bad idea, then, for a man to have an eye exam every two years thereafter.

The next logical question is, whom should you go to? There are ophthalmologists, optometrists, and opticians—each with their own specialties and degrees of training. A general rule of thumb in eye care is that the longer the title, the more professional training that eye specialist has had.

Ophthalmologists are M.D.'s who have attended medical school for four or more years, followed by one year of general medical internship. They then complete a hospital residency of at least three years while specializing in eye-related disorders. Once trained, ophthalmologists are able to prescribe glasses, contact lenses, and drugs for eye diseases. Some but not all ophthalmologists go on to practice surgery (and, lately, to perform laser treatments).

Optometrists generally have attended a four-year school of optometry after four years of college, leading to the designation of O.D., or doctor of optometry. They become specialists in the physical properties of the eye as well as in the properties of corrective lenses—both glasses and contacts. Typically, optometrists prescribe corrective lenses for visual faults such as nearsightedness, farsightedness, and astigmatism, but unlike ophthalmologists they are not licensed in most states to dispense drugs.

Opticians have been trained for one or two years (depending on state requirements) in lens technology. No college degree is required, but the Opticians Association of America does have ongoing certification and licensing requirements for its members. It is to an optician that you would go normally for the corrective lens that has been prescribed by the ophthalmologist or the optometrist.

In past years there has been rivalry between the two professions of ophthalmology and optometry, but much of the competition for patients has since turned to cooperation. Dr. Eleanor E. Faye, a leading New York City ophthalmologist, regularly works with one optometrist and envisions more such team efforts in the near future. "The controversy isn't viable to me anymore," Dr. Faye says. "The standoff is really outmoded."

Harvard the amount of myopia increased for each year spent in graduate school."[6]

And the risk is there at any school of higher learning, adds Dr. Robert L. Stamper, associate professor of ophthalmology at the Pacific Medical Center in San Francisco and at the University of California at Berkeley. People who spend inordinate amounts of time fixing their eyes close-up on books, video screens, paper, or whatever may in time suffer "ciliary spasm," a sort of charley horse of the accommodative eye muscles. The good news here is that *after* graduate school or other long periods of near-point visual stress, the eyes can correct themselves.

Another finding that may surprise nearsighted persons is that genetics do not account for faulty vision perhaps as much as had been thought. Repeated tests on animals and humans have debunked much of the myth of inherited myopia. More important, eye doctors say, is the fact that nearsightedness is relatively rare in cultures where book learning is not rewarded. Healthy eyes at rest naturally gaze into the distance; they are not fixed on near objects. As optometrist Kavner intones: "Distance vision is relaxed vision." We would do well at any age to recall that. It makes sense to mix reading, writing, working, or watching television with outdoor activities and far-off glances. The eyes will appreciate it.

GLAUCOMA

Up until the age of 40, most people don't think much about glaucoma. At the four-decade mark and later, though, glaucoma becomes a leading cause of blindness. Briefly, it is a condition that results when an imbalance of eye fluid creates excessively high pressure in one or both eyes. If this "intraocular pressure" is left untreated over a long time-span, serious damage and blindness can follow. Informally, glaucoma has been called "tunnel vision," because peripheral vision is the first to be affected by the condition. In most cases, both eyes are affected. And although glaucoma cannot be entirely cured, early detection and treatment can control it. Nearly all blindness due to glaucoma can, in fact, be prevented. Typically, treatment with prescription eyedrops and other pressure-reducing drugs can arrest the expected debilitating visual effects—if, that is, the condition is detected early on.

When the eyes are healthy and clear, the front part of each eyeball is filled with aqueous fluid, which regulates the proper pressure of the eyeball. If this fluid doesn't drain properly, pressure slowly builds, which eventually compresses crucial nerve fibers and blood vessels in the optic disc. This might not be painful, but it is potentially vision-threatening. The optic disc surrounds the optic nerve, whose job it is to carry visual messages to the brain. The two most common types of glaucoma are *chronic* and *acute,* though some eye doctors refer to them as *open-angle* and *closed-angle,* respectively. (Their preference stems from knowing that some cases of acute glaucoma also can be "chronic" in that they never recede.) In the United States, where more than 2 million people suffer from the disease, chronic glaucoma is the most common type. It is painless as it slowly erodes one's vision. Acute glaucoma is unusual and much more painful, commonly bringing on nausea, vomiting, and sharply decreased vision. Surgery is usually required to correct this condition, which for reasons unknown is the more common type of glaucoma reported by Asians.

The haunting aspect of glaucoma is that symptoms are rare. In most cases, by the time it is diagnosed, irreversible damage already may have occurred. Glaucoma also tends to be hereditary. On the positive side, better pressure-lowering eyedrops and pills have been developed recently. Timolol, one new drug used to treat chronic open-angle glaucoma, is especially beneficial for elderly persons who have both glaucoma and cataracts. Marijuana, hardly a new drug, is now used medicinally in treating glaucoma (experimentally) in about 30 states. It has been shown to help slow the progress of the disease by preventing excessive fluid pressure from building up in the eyes. It remains to be seen whether marijuana will actually enter the mainstream of glaucoma treatment, for it is still allowed as treatment only on a "research basis."

Laser treatments, meanwhile, have moved beyond "research basis" status and are now used by ophthalmologists in place of surgery to relieve chronic eye pressure. If a glaucoma patient doesn't respond to prescribed drugs or oral medication, says Dr. Eleanor E. Faye, "you can treat the area of the eye where fluid is drained. If blocked, it can be opened with applications of one hundred tiny laser burns." Dr. Faye, who was the first female ophthalmological resident at Manhattan Eye, Ear, and Throat Hospital in 1956, nonchalantly explains that the laser she uses in New York is a mere five blood *cells*—not blood vessels—wide. "What this means is that now you will have a new group [of future glaucoma patients] who won't lose their vision."

CATARACTS

In an uncrowded area of Baltimore, at the National Institute on Aging's Gerontology Research Center, a youthful researcher, Neil S. Gittings, regularly screens subjects as part of the center's long-term studies on aging. His job is to search for signs of visual defects and to track how well certain pairs of aging eyes are doing. Something has occurred in the past decade, though, that has thrown Gittings's routine out of whack. That something concerns cataracts in the eyes of the aged, and a drastic means of correcting the defect. Subjects in the National Institute on Aging study and across the land have been showing up at vision screening exams with plastic lenses in their eyes. These are not regular contact lenses, but "intraocular lenses" (IOLs), which have been described as the most important and interesting development in ophthalmology in the past ten years. They have been surgically implanted in hundreds of thousands of patients whose natural lens has turned cloudy because of cataract. Says Gittings, "The people I know in the study who have them [IOLs] are tickled to death. There are others who say, 'I wish I were older so I could have them.'" Because intraocular lenses have such a drastic effect on improving eyesight, Gittings in effect now excludes those with IOLs from data reports concerning normal, aging eyes. A new category of experimental subjects at the National Institute on Aging has clearly emerged.

Although people of any age can get cataracts, they are much more common among the aging. Over time, the normally transparent lens becomes cloudy or hazy, which eventually can block light from entering the eye and cause faint or blurred visual images. Bruce Rosenthal, O.D., a specialist in treating low vision at the State University of New York School of Optometry, compares the clouding of the eye lens with adding drops of milk to a glass of pure water. The formation of a cataract, he says, is not unlike adding one milk drop to the glass each year; eventually the glass will become murky. Usually evident in some form when a person reaches 65, cataracts are not bothersome in their earliest stages. Eye doctors cannot precisely predict at what age cataracts will first form, partly because they seldom develop at the same rate in both eyes. "I had a one-hundred-and-seven-year-old patient who had no lens change in one eye lens, but needed the other one taken out due to cataract," Dr. Rosenthal says. The most frequent symptom is blurred or dimmed vision. The only treatment is to remove the clouded lens surgically to allow light to enter the eye freely.

Up until about 1970, people who had cataracts removed were fitted either with thick, unwieldy cataract glasses or with contact lenses, which took over part of the focusing function of the previously healthy lens. The catch was, neither the glasses nor the contact lens could actually simulate the exact function of the lens. In the past decade, however, the transparent IOL has gained wide acceptance in ophthalmological circles. In 1978, ophthalmologists performed between 25,000 and 40,000 such operations in the United States. By 1982, more than 400,000 lenses were being implanted annually.[7] Unlike a contact lens placed over the eye, an intraocular lens is inserted into the eye where the clouded lens was removed. The artificial lenses are often made of a material called polymethyl methacrylate, or PMMA—or, as many patients and doctors say, plastic.

"'It's a miracle! It's a miracle!' Patients say that all the time," says Dr. Faye. "Instead of six or seven weeks of rehabilitation with one eye out of balance, as in a normal cataract removal, people feasibly can be home in three days doing their own shopping and cooking." Discounting the fact that the procedure is not a panacea (the possibility of more complications exists), eye care experts describe its effect as wondrous. Dr. Stamper of the Pacific Medical Center tempers that enthusiasm, but only slightly: "We should keep in mind that IOLs have only been implanted successfully over a twenty-year maximum span. For instance, if we implant an IOL in a forty-year-old man, we don't know how he will react in thirty years. After all, it is a foreign material—it's plastic. Some people do not tolerate it." Still, the IOL certainly has been a boon to patients who are able to have the procedure. It bodes well, too, for future generations of elders who expect to live well into their 70s or 80s and beyond—and who wish to keep their dominant sense fully alive.

HOLISTIC EYE CARE

Tracking the decline of the dominant sense can be threatening to, say, a 36-year-old man who has fine vision and regularly eats his carrots. And yet, he has reasons to be optimistic. The more obvious are technological: Extended-wear contact lenses, bifocal contact lenses, intraocular lenses, and laser treatments are fast becoming commonplace. It used to be that optometrists and ophthalmologists had a rather limited view of treating cataracts, because they mostly affected only their oldest patients, and because shorter life expectancies meant that many would-be cataract patients never lived to the point where their eyes grew cloudy. Of course, this is not meant to imply that aging eyesight is something to look forward to; rather, it suggests that the prognosis need not be entirely bleak.

Research has recently brought new thinking to the relationship between nutrition and older eyes. Just as vitamins and minerals are nutrients for the rest of our bodies, they are also necessary for healthy eyes. "Traditional medicine is anti vitamins and supplements, but I don't buy that," says Dr. Faye, who is also a specialist in treating those with extremely poor vision. "I put all my patients on a nutritional diet." Probably for good reason. Dr. Roger Williams, a University of Texas biologist, has demonstrated that in the case of laboratory animals, the number of cataracts was directly related to the lack of certain nutrients in the diet.[8] Without extrapolating his findings too far, Dr. Williams suggests that a healthy diet supplemented by vitamins and minerals may help prevent cataracts from forming. While the healthy eye lens is rich in vitamin C, a diseased eye lens contains hardly any. In addition, Dr. Richard Kavner reports, glaucoma and cataracts are associated with low levels of vitamin C in the lens. While vitamin A is usually cited for its vision-aiding

Workouts for the Eyes

Day after day, in health and fitness clubs across the land, hundreds of thousands grimace and sweat as they strive to strengthen their bodies. For the most part, they give little thought to strengthening their eyes. The eyes will take care of themselves, it is thought, until, inevitably, the decline comes. But among certain eye care professionals, especially behavioral optometrists, eye exercises are seen as an essential part of any effort to prevent decline. The goal of exercises is not to replace glasses or contact lenses, but to help people make the best possible use of their vision systems.

More than 40 years ago, Aldous Huxley, science writer and novelist, wrote *The Art of Seeing* to further research into what he called visual reeducation. Huxley espoused the principles of Dr. W. H. Bates, who recommended such practices as "palming" and regulated blinking as preventive therapy for the eyes.

Palming: Simply put, palming is a technique used to keep light from entering the eyes and thus relax them. First the eyes are shut, then covered by one's palms, with the lower palm resting on each cheekbone. That way, the eyeballs are never rubbed or pressed as light is excluded. To heighten the relaxation, elbows can be placed on a desk or table during the exercise. Palming, Huxley wrote, "keeps the mental powers of attention and perception at work in the effortless, freely shifting way which is natural to them, at the same time as it rests the eyes." Besides relieving strain and fatigue, vision is said to improve for a time following the technique.

Blinking: Not surprisingly, most people don't think a lot about blinking. Yet if they did, they might see better. Blinking does two basic things: It lubricates the eyes with tears and regularly rests them by shutting out light. According to Huxley, those whose work demands close, detailed attention could help their eyes by performing a brief blinking drill. First, try a half-dozen light "butterfly wing" blinks; then close the eyes for a few seconds. During a tough day on the job, repeating the drill occasionally can help the eyes battle the effects of aging. And perhaps boost productivity a bit to boot.

Focusing Pursuits: Today's vision therapists talk about boosting productivity of the entire visual system, not just the eyes. Though there are only a few hundred behavioral optometrists scattered across the country, they are prominent in high-level athletics, where a slight increase in visual acuity can shave microseconds off a skier's time, or help send a baseball soaring over the fences. Richard S. Kavner, O.D., has taught vision therapy to professional hockey players and is former chairman of the Department of Vision Therapy at the State University of New York. As part of his practice, he provides visual games for patients to do at home. In one exercise, called "focusing pursuits," patients practice focusing accurately on a moving target. To try this, tape a couple of words from a newspaper on a small stick (or ruler). Hold this out about 16 inches in front of you with the letters visible. Next, slowly swing the stick around in a circle—first closer to you, then away—in constant motion while trying to keep the words in focus. Try this clockwise, then counterclockwise. Over time, the circumference of the circular motions should increase, giving the eyes a more complete, well-rounded workout.

properties, one newer finding is that vitamin D and calcium treatments in some studies markedly improved myopic vision and other eye ailments.[9] Similarly, vitamin E treatments apparently have been shown to help arrest degenerative conditions in aging eyes, including presbyopia. In light of such findings, nutrition is gaining a higher profile among eye care professionals in the 1980s.

In the early part of this century, years before he wrote *Brave New World*, Aldous Huxley faced a bitter prognosis. While in his teens he suffered from "keratitis punctata," an eye disease that left him nearly blind. Frustrated and determined to keep his sight, he happened upon the works of a Dr. W. H. Bates, who proffered a method of "sight without glasses" that could be considered one of the earliest forms of vision therapy, or behavioral eye care. Huxley wrote *The Art of Seeing* in 1942 in gratitude to Dr. Bates and his method, which the novelist said restored much of his sight. The book was peppered with lines such as "Sensing + Selecting + Perceiving = Seeing," and "... the acquisition of habits of proper use will generally produce a certain improvement in the organic condition of the eye." Eye exercises were described, such as "palming," "shifting," and regularly blinking—and the book was viewed with healthy skepticism. In 1975, however, due to a reported new interest in preventive eye care, *The Art of Seeing* came out in paperback.

Meanwhile, "behavioral optometrists" have meshed the beliefs of Huxley and Dr. Bates with late twentieth-century technology to offer more holistic and prevention-minded eye care. In addition to eye exercises, a behavioral optometrist might prescribe eye-resting regimens. Also in use are microcomputers that measure one's entire visual field, or devices called soccadic fixators that measure one's eye-hand coordination and reflex time. Already there are machines that can tell a person instantly what sort of prescription lens he needs as soon as he looks into a viewer. Peering a bit further ahead, Dr. Stamper raises the possibility of a complete automated diagnosis: "With all of these automatic devices," he says, "in five, seven, ten years, perhaps, the average Joe may be able to step into the local five-and-dime, plunk one dollar into a Polaroid-photo-type booth, and have his glasses prescribed by machine." Dr. Stamper—a Cornell graduate, former Peace Corps volunteer, and now an oft-quoted member of the American Academy of Ophthalmology in San Francisco—appears somewhat bemused by the prospect.

MAINTENANCE: THE EYES

After the age of 40, it is a good idea to have your eyes examined every two years. Don't ignore the inevitable weakening of your eyes. When eye exams and the telltale loss of sharp, strong vision point to a need for glasses, get them. Here are some other suggestions for protecting your vision over time:

- Do the palming, blinking, and focusing exercises described on page 51 to relieve fatigue and strengthen the eye muscles.
- Get enough sleep. The body as a whole needs rest. Lack of it will be particularly noticeable in the eyes.
- Don't rely on fluorescent overhead lamps to light your desk when your work requires close reading. Equip your work space with a table-top lamp to prevent eyestrain.
- Wear shatter-proof safety glasses or sports eye protectors for racquet sports, especially those played on a closed-in court, and for yard and workshop jobs where a power mower, paint sprayer, or saw could spray material into the eyes. When you swim in a chlorinated pool or in a pond (where bacteria can infect the eyes), wear goggles.
- In bright sunlight, wear good sunglasses with dark lenses. Research indicates that eyes suffering from years of overexposure to ultraviolet rays are more likely to develop cataracts.
- If you get a foreign object in your eye, use an eyewash in a clean eyecup to wash it out.
- If a harmful substance gets in the eye, immediately flush the eye with water for at least 15 minutes. Do not rub the eye.

Eye care professionals list the following nutrients as particularly important in maintaining healthy vision:

- *Vitamin A* has traditionally been credited with aiding night vision. It also helps prevent drying of the eyes. Best sources: yellow, orange, and dark-green vegetables (e.g., squash, carrots, spinach), fortified milk, eggs, and liver.
- *Vitamin C* is found in abundance in a healthy eye lens, but in scant quantities in a diseased eye lens. Best sources: citrus fruits, tomatoes, dark-green vegetables.
- *Riboflavin* (vitamin B_2). One symptom of riboflavin deficiency is a sensitivity of the eyes to light. Best sources: whole-grain and enriched cereals, pasta, and bread; dark-green vegetables; milk and meat.
- *Vitamin D and E* are being studied now for their therapeutic uses. Vitamin D in conjunction with calcium improves myopic vision (best sources: fortified milk, liver, egg yolk) while vitamin E has been linked with success in arresting degenerative conditions in aging eyes (best sources: margarine, whole-grain cereal and bread, and green, leafy vegetables).

Hearing
About Ears

The voice rang clearly through the TWA wing at La Guardia Airport. "Ladies and gentlemen," ticket agent Brendan Callendar announced, "this is your final boarding call for Flight 579 to St. Louis and Phoenix." As daylight turned to dusk, passengers on their way out of New York that summer evening offered up their flight envelopes and tickets for inspection at Gate 24. Below, on the tarmac and in the bowels of one of the nation's busiest airports, the TWA ground crew readied Flight 579 for the air. Workers loaded baggage and precooked meals. The flight crew ran an instrument check as the fuel crew filled the tanks. And ramp supervisor Dick Ayalo, 46, filled out a preprinted flight log sheet with numbers. All the while, engines of the Boeing 727 whined in anticipation of takeoff. "We are outside five, maybe six hours a day," Ayalo said, "depending on the traffic." As he spoke, a TWA crewman wearing a headset stepped inside the all-purpose office for a Styrofoam cupful of coffee. "Out there," Ayalo said, pointing his nose at nearby idling jets, "you are more prone to immediate aircraft noise."

A couple of gates over, in the American Airlines area of La Guardia, Bill Kellaher, 50, supervisor of ramp services for American, awaited the arrival of Flight 202 from Detroit. Within minutes, the pilot brought the jet to a halt, its front wheels straddling the painted yellow parking line under the tarmac. Although the plane had stopped, its parts hadn't. The whoosh, whine, and high-pitched hiss of engines filled the runway like a tremendous roll of ocean waves crashing on shore, only louder. Jerry Riggs, 53, an American employee for 30 years, stood at attention under the plane with a sleek, trim headset firmly in place, plugging both ears. The ear protection was as much part of his uniform as his shiny metallic tie clasp shaped like an airplane.

Once a year, in the medical units of TWA, American, and other major airlines, ground crew workers such as Riggs, Kellaher, and Ayalo submit to a battery of tests for vision, depth perception, blood pressure, and, of course, hearing.[1] Even though standard-issue headsets are part and parcel of every maintenance worker's uniform, the tests are precautionary, and wise, for at the loading gates the noise level regularly tops 100 decibels. If the average 55-year-old executive working in an office starts to lose some of his finer points of hearing simply because of age, surely a 55-year-old ramp supervisor at a major metropolitan airport will be at greater risk. He deserves a periodic good look and listen by a hearing specialist.

Missed Notes

A child can hear sounds reaching as high as 20,000 hertz, but in early adulthood the range starts decreasing. This seems to be a direct result of a breakdown of cells in the organ of Corti, the part of the inner ear that transforms the vibrations picked up by the outer ear into nerve impulses, as well as of deteriorating nerve fibers. Fortunately, hearing diminishes least in the range of everyday human speech—the average old man can hear conversations fairly well. To the young, an old man often seems deafer than he really is simply because he's not paying attention (perhaps with very good reason).

Age 30: Has trouble hearing above 15,000 hertz (a cricket's chirp).
Age 50: Can't hear above 12,000 hertz (a "silent" dog whistle).
Age 60: Can't hear above 10,000 hertz (upper range of a robin's singing); has trouble distinguishing among tones in range he can hear.
Age 70: Misses some words in normal conversation; can't hear above 6,000 hertz (high notes on a pipe organ).

Toward the end of the Carter Administration, on the same January day in 1981 on which the National Transportation Safety Board reported that the nation's airlines had set a new safety record for lowered accident and death rates, the Occupational Safety and Health Administration (OSHA) ordered various industries to provide hearing protectors for more than 5 million workers across the country, as part of a new "hearing conservation program."[2] Specifically, the regulations were designed to protect those who work in places that commonly average 85 decibels over the course of the day, where the risk of material impairment rises significantly in the absence of hearing protection. As many as three-fourths of the workers in the textile industry, for example, work in a potentially harmful, noisy environment. The OSHA orders, according to agency spokesmen, would also improve safety and reduce absenteeism, workers' compensation payments, and, possibly, heart disease. After a few delays by OSHA staffers under Reagan, the second phase of the conservation program, which called for stepped-up testing and annual monitoring of the affected workers, became law in March of 1983.

HEARING AND ITS LOSS

Modern explanations of hearing and speech pathology often compare our hearing apparatus with a stereo sound system. Since each of our ears picks up distinctive sound cues from the air, a stereo effect is produced. The

The Ear: A Built-in Amplification System

Sound waves enter the auricle of the outer ear, travel through the auditory canal to the eardrum and then on to the tiny bones of the middle ear—the hammer, anvil, and stirrup. In the inner ear, the vibrations stimulate minute sensory organs that send electrical impulses along the eighth cranial nerve to the brain. When presbycusis (age-related hearing loss) occurs, it is because these sensory organs, known as hair cells, have degenerated.

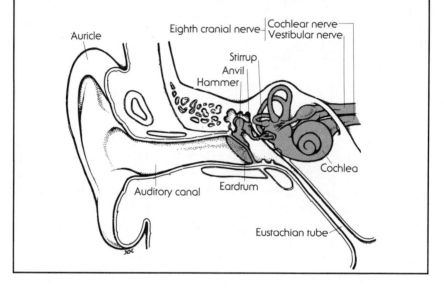

powerful electronic equipment that we buy and aim at our ears only magnifies the effect of our built-in stereo receivers. No imported headphones needed.

We hear when sound vibrations, traveling through space on air molecules, wend their way through the outer ear, middle ear, and inner ear to the brain. The outer ear consists of the fleshy funnel-shaped protrusion on each side of the head known as the auricle, or pinna, and also includes the auditory canal that leads to the eardrum, or tympanic membrane. As sound passes through the three separate parts of the ear, various hearing structures go to work picking up the vibrations, amplifying them, and sending them along the eighth cranial nerve, or auditory nerve, en route to the brain.

When the sound runs smack into the eardrum, the vibrations set off a chain reaction in the small bone-enclosed middle ear. Here, three tiny bones

—casually called the hammer, anvil, and stirrup—snatch the wobbly sounds, amplify them, and send them galloping toward the inner ear. (It is also in the middle ear where the Eustachian tube connects the ear passages with the top part of the throat to equalize the air pressure around the eardrum. The importance of this tube becomes quite apparent in descending airplanes or rapidly rising elevators.) Fluid-filled passages, cavities, and the snail-shaped cochlea comprise the complex inner ear, where sounds finally stimulate the special minute nerve endings known as hair cells. The organ of Corti also is located here, as are the vestibular nerves that help us keep our balance. Those suffering from age-related hearing loss tend to have, along the cochlea, abnormal or degenerated hair cells, which, as extremely delicate sensory organs deep inside the head, are crucial to proper hearing. From the hair cells, electrical impulses shoot along the auditory nerve to the brain for final processing.

Disturbances within these channels of the ear can be classified by hearing specialists as either conductive hearing loss or neurosensory (nerve-type) hearing loss. The first includes hearing loss due to an ear infection, a punctured eardrum, or an excessive buildup of earwax, which will cause the structures in either the outer or middle ear to malfunction. As a result, the ear's ability to pick up and carry sound vibrations to the inner ear is hampered. Fortunately, conductive disorders can be medically or surgically treated and cured. Of these conductive problems, earwax buildup is particularly common among older people.

Oddly, both the wax and hairs inside our ears have evolved over millennia in part to discourage insects from nesting and laying eggs, of all things, in our ear canals. But the wax, while necessary, can cause problems, and occasional cleaning of the ear canal by a physician may be necessary to prevent impaction.

"In our program," says Cheryl Hamat, 32, a speech/language pathologist in the communicative disorders department of Rehabilitation Hospital in Honolulu, "our audiologists check to see that nothing is blocking the auditory stimulus—like earwax. It is amazing how many individuals fear going to a physician when they have a problem that is medically treatable. They don't realize that the problem can be just impacted wax."

Tougher to correct are hearing disorders that have to do with how sounds are processed and sent to the brain. These are grouped under the rubric of neurosensory hearing loss. Though it often can be caused by diseases such as German measles and mumps, by antibiotics, or by tremendously loud noises, probably the most widespread cause of neurosensory hearing loss is aging.

Even as his earlobes have grown with the help of age and gravity, so too has a man in his 50s begun to lose some discrimination in his hearing. While great variation in hearing ability exists among the aging, in most cases the first loss of hearing occurs in the higher pitch tones (or frequencies) in the soprano range and above.[3] Sounds or tones that have lower pitch generally are better heard. This age-related loss of hearing is called presbycusis (of Greek origin from *presby-,* meaning "old," plus *cusis,* meaning "ear"), and it mostly, but not exclusively, affects those over 60 years of age. Presbycusis is caused by the normal aging of the hearing nerve in the inner ear, for which there is no cure or effective medical treatment yet available. By age 65, some 5 percent of all adults have a recognizable hearing impairment. As one might expect, this percentage rises with age. At last count, more than 16 million Americans had some noticeable hearing impairment, most commonly presbycusis.[4] Most of the hearing aids in this country are worn to help correct hearing loss due to age-related presbycusis. While the various forms of hearing aids cannot actually *cure* presbycusis, they can help compensate for broken-down hair cells of the cochlea. In a degenerated state, these tiny cells can only send rather weak or distorted electrical impulses to the brain.

As Jack Botwinick, professor of psychology at Washington University, writes in *Aging and Behavior,* "While the decline with age in hearing tones lower than 1000 Hz [hertz being the frequency of one cycle per second] is slight—it is only about five decibels from age 25 to 50 years—it is progressive; that is, the decline is somewhat greater, for example, between ages 75 and 85 than it is between 25 and 35. Presbycusis becomes readily apparent after age 50 with pitches above 1,000 Hz. As the frequencies are increased, loudness levels must be raised progressively for the older person to hear the tones at all."[5] Botwinick points out that men at age 50 often have a slight hearing loss of 17 decibels or more with tones in the 4,000 hertz range—the equivalent of the highest note on the piano. At age 75, the loss on average is about 47 decibels. This decline in hearing with age tends to be more dramatic among men than women, for reasons not completely understood, although exposure to louder workplace environments might have some bearing on the disparity. One reassuring note: For pragmatic purposes high-tone hearing loss for frequencies above 4,000 hertz does not have much of an effect on the average man's life-style.[6]

WHAT EAR EXPERTS LOOK AND LISTEN FOR

At Rehabilitation Hospital's communicative disorders clinic in Honolulu, as well as hearing clinics across the mainland, physicians who specialize in treating disorders of the ear, often called otologists, examine patients on a referral basis. The relationship between otologists and audiologists echoes that of ophthalmologists and optometrists (see chapter 4). Otologists typically concentrate on detecting disease and treatment, while audiologists, who are licensed but are not medical doctors, for the most part measure and evaluate hearing abilities. Audiologists also help people select hearing aids.

The two tests most commonly performed in hearing clinics are a pure-tone hearing test and impedance audiometry. In the pure-tone test, a person sits inside a specially equipped soundproof room where he dons a set of earphones. The audiologist then plays through an "audiometer" a series of pure tones that range in frequency from 125 to over 8,000 hertz. Because these sounds are in a larger frequency range than the 500-to-4,000-hertz range of most speech, pure-tone testing can provide more refined information to the clinician than an orally administered test. Based on a person's responses, audiologists plot the results on an audiogram, which is the individual's personal "hearing map." Clinicians typically follow the mechanical part of this test with an oral test of sorts by reading lists of words softly, loudly, and in a normal voice to the person in the booth.

Probably the biggest drawback of the pure-tone test, audiologists say, is that it requires a forthright, patient response, which can depend at times on the confidence of the person being tested. Some elderly people, for instance, may not respond to certain sounds during the pure-tone test because they are not "certain" they heard a particular cue. They may prefer to err on the side of caution by not responding, rather than by raising a hand and being "wrong."

The other common procedure conducted at most hearing clinics is impedance audiometry, which is inherently more objective than pure-tone testing. Impedance audiometry measures how well each part of the middle ear functions as sound waves pass through the central auditory pathways. Some older people are affected by a shrinking supply of blood to the brain that impairs the auditory pathways; impedance audiometry will pick up this impairment. It is used primarily, however, to look for disease.

One disease of the ears causes young adults and middle-aged people to appear to have hearing that is aging before its time. This is called otosclerosis, and it is thought to have been responsible for Beethoven's progressive hearing loss. The bone surrounding the inner ear turns spongy and continues to grow abnormally; one's hearing is irrevocably affected. But unlike presbycusis, otosclerosis is not a normal consequence of aging.

If, after examination, a hearing aid is required, the patient can choose from among four different types that are usually available. These are identified by where they are worn—behind the ear, all in the ear, eyeglass aids, and body aids. Basically, a hearing aid is a miniature flesh-colored amplification system consisting of a microphone, amplifier, battery, speaker, and volume control. Most also include a separate ear mold that fits in the ear to prevent sound from "leaking" out of the ear when the aid is in operation (the all-in-the-ear aid has the ear mold built in).

Hearing aids are miniscule, but their cost is not. They generally run between $300 and $650; cosmetic differences account for much of the variation in price.

BEYOND HEARING AIDS

"Because of increased longevity," says Herman Hertzberg, a New York City audiologist, "there is going to be a lot of research in this area. It is already on the way." Summarizing recent trends in hearing research, Hertzberg says the newest testing equipment that has been developed is "totally nonsubjective." One new gauge, Brainstem-Evoked Response Audiometry (BERA), works by picking up and measuring the brain waves that are formed in the processing of sound. BERA is not helpful in measuring all types of hearing loss, and it is not widely used in the average hearing testing center, but it has started to make its way out of experimental labs and into leading otologists' and audiologists' offices. Another development is the cochlear implant, an artificial hearing device, which, as the name implies, is surgically implanted in the cochlea. Both Hertzberg and Hamat of Rehabilitation Hospital cite the cochlear implants as the most exciting area of research into hearing devices that are more sophisticated than the standard hearing aids.

With so much talk in the business and medical communities about high technology developments, leaders in the hearing-services field are understandably eager for news of some kind of artificial ear. Even as hearing aids get smaller, more durable, and more powerful, and even as cochlear implants become more common, the search continues for an even more effective device to correct hearing loss. Gerald Merwin, a researcher at the University of Florida, for instance, reported in 1981 that he had replaced the microscopic bones of the inner ears of mice.[7] The bones implanted were made of "Bioglass," a sturdy ceramic material that has the welcome property of not being rejected by the body's immune system. No concise predictions concerning use of the artificial inner-ear bone material implants in humans have yet come out of Merwin's laboratory. However, his and other similar experiments bear close watching.

Meanwhile, at the University of Utah Medical Center (where Barney Clark underwent his historic artificial-heart implant operation) and at Columbia University, researchers have been making platinum wire devices that simulate branches of the normal inner ear. When inserted, the devices go one leap beyond cochlear implants. Attached behind the ear, the wires are fed into the inner ear where they deliver computer-driven electrical signals to the brain so that deaf persons can "hear" loudness, rhythm, and some degree of pitch.[8] Still, human speech cannot yet be understood with the aid of the device.

Recent psychological and neurological research has also suggested some surprising facts about aging and hearing. A few years ago, in an experiment conducted on college students, Dr. Philip G. Zimbardo, a Stanford University psychologist, found that when otherwise healthy individuals were told under hypnosis that they had a hearing loss, they exhibited paranoid tendencies. Zimbardo believes that much of the behavior that is commonly called paranoid among the elderly is misdiagnosed, or at least mislabeled. Zimbardo and his team found after months of carefully designed experiments that when hypnotized students "experienced" significant hearing loss, they tended to project behavioral symptoms of paranoia that resembled those exhibited by the aged—including delusions of grandeur or persecution. A newspaper account of these findings, which were later more formally published in *Science* (June 25, 1981), reported that Zimbardo believes many elderly people have symptoms of paranoia because they have been losing their hearing but were not aware of it.[9]

Another suggestive opinion comes from Dr. Frank Wilson, a California neurologist, who believes that making music can have a beneficial effect on one's hearing at any age. Admittedly, learning to play the cello at age 55 will not cure presbycusis, yet, according to Wilson, "the musician can continue to improve, no matter what his age. He may not be able to do some things as he gets older, when he gets arthritis and everything else, but he can continue to enjoy a love affair with his instrument."[10] Wilson, a boyish 44, with shaggy brown hair and a warm smile, is chief of the Department of Neurology at the Kaiser-Permanente Medical Center in Walnut Creek, Calif., and a special consultant to the American Music Conference, a nationwide, nonprofit organization. Wilson's neurological research suggests a correlation between music study and muscular development, coordination, mental concentration, sense of timing, memory skills, and visual, vocal and, finally, aural development.

Writing on the subject of age in his *Esquire* Ethics column in April, 1981, Harry Stein told of one aging fellow who seemed to be handling a hearing problem resolutely:

> There, one evening not long ago, on Johnny Carson's couch, sat Jimmy Stewart, acting like a caricature of Jimmy Stewart. Still boyish-looking, endlessly befuddled in that chipper way, he hemmed and stuttered through ten minutes of small talk, and then Carson, obviously charmed, departed from his question sheet. "Do you feel old?" he asked.
>
> "Sure!"
>
> The answer, so unexpected in its lack of equivocation, brought forth a big laugh, which seemed to baffle the actor even more. "I . . . I look in the mirror and I'm *old,*" Stewart explained.
>
> And a moment later he went on to prove it, telling of his contemporaries, their hearing gone, futilely trying to engage in conversation. "I can stand so much, and then I say"—suddenly he jerked a hearing aid from his ear—"Get one; they work!" . . .
>
> We're simply not used to that kind of candor in television, certainly not on a talk show, and absolutely not on the subject of aging. On a medium that has become the principal instrument for promoting the ideal of personal youth, the sight of an elderly person addressing himself to the subject of physical deterioration and being witty about it to boot is about as surprising as it would be to catch Michael Landon abusing a puppy.

Broadcast over the television airwaves, the message came in loud and clear.

MAINTENANCE: THE EARS

Unless there is evidence of hearing loss or a family history of hearing disorders, a checkup every few years is often enough for most adults. After 55, a hearing examination every year is a good idea.

Professionals also recommend common sense in ear care to keep ears healthy:

- To clean the outer ear, use a cotton swab. Never insert the swab into the ear canal, as it will push earwax down deeper into the ear. Some people produce excessive earwax and must have it cleaned out by a physician.

- To prevent your ears (actually the Eustachian tubes) from plugging up when flying, try yawning and chewing gum or sucking on mints (to induce swallowing). Avoid alcoholic beverages before or during the flight: Alcohol will cause the mucous membranes in the Eustachian tubes to swell. If you're flying with a cold or sinus trouble, the mucous membranes are probably already swollen. Use a nasal decongestant before the plane's descent.

- Exposure to excessive noise can cause irreversible damage to the ears. When using a power saw or lawn mower, wear ear plugs or ear muffs. If you use earphones, keep your stereo tuned to the lower- or mid-volume level.

- Protect your ears against the elements; they are particularly vulnerable to frostbite and sunburn. Cover your ears in the winter and apply a strong sunscreen to the tops and backs of them when you're out in the sun.

At last count, more than 16 million Americans had some noticeable loss of hearing. The symptoms below are indicative of a hearing loss in its early stages. People over the age of 60 are more prone to develop hearing loss, but these symptoms can appear at any age:

- A consistent difficulty in conducting a telephone conversation might indicate that you rely more than you realize on reading lips to "hear."

- Ringing, buzzing, or whistling sounds that others can't hear are internally produced, and are symptoms of tinnitus, itself a symptom of many ear disorders.

- Leaning forward to hear is equivalent to squinting to see better: Your body tries reflexively to help the impaired organ.

- Frequently asking others to repeat themselves or giving inappropriate responses because you've misunderstood is indicative of a hearing loss, as is difficulty in locating the source or even direction from which a sound is emanating.

If any of these occur on a regular basis, have your ears examined. Much loss of hearing can be simply corrected with a hearing aid.

The Mouth and Its Telling Role

Unquestionably, one of life's little pleasures in adulthood comes when the dentist flicks off the fluorescent light aimed at your face and tells you, as you lie back in the chair like an astronaut, that once again you have no cavities. An unexpected benefit of age is that the enamel on your teeth toughens, and you tend to develop fewer cavities. But as anyone who takes a good look at a smile knows, there is more to a mouth than teeth. Which means there is more to maintain and protect, where the oral cavity is concerned. After age 30, the focus on mouth care should shift away from concern about cavities toward an enlightened concentration on the gums. Although the prime cause of losing teeth in those under 30 is decay, the main reason for tooth loss in those 30 and over is gum disease.

The decrease in cavities is partly the result of preventive dental care—which really only began in the 1950s—and partly the result of the addition of fluoride to municipal water supplies. While the babies of the baby boom generation were wailing and screaming as newborns, some concerted dental research was making noise of its own. In 1955, three ten-year pioneering studies of water fluoridation and tooth decay came to a close with good news for the future.

In December of that year, *The Journal of the American Dental Association* reported that in the fluoridated communities of Grand Rapids, Mich., Newburgh, N.Y., and Brantford, Ontario, the overall rates of children's tooth decay showed a nearly 60 percent drop when compared with prefluoridation findings. "The results from these three cities evidence the gradual transmission of the theory of fluoridation into a scientific law," wrote Dr. H. Trendley Dean of Chicago, secretary of the association's Council on Dental Research.[1] For example, ten-year-old children in Newburgh, N.Y., were shown to have an average of just over two decayed, missing, or filled teeth compared with children in neighboring Kingston, N.Y. (which did not have fluoridated water), who had just over four teeth that were decayed, missing, or filled. But there was still much work to be done. Scientific studies were one thing; convincing actual cities and states to go the fluoride route was quite another. Up through the 1960s, city councils fought over what—if anything—to add to the water, how much, and when. It took New York City ten years from the completion of the Newburgh-Kingston study to start fluoridating its water.

The Diminishing Tooth

Eating gradually files down a tooth, but not enough to make any significant difference to anyone under the age of 200. The problem is keeping the tooth, and it is one problem a man can control. Despite the fact that the amount of enamel on the surface will decrease with age and the layer of dentin underneath will become more translucent, most tooth and gum decay is a result not of aging but of neglect and disease. The average 70-year-old man today has lost a third of his teeth; because of fluoridated water and better dental care, his descendants should fare better.

Age 30: 2 teeth missing
Age 50: 7 teeth missing
Age 60: 8 teeth missing
Age 70: 10 teeth missing

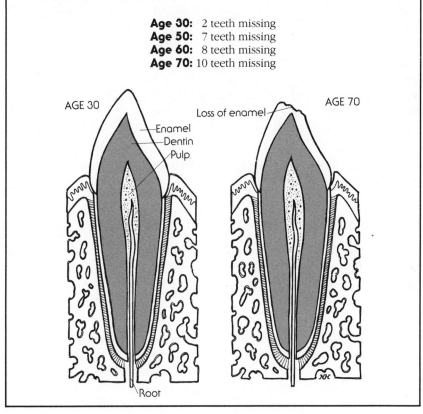

There were doubters in 1965, and there are doubters today, but they don't happen to be among the elite of the dental profession.

"Cavities are rapidly becoming a thing of the past," says Dr. Roger Stambaugh, professor in the department of periodontics at the University of Southern California in Los Angeles. "The dental profession is moving away from filling teeth to becoming more involved in cosmetics, periodontics, and oral surgery." Stambaugh believes there is a valid connection between the 1955 fluoride results and the shift he sees today. In regard to aging and dental health, drinking fluoridated water in one's youth can only bode well for one's teeth in adulthood. "We're already seeing a tremendous impact," he says. "It looks like more of the children of the Fifties will have their teeth when they're older, and fewer will have dentures and removable prosthetics." This is already happening. Dental schools in various cities are having trouble these days finding patients who need complete sets of dentures for dental students who need to make them as part of their state licensing exams. People just aren't losing as many teeth as they used to.

Dr. Robert Gottsegen, professor of dentistry and director of the division of periodontics at Columbia University's School of Dental and Oral Surgery, agrees that this is a strong future trend. "You will see more teeth with fewer cavities," he says. What Gottsegen and his colleagues can't say, though, is that the addition of fluoride to drinking water will result in a decrease of common gum disease as the children of the baby boom reach middle age. Periodontal disease is still a big problem, and baby boomers are just now having to pay more attention when the dentist talks about gingivitis, periodontitis, and plaque control.

TEETH AND GUMS TOGETHER

When a boxer connects a right hook to the jaw of his opponent, he typically drives his gloved fist into *two* jaws, the upper and the lower, or the maxilla and the mandible. The arch of the teeth in the upper jaw is generally larger than the lower jaw, as are the upper teeth themselves. When glove meets flesh, the aggressor usually doesn't knock any teeth out of his opponent's mouth. This is not only because the opponent wears a protective mouthguard, but also because teeth are composed of tough, bonelike dentin and are coated with enamel, the hardest substance of the body.

An adult who has not lost any teeth should have 32 of them, each consisting of three parts: the crown (the visible portion), the neck (embedded in the gum), and the roots (the anchors). Deep inside the tooth is the pulp, where blood and nerves reside. If a cavity is the cause of a toothache, this means the decay has been attacking the tooth's coating for some time and has reached the sensitive pulp beneath. Deeper still, the roots of the tooth are anchored firmly to the jawbone, fastened by strands of gum tissue, or periodontal membrane and ligament. The roots are coated with cementum, a bony material slightly softer than enamel.

Over the years, chewing gradually files down the crowns, but not enough to make any significant difference. Yet, hard as it is, enamel does diminish a bit each decade after age 30, and the layer of dentin underneath becomes more translucent. Nothing can be done about that, but keeping the tooth is something over which a man can exert some control.

HEALTHIER OLDER TEETH AND GUMS

Not surprisingly, pummeled boxers are not the only people who suffer from sore mouths. Gum disease and the frequent minor bleeding it causes is the bane of middle-aged citizens from all walks of life. Professional golfer Calvin Peete, 40, was feeling pretty good after firing a first-round, four-under-par 68 in the 1983 Georgia-Pacific Atlanta Golf Classic. The next day, however, he shot an unimpressive 75. "It's just that I have this gum infection that flared up and I lost my concentration," he said. "I just wanted to get the round over with and get in for some medication."[2] If Peete had devoted as much attention over the years to gum-cleansing strokes as golf strokes, he might not have been so distracted in Atlanta. However, the medication must have helped. Twenty-four hours later, in the third and final round, he shot a nine-under-par and won the tournament by two strokes. With his gums and clubs under control, Peete smiled widely for photographers as the event drew to a close. He was $72,000 richer.

Peete is one of millions of Americans who suffer from periodontal disease. According to a 1983 report prepared for the American Academy of Periodontology, more than 90 percent of the population will get some form of gum disease during their lives, making it second only to the common cold among the most prevalent illnesses.[3] In short, of 125 American adults who still have their teeth, about 100 have some form of gum trouble, most of which is undiagnosed.

Writing in *Harper's,* David Owen pointed out, "As virtually any dentist will tell you, there is enough untreated dental disease already in existence to keep the world's dentists busy until they all drop dead."[4] More than 30 million Americans are said to suffer severe cases of periodontal disease, and together they spend $350 million annually to treat it. It is interesting to note that there are only some 3,500 trained periodontists in the country available to treat those 30 million-plus advanced cases.

Perhaps this is why Paul Keyes's regimen for treating gum disease has received widespread attention recently. At 67, Keyes sits as chairman of the International Dental Health Foundation in Reston, Va., which he set up with an associate in 1981 after an eight-year stint on the Harvard faculty and after

27 years of research with the National Institute of Dental Research. While still at NIDR, Keyes (rhymes with guise) began touting an alternative treatment for bleeding gums and periodontal disease. Today, he concedes that his ideas are not even new, and remarks that their elegance lies in their conservatism—not in newfangled, "radical" dental thought.

Yet his method seemed new enough to the editors of *American Health,* who devoted four pages of its premier issue in 1982 to an article called "To Avoid $2,000 Gum Surgery, Acid Breath, and Loose Teeth." In it, writer Judith E. Randal described the Keyes method as an alternative to expensive and often painful oral surgery performed to control advanced cases of gum disease. At the heart of the Keyes method are three simple measures: brushing with a homemade paste of baking soda and hydrogen peroxide; rinsing the mouth with a salt solution using a water irrigation device such as a Water Pik; and regular professional cleaning and microscopic evaluation.

After the article ran, dozens of dentists, including periodontal specialists, called the magazine to praise or complain about the Keyes method or the article. Eventually *American Health* ran a follow-up report that listed more than 200 dentists in 28 states and the District of Columbia who support and practice the "salt-and-soda" method.[5] In the normally staid world of dentistry, however, the debate still rages: Is Keyes's method truly an alternative to surgery for diseased, aging gums?

In 1983 William Killoy, of the University of Missouri, Kansas City, summarized four studies of 72 patients at four different universities, concluding that the Keyes technique might not be as effective as had been claimed. "I believe this is leading the patients and dental profession into a false sense of security," he said. "Baking soda is not the magic pixie dust some of the lay writers would like you to believe."[6]

"They're arguing about the wrong thing," Keyes says of his critics. "They're arguing over how you treat the defects." Keyes wants them to look more closely at the causes of periodontal disease. "We have gotten tremendous coverage," he says, ticking off such publications as the *Saturday Evening Post, Woman's Day,* and *People.* "And I keep asking myself, Why is there so much interest? The reason is that the public has been disappointed. They are damn disgusted with what has been happening to them. The periodontist is not to blame. . . . It is the general dentists who have not detected all this trouble earlier. They have passed the buck. Their diagnostic procedures haven't picked up the disease."

For an effective dental cleaning and examination, Keyes urges a visit to a dentist who uses a phase contrast microscope, which, because it has a video display screen, allows the patient as well as the dentist to see the bacteria in

A Solution in a Solution?

The method of plaque control recommended by Paul Keyes, D.D.S., chairman of the International Dental Health Foundation in Reston, Va., consists of the following steps:

1. Have an examination, a thorough cleaning and scaling, and if possible have the dentist (or periodontist) use a phase contrast microscope to detect and chart the presence of excess bacteria.

2. Once a day, mix about two tablespoons of baking soda with a small amount of hydrogen peroxide to make a thick paste. (Epsom salts can be substituted for baking soda if high blood pressure is a factor.)

3. Massage the paste in and around the front and back of the teeth and gums, as well as in the crevices between the teeth, using a rubber applicator or stimulator—the kind often found on the end of toothbrushes.

4. Brush the front, sides, and back of the teeth and gums with a toothbrush.

5. Add salt to a glass of water until it is saturated, and pour the solution into a water irrigation device such as a Water Pik.

6. Rinse the front and back of the teeth and gums with the solution; then run clean water through the device to flush the salt residue from its parts.

Those who do all this diligently say it takes no longer than ten minutes a day. Some who don't like the aftertaste of baking soda and peroxide brush their teeth afterwards with "regular" toothpaste.

Whether or not it effectively controls gum disease, baking soda is incontrovertible as an effective dentifrice. As an antacid, it effectively neutralizes the corrosive acids found on the teeth and gums, freshens the breath, and polishes the teeth.

the mouth. Keyes believes the most important part of preventing gum disease is controlling the spread and growth of bacteria. Most mainstream dentists do not use the microscope. To hear Keyes state the problem, it seems an uncomplicated task. Find the bugs in the mouth. Kill them daily. Control the accumulation of plaque.

Everybody has plaque, even the people you sometimes see in the office who trundle off to the restroom after lunch, toothbrush and toothpaste in hand. Plaque forms within 12 to 24 hours after the last brushing, especially in the areas toothbrush bristles can't quite clean. A soft, colorless material, plaque sticks to the teeth particularly along the gum line. When it accumulates and hardens, it mineralizes into calculus, a, sticky substance and irritant that promotes the growth of still more plaque. Unchecked, relatively common and painless bouts of swollen gums, gingivitis, can turn into more serious cases of periodontitis. Eventually, the bacteria in plaque can corrode the gum tissues to the point where the gums and teeth start to separate. When gum disease is advanced, the result is a host of unwanted periodontal pockets, described in this manner by New York dentist Vincent M. Cali: "What we have in a periodontal pocket is an extremely narrow space that's almost impossible to clean, which is filled with bacterial wastes and other debris suspended in a slimy solution."[7]

Most dentists would agree with Keyes that cleaning plaque from the teeth and gums is an essential part of dental care. Even Robert Gottsegen, perhaps Keyes's most outspoken critic, says that scaling is part of any sound treatment to remove and control bacteria. Gottsegen, a 1938 graduate of Columbia University, is slightly built, and wears a knee-length medical coat as he talks in his cramped office at Columbia's dental school. Of Keyes, he says: "He has latched onto rediscovering the wheel." Like Keyes, Gottsegen insists that bacteria—not aging—cause gum disease, but, he says, that is not a new idea. And, he adds, it is not necessary to use a phase microscope, since a good periodontist is able to detect the presence of microbial organisms by probing alone. But his major argument with Keyes is that his technique wrongly implies that oral surgery can be eliminated.

Keyes insists, "We're not anti surgery. In its place it can be very useful, but I prefer to start with conservative measures."[8]

It is not the intent of this chapter to try to solve the ongoing debate, but rather to report the merits of good gum care that experts agree upon, and to promote better maintenance of the teeth and gums through middle age. Because of contributions put forth in dentistry and oral surgery in recent decades, the public simply has more choices for mouth care today. If the choices stir up debate in the dental profession, there is still the common ground of better oral hygiene to stand on. As Dr. Morris Yarosh, an instructor at the Mount Sinai dental school and a general practitioner in New York City, says, "Think of all the people who are jogging every day for their bodies. What if they put the same effort into taking care of their teeth?"

In addition to regular professional cleaning and regular brushing, dentists almost universally recommend daily flossing as part of any good dental care plan, regardless of one's age, because flossing helps defend teeth and gums against plaque and periodontal pockets. Some dentists also suggest that in addition to brushing one's teeth, one should use a tongue depressor, popsicle stick, or toothbrush to scrape additional troublesome bacteria from the tongue.

The point of all home care is for normal, healthy adults to be able to keep their teeth well into their 50s, 60s, 70s, and beyond—and, if possible, to avoid the pain and expensive treatments or surgery associated with periodontal disease. A generation ago, millions simply assumed that they would need dentures in old age. It was assumed that gum disease was part of the aging process. We now know better.

AGING YOU CAN SEE, TASTE, AND HEAR

Even among people who avoid the various forms of gum disease, certain age-associated changes will occur in the mouth. Besides the gradual attrition of enamel, teeth slowly change color from off-white to near-yellow because of a steady accumulation of brown pigment. While this may not be welcome, aesthetically, the added pigment helps the tooth become more resistant to decay. At the same time the tooth is getting extra protection on the outside, on the inside it is getting weaker. As early as age 40, the blood vessels in the tooth pulp tend to become less efficient, more clogged and arteriosclerotic. About the only thing positive to be said about *these* changes is that as blood flow and nerves diminish within the teeth, future dental work could be less painful than it was in one's childhood.

However, even that is debatable. Dr. Sidney L. Horowitz of Columbia University's School of Dental and Oral Surgery contends that among those who undergo orthodontic treatment (many of whom are his patients in private practice), middle-aged adults have a rather low pain threshold. He says, only half in jest, "You just can't ratchet them up the way you can with children." Horowitz treats a number of adults for malocclusion (abnormal bite) by applying braces to the teeth. Referring to the rise in the number of adults who wear braces, he notes that both men and women are tremendously concerned with making a good impression in their jobs. In addition to its cosmetic value, correcting malocclusion, he says, is part of good preventive care. "I hesitate to say that malocclusion leads to periodontal disease," says Horowitz, "but on the other hand we can set a patient up so that, given a reasonable amount of home care, it will be easier for him to maintain good health. There is no question that crooked teeth are more difficult to clean effectively."

Eventually, however, no matter how clean the teeth may be, even well-tended gums recede. Given enough time, the roots of the teeth can be exposed, cavities can again become a problem, and root decay can occur. So while it's true that most tooth and gum decay is the result of neglect and disease, for a man in his 70s or 80s, time itself may be a cause.

Protected by the teeth, gums, and an ever-present coating of saliva, the tongue holds up pretty well over the years. Inevitably, however, as a man

Taste and Talk

As a man ages, he tastes less. When he's 30, each tiny elevation on his tongue (called a papilla) has 245 taste buds. By the time he's 80, each has only 88 left. His mouth gets drier as the mucous membrane secretes less. His voice begins to quaver, apparently because he loses some control over his vocal cords. He talks more slowly, and his pitch rises as the cords stiffen and vibrate at a higher frequency: After 50 his speaking voice rises about 25 hertz (cycles per second). If it was once pitched at C below middle C, it will have risen to E-flat.

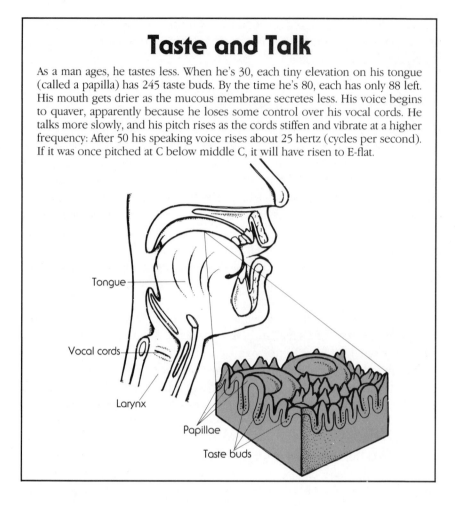

Tongue

Vocal cords

Larynx

Papillae

Taste buds

ages, he grows to taste less than he did as a child. In a normal man of 30, there are some 245 taste buds on each tiny elevation of his tongue, or papilla. When he reaches 80, each papilla will have an average of only 88 taste buds. That doesn't necessarily mean he tastes only a third of what he did as a child, but it does signify a noticeable taste loss. Taste buds atrophy in old age and then fail to regenerate. Then, too, mucous membranes begin to secrete less with age, drying out the tongue and mouth. But when one considers that everything that enters the mouth moves over the tongue, it is remarkable that the healthy mouth at 80 still contains a myriad of taste buds and that the sensation of taste is still very much alive.

Behind the tongue, at the very back of the mouth and below, are the pharynx, the epiglottis, and the larynx, which enable us, respectively, to breathe, to eat, and to speak. The larynx houses the Adam's apple and the vocal folds, which in turn enclose the vocal cords. As a man ages, the pitch of his voice rises as the vocal cords stiffen and vibrate at a higher frequency than before.

The difference between a voice's pitch and frequency is that the pitch is an *interpretation* of the number of times the vocal folds, or membranes, rise and fall in one second, while the frequency is the *actual* rate of vibration of the vocal folds. As humans, we can interpret frequencies of sound that range from vibrations as slow as 16 hertz (cycles per second) to those as swift as 20,000 hertz.[9] Sounds below or above that range are undetectable to our ears. A low male voice has what is called a "pitch range of fundamental frequency" of 65 to 312 hertz, while for the sake of comparison the middle C note on a piano has a frequency of 256 hertz.

After age 50, a man's voice rises as many as 25 cycles per second, for example from a C to an E-flat in the octave below middle C. Speech and hearing experts say the reason for this is a decrease in the mass of vocal folds. The connective tissue and ligaments that make up the vocal folds and cords, respectively, eventually lose their elasticity. As a result, there is more jitter in the voice and more perturbation.

In sum, these are the changes one notices in an older man's voice: He speaks more slowly, his voice is higher, and it quavers a bit. They are gradual, barely perceptible, changes, although people trained in speech and voice therapy can guess a man's age fairly accurately just by listening to him speak. As for the man himself, he's likely to notice that his command over the pitch of his singing voice has diminished. Aiming for the D below middle C, for instance, his voice is likely to wobble. And, when he stands to refute an argument, he'll have to rely on reason more than vocal power. Nevertheless, he'll find that the voice of wisdom can afford to quaver a bit.

MAINTENANCE: THE TEETH

Here's the good news:

- Your teeth can last a lifetime.
- Dentures are not an inevitability.
- Periodontal disease can be prevented.

However, to realize your potential for a lifetime of dental health, a good dental program must be established.

- First, you should know that bacteria, not aging, is responsible for most gum disease and tooth loss. The buildup of debilitating plaque cannot be controlled completely at home. Depending on how rapidly tartar (hardened plaque) builds up on your teeth, you should see a dentist one to three times a year.
- Brush with a soft or medium bristled toothbrush at least twice a day. Replace your toothbrush when it loses its shape (usually once every three or four months).
- Floss at least once a day to remove plaque between the teeth.
- Some dentists recommend scraping the tongue with a tongue depressor or toothbrush to eliminate bacteria there.
- Others suggest rinsing with an antiseptic mouthwash twice a day for 30 seconds to help retard plaque formation.
- Meet the adult requirement for vitamin C: It can't prevent gum disease but a vitamin C deficiency can result in gum deterioration. Good sources are citrus fruits and juices, tomatoes, and dark-green vegetables.
- If it is impossible for you to banish sweets from your diet, choose natural sweets like fruit, or slippery sweets like flavored yogurt or ice cream. Stay away from sticky or chewy candies: They are ground into your teeth and can actually pull out fillings.
- Smoking results immediately in stale breath and ultimately in tobacco-stained teeth. Best solution: Don't smoke. But if you do, you can use "smoker's tooth polishes," which help reduce stains on the teeth.

Helping Bones
and Muscles
Through Time

$\mathbf{A}$s a 19-year-old rookie pitcher at spring training in 1955, Sandy Koufax of the then Brooklyn Dodgers was understandably edgy: "I was so nervous and tense I couldn't throw the ball for ten days," he told *The New York Times*. "When I finally started pitching, I felt I should throw as hard as I could. I wound up with an arm so sore that I had to rest for another week." Eight years later, in the throes of the National League Pennant Race, Koufax performed brilliantly, pitching his way to a record of 25 wins and only 5 losses. He struck out 306 batters in 311 innings and was named the National League's most valuable player. The "Man with the Golden Arm" went on to beat the New York Yankees twice in a swift four-game World Series sweep and won the 1963 Cy Young Award as outstanding pitcher in the Major Leagues. But in 1966, after striking out 317 batters and posting a 27-win, 9-loss record, Koufax retired from baseball because he feared he might permanently injure his arthritic left arm. He was 30 years old.

In X rays taken at the time, his left elbow appeared to belong to someone much older, perhaps a man in his 60s. Dr. Robert Kerlan, who was then orthopedic surgeon for the Dodgers, said the type of arthritis that plagued Koufax was osteoarthritis, believed to be caused by direct injury or constant abuse. (Considering that Koufax injured his already aching elbow in a slide into base in 1964, both causes seemed to apply.) Instead of the normal amount of synovial, or lubricating, fluid in the elbow joint, Koufax's arm contained an excess of this fluid, which caused swelling and throbbing pain through innings full of 90-mph fastballs and arcing curves. Eventually, Koufax lost mobility in the elbow, and his condition reached the point where he had to have the left sleeves of his coats shortened. Despite the repeated soaking of the elbow after each game, it became overwhelmingly painful, and he was forced to retire while still in his prime.

Sandy Koufax's case is anything but typical, but it highlights the kind of problem that can affect the bones and muscles of anyone who happens to live long enough. Everything about a man's joints and musculature becomes trickier to maintain with advanced age. His bones lose calcium, and become more brittle and slower to heal. Of the growth, development, remodeling, and repair functions normally handled by the body's skeleton, it is the reparative function that is most negatively affected by aging.

However, people who remain active tend to develop bodies that can effectively combat the effects of degeneration. Not long ago, Dr. Kerlan, who is now the orthopedic surgeon for the Los Angeles Lakers, offered some positive thinking in the battle against aging. While overuse can cause the kind of damage Kerlan had seen inflicted on Koufax's arm, Kerlan points out that reasonable, regular exercise is beneficial because it helps to increase bone mass over time. The reason? Coarse fibers of the bone enlarge in reaction to the stresses placed upon them. In an unofficial review of his patient list (excluding the Los Angeles Lakers), the noted orthopedic specialist says that middle-aged and older men are a rather hardy lot. Dr. Robert Addison, 61, a Chicago orthopedist who happened to intern with Kerlan years ago, concurs. And, he adds, a man's general physiology and mental state improve with activity when exercise is directed and productive. Addison, who created the Center for Pain Studies at the Rehabilitation Institute of Chicago, is also associate professor of orthopedic surgery at Northwestern University Medical School in Chicago. "Unless you use your body, it can literally waste away," says Addison. "Bones become more porous and more susceptible to damage. This, in brief, is aging."

In terms of the future elderly—those who are now in their 20s, 30s, and 40s—there are indications that aging will be thought of as a healthier process than it is today. The current generation of young adults and those in mid-life aren't quite so set on slipping into a sedentary sort of life. "Years ago," says Addison from his office at the Rehabilitation Institute, "when you were thirty-five or forty, you raised a family and did little in the way of exercise—like some sort of idiot. You adopted an old person's life-style." These days grandfathers go jogging.

Contrary to popular speculation, Kerlan hasn't noticed any increase in the number of stress fractures among still active aging men. That is not to say, though, that men in their 40s and 50s are invincible. "There are numerous soft tissue and joint problems," he says, particularly in the joints—where two ends of bones are joined by cartilage at a point of friction. The "articular" cartilage of elbows and knees, especially, tends to grow thinner with age.

Dr. Kerlan, quoted in an October, 1980, *Esquire* story, "The Knee," explained the knee's vulnerability. "The joint itself hasn't changed in millions of years," he said. "In the earliest skeletons found, the knee joints are pretty much the same as they are today. The fact is, the human anatomy is simply not constructed for the games men play today." Going one step further, Dr. James Nicholas, the New York orthopedist who operated on Joe Namath's knees four times, says that given the loads and torques it must handle, the knee is the most poorly constructed joint in the body. Perhaps that is why professional football players' knees tend to resemble, at times, Sandy Koufax's left elbow.

BONES OVER TIME

There are 200 distinct bones in the entire adult skeleton. Proportionally, the bones of the body average only about 14 percent of a man's total weight, assuming a man of average build of about 175 pounds. The 650 muscles of the human body, meanwhile, make up nearly 45 percent of a man's mass. In *Gray's Anatomy,* the bones are typically divided into four classes: long, short, flat, and irregular. For example, the femur, or thighbone, is considered a "long" bone (it happens to be the longest bone in the body). The bones of

The Less Flexible Joint

As he gets older, a man's bones lose calcium. They become more brittle and slower to heal. Relatively few men suffer from rheumatoid arthritis, but after 60, chances are good that a man will develop a less serious condition called osteoarthritis. Years of flexing have worn down and loosened cartilage around the joints; the presence of this stray cartilage, coupled with depleted lubricating fluid in the joints, makes for a slower-moving, stiffer man. Movement is further restricted by ligaments that contract and harden with age. The hardened ligaments are more liable to tear.

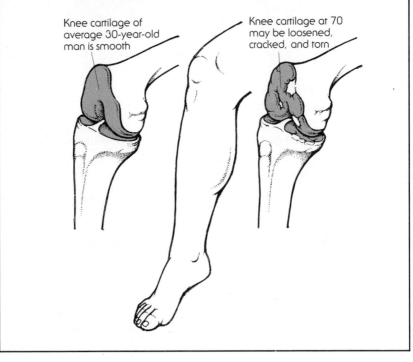

Knee cartilage of average 30-year-old man is smooth

Knee cartilage at 70 may be loosened, cracked, and torn

the ankle joint are considered short bones. An example of the so-called flat bones would be the shoulder blades. And vertebrae are probably the best known of the irregular, or mixed, bones. Together the four classes of bone form the skeleton.

The stuff of which bones are made might surprise the uninformed. In a young, healthy man of 30, about one-quarter of his bone weight is water. Another quarter of bone matter is organic material, largely connective tissue called collagen. The balance—nearly 50 percent of bone weight—is a hard mineral that is basically calcium phosphate. The tough outer portions of the bones are pinkish white in color. Inside, because of the blood vessels, nerves, and marrow, which combine to keep the matter healthy and strong, the color is deep red. Even if the bones were hollow cylinders, they would be pretty strong. In *The Human Body,* Isaac Asimov compares their strength to that of "a sheet of ordinary writing paper, rolled into a loose cylinder and bound so by a rubber band, [which] will support a fairly heavy textbook."[1] To carry the analogy a step further, think of weakened aging bones as erasable onionskin, which would have a tough time supporting a hefty textbook and could, in fact, be dented by a strong rubber band.

Men are typically taller than women because their long bones tend to grow for longer portions of the life cycle than do women's bones. A man's bones are the thickest and strongest from the ages of 21 to 30.[2] Around age 40, men and women begin to lose bone mineral, but at different rates. In most cases, a woman's bones will weaken much sooner than a man's, partly because of hormonal differences. Researchers in the fields of orthopedics and bone metabolism don't have all the answers about the causes, yet they report that many more women than men suffer from osteoporosis. This condition primarily affects postmenopausal women and elderly men, and can briefly be described as one in which the bones do not properly absorb needed calcium, leading to atrophy and increased porousness of the bone tissue.

The result is a skeleton that is more susceptible to fractures, to loss of height, and to an uncomfortable, unsightly curvature of the spine as bones become more brittle. Of the 200,000 people in middle age or older who suffer broken hips each year, and the 100,000 people of similar age who break their wrists, at least half of them are likely to have osteoporosis as an underlying condition.[3] Yet, although many doctors continue to believe that osteoporosis is an unavoidable part of the aging process, others are beginning to view the condition as both treatable and preventable, as more is learned about what causes the loss of bone strength.

Many of the aging men who suffer from osteoporosis are alcoholics.

They can be treated successfully as long as they refrain from drinking, says Dr. Joseph M. Lane, associate professor of orthopedic surgery at Cornell Medical Center and chief of the Metabolic Bone Disease Service at the Hospital for Special Surgery in New York City. Lane recalls one male alcoholic who was treated with a calcium supplement and increased his bone mass four times. It was not, says Lane, an isolated incident: "Most people are less and less able to meet their calcium requirements as they age. If we could improve their diet, we could help them prevent [osteoporosis] from occurring." Vitamin D as well as calcium plays a significant role in the maintenance of bone strength.

The loss of bone mass may not seem an important problem to a man who is 65 years old, says Lane, but it should, considering that more and more people are living beyond their 60s and become increasingly vulnerable to leg and hip fractures.

THE BACK FIELD

If there is another part of the anatomy that tends to give an older man trouble, it is his back. In the United States, roughly 75 million people suffer from back problems, and some 7 million new sufferers are added every year.[4] The spine is a complex structure, and it has plenty of chances to go out of whack during a lifetime. It supports the trunk and houses the spinal cord, canal, and nerves. It is formed by 33 vertebrae piled one upon the other in a curving double-S shape, connected by discs and cartilage and ringed with layers of muscle. Ligaments, tendons, and muscles team up to keep the spine from collapsing and also allow the body to move. There are self-contained sacs of fluid in the circular discs that function as shock absorbers for the spine. Whenever you stretch—to sidle into a tight airplane seat or bend over to lace your shoes or lunge forward to catch a softball—some fluid is displaced from the discs. Eventually, the discs shrink and the vertebrae compress.

The back absorbs a lot of abuse in its mission of antigravity support. At its best, the back is generous about allowing a good bit of contorted body movement without long-lasting injury. But, after age 20, the blood supply of the discs starts to diminish, and by age 30, the growth cycle having been completed, there is no blood left. The discs from then on must get their nutrients only from lymph, the transparent fluid collected from various body tissues. This loss of nutrients is one reason why back injuries tend to heal more slowly in older men. Among middle-aged and older individuals, back

Height and the Compressed Spine

A man is able to withstand gravity only so long. As his muscles begin to weaken, his back will begin to slump. And as the discs between the bones of his spine deteriorate, those bones move closer together. The result: the inexorably shrinking man.

Age 30: 5′10″
Age 40: 5′9⅞″
Age 50: 5′9⅝″
Age 60: 5′9¼″
Age 70: 5′8⅞″

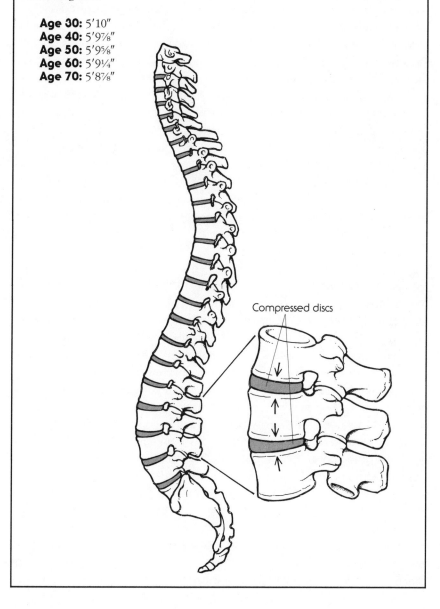

Compressed discs

injuries can too often lead to chronic pain. And every few years, it seems, new forms of therapy emerge to catch the eyes of those chronic sufferers.

The Wall Street Journal does not sell newspapers for the same reasons the *National Enquirer* sells newspapers. It was perhaps surprising, then, for some *Journal* readers when a cartoon of sorts appeared on the editorial page one day in the fall of 1982.[5] In it, a young woman was pictured hanging by her ankles in a tight leotard, with little explanation and this unhelpful headline: "See Pic Below, Read Text for Explanation." Subtitled "On Sports," the article, by Frederick C. Klein of the *Journal*'s Chicago bureau, explored the country's seeming fascination with a trendy item called Gravity Boots. As it happens, Gravity Boots aren't boots at all, but ankle collars made and marketed by Gravity Guidance, Inc., of Pasadena, Calif., a firm that promotes hanging upside down for a healthier back, healthier bones and joints, and a healthier frame of mind. This is called "inversion training" or "inversion therapy." Klein quoted Dr. Robert M. Martin, 73, the orthopedist who founded Gravity Guidance: "All day we're either standing or sitting with gravity pressing down on us. Hanging by the feet allows our bodies to decompress, our spines to be realigned, and our joints to separate. A little inversion goes a long way." After testing the product himself with the aid of an expert, a slightly skeptical Klein wrote, "The overall sensation was pleasing, my back felt better and I think my left knee was a bit less sore than it has been. I just might try it again sometime." After the article ran, Klein went out and spent "$100 and change" for a set of Gravity Boots and a bar to hang them from in his home. The ankle collars hadn't drastically altered his sense of well-being by the spring of 1983, though he did say they helped his children discover new forms of entertainment. On the other hand, they certainly haven't caused him any pain. Gravity Guidance didn't need Klein's halfhearted endorsement: In 1982 it sold more than $12 million worth of the product, and Paula Johnson, a corporate spokesperson, estimated 1983 sales at over $35 million. The Gravity Boots, or ankle collars, sell at the low end for about $100, while variations of the system can cost up to $900.

Most of the boom followed the 1979 movie *American Gigolo,* in which Richard Gere hoisted dumbbells, did sit-ups, and puffed a lot while hanging from a pair of ankle collars. He was sweating at the time (not to mention throughout the film), but he did not appear to be suffering from back pain. In fact, back pain sufferers are among those who claim that inversion therapy works. There is also a growing market for various types of inversion therapy systems among people who want to prevent back pain from ever occurring. One kind, called Back on Track, made by the Lossing Orthopedic Co., suspends the body from the waist instead of from the ankles. It costs about $600. With fitness and rehabilitation facilities increasing, and with many more scheduled in the future to accommodate middle-aged and older adults, inversion therapy is getting a close look from physicians and the health industry alike.

"We have had [inversion systems] at our center," says Dr. Robert L. Swezey, medical director and founder of the Arthritis and Back Pain Center in Santa Monica, Calif. "We found about fifty patients who wished to try inversion therapy under our observation. Ten went ahead and elected to rent their own units—and two people elected to stay with it for long-term therapy. We were unimpressed." Swezey warns that there are possible dangers arising from inversion training, and says that he would not recommend it for anyone with a detached retina, or for anyone who has a history of high blood pressure. Getting in and out of the apparatus can pose a problem for beginners or the elderly. For their part, the people at Gravity Guidance point out in the owner's guide that people with hypertension, retinal problems, or certain types of back problems are warned to refrain from inversion training without their doctor's approval. Several orthopedic and pain specialists believe that Gravity Boots and other products like them belong to the class of "vogue therapies." Dr. Robert Addison of Chicago, for one, says, "I can show you illustrations of inversion therapy in medical history texts dating back to 200 A.D. There's not much new in this world."

HELPING MUSCLES

The problems a man can have with his back are not by any means confined to the spine itself. According to Dr. Hans Kraus of New York, a world-reknowned expert on back ailments, more than 80 percent of all back pain is caused by muscular weakness, which is aggravated by muscular imbalance. Inside a 30-year-old healthy man's body, all the nearly 650 muscles team up to give the bones and joints mobility. They are made up of approximately 75 percent water, about 20 percent proteids (protein), about 2 percent fat, 2 percent salts (mainly potassium phosphate and carbonate), and about 1 percent carbohydrates and nitrogenous extractives.[6] Unused muscles, like bones, atrophy. With age, and the increased chances of immobility caused by illness or injury, muscles can quickly deteriorate. But even a healthy, active man loses muscle mass in time. And with it, he loses storage capacity for glycogen. Derived from carbohydrates, glycogen resides in the muscles and elsewhere until the body is called upon to act vigorously, such as in sports or in threatening situations. The loss of glycogen is one reason older people do not have as much endurance.

It has often been said that virtually all of man's lower-back problems can be traced to that point in evolution when the first hominid stood erect.[7] If we had continued along the evolutionary track as stooped-over, knuckle-walking, hunting primates, we would probably suffer far less back pain. Still, there is much that *homo erectus* can do to improve his posture and thus improve the musculature of the back. Writing in the December, 1981, *Esquire,* in "The Unracked Back," Thomas DeCarlo first suggests stretching before and after any athletic activity. Stretches of the hamstrings and hip flexor muscles should be especially helpful, because these muscles oppose the back muscles in activity and can help keep the machinery in tune. Abdominal and back muscles also are important ones to work on, at least three times each week. Bent-leg sit-ups and back arches are helpful. In terms of long-range fitness programs, swimming, gymnastics, ballet, and yoga generally are most effective in helping to take the burden off the lower back.

Nowadays, one of the most debilitating activities of man is sitting. When you sit, the height of your chair should allow your feet to be flat on the floor with your knees at or above hip height. By crossing your legs and using armrests, you can further reduce the stress placed on the curved spine. When possible, it is better for your back if you stand rather than sit, as long as you can move around a bit. At the local bar keep a foot on a barroom rail or stool. At work, emulate a boardroom full of the country's top corporate planners who over the years have taken to working while standing. C. Peter McColough, of Xerox Corp., is one of the many corporate chairmen who prefer to work without a chair. While McColough has used a stand-up desk for some 20 years, Xerox President David T. Kearns acquired one in 1981 to help his aching back. George Shinn, chairman and CEO of First Boston Corp., Roger Birk, chairman of Merrill Lynch & Co., and Fenwick Crane, chairman of the Family Life Insurance Co., are among other upright top execs following in the footsteps of Edward Allen Pierce, a founder of Merrill Lynch who worked standing up until he was 90.[8]

It is true there are many causes of back pain, but overworked muscles and slipped discs are the most common complaints. In the slipped, or "herniated," disc, the squishy pulp, or core, of the malleable disc bulges out past a ring of cartilage and puts pressure on the spinal canal and spinal nerves. To explain to patients how a disc ruptures, Dr. Ronald S. Taylor, 36, of Detroit's Troy-Beaumont Hospital tells them the shock-absorbing disc is like a jelly doughnut. He shows them a model skeleton he keeps on hand and says, "When the jelly squirts out, it puts pressure on the nerves." In surgery on the disc, the surgeon takes out the protruding jelly to get the stress off the spine. Today, fortunately, surgery and bed rest are not the only available remedies for herniated discs. (In the past, some 200,000 persons annually have had surgery to repair ruptured discs.[9])

In late 1982, however, the U.S. Food and Drug Administration approved the use of injections of chymopapain, an enzyme derived from the papaya plant, to treat slipped discs. "The drug, chymopapain, is for use in treating herniated lower-back discs when more conservative measures such as bed rest and traction fail," read the announcement. "It is intended to be injected into the disc in a hospital setting by physicians experienced in the diagnosis and treatment of lumbar disc disorders and specially trained in this particular injection procedure. In a clinical study of the drug involving 108 patients, the success rate relieving disabling pain was 75 percent."

Before the drug was approved, thousands of Americans used to go to Canada to receive chymopapain treatments. First used in treatment in 1963, chymopapain was developed by Dr. Lyman Smith, an orthopedist from Elgin, Ill. The substance resembles an ingredient found in meat tenderizers. Chymopapain dissolves protein as it acts, and when it is injected into the disc, it relieves pressure on the spinal nerves. The procedure is simpler than surgery and costs about one-third to one-fourth as much. But it is still controversial: Some people are allergic to chymopapain, and it is not 100 percent effective. According to Dr. Swezey of the Santa Monica Arthritis and Back Pain Center, it can only be injected once into a ruptured disc. Still, Swezey says: "I've referred patients to Vancouver for years. Chymopapain is useful in very selective cases."

As an alternative to conventional surgery, this drug promises to change —if not revolutionize—treatment for slipped discs throughout the land. But Dr. Taylor, among others, reminds men in their middle to later years that the best medicine for back problems is preventive. Weight control and regular exercise are excellent ways to prevent ruptured discs in the first place. When a man is out-of-shape, his back is forced to absorb extra stress. "Losing weight can easily take half the stress off the spine," Taylor says. "The back problem is an aging phenomenon," adds Dr. Joseph Lane of the Cornell Medical Center. "You need exercise to keep yourself supple." In an article in July, 1980, *Time* magazine quoted New York orthopedist Leon Root, who puts things even more bluntly when discussing lower-back pain, weakness, and exercise: "Seated across the desk from a patient, [Root] outlines the exercise routine, then picks up a small scalpel and hones it a few times on a small whetstone. 'Remember,' he says, 'if you don't want to be bothered with exercise, I also do surgery.' "[10]

WHEN ARTHRITIS CALLS

If it is any consolation to the aging man of the 1980s, the fossilized remains of dinosaurs show evidence of stiffened joints. Creaky joints were also apparently common in man's ancestor of the Neolithic Period around 6000 B.C. Arthritis, which causes so much misery among the aging, has had a long history. It affects more than 10 percent of the world's population, more than 30 million people in the United States alone. Of the various types of arthritis, the two most common forms are osteoarthritis—the affliction that caused Sandy Koufax's early retirement—and rheumatoid arthritis. The rheumatoid type is more serious and brings with it the threat of crippling. It can strike children and adults alike, and causes more pain and deterioration in the joints than does osteoarthritis. The rheumatoid type most often occurs in women aged 20 to 40. Doctors still do not completely understand its cause.

Osteoarthritis is the form of the disease referred to when one hears: "Everyone gets some arthritis if he lives long enough."[11] Rarely seen in those under 35, it is quite common in those over 65. As in Koufax's case, when osteoarthritis strikes, it tends to progress slowly at first. The cartilage, or tough shock-absorbing pads between two mobile bones, begins to degenerate and, finally, to show a series of cracks. The bones try to compensate by laying down extra calcium, but this is not a comfortable, acceptable substitute for the cartilage that has worn away with time. The body responds, angrily, with pain at the ends of the bone where it attaches to muscles and ligaments. The joint swells, with excess synovial fluid and bony spurs, or osteophytes. The swelling typically is followed by stiffness, the stuff of arthritis, then recurring but unpredictable pain.

Besides simple wear and tear, heredity contributes to the likelihood of contracting osteoarthritis. There simply are too many spry 70- and 80-year-olds running around to blame the onset of the disease on age alone. But how do you know if you might be among the future afflicted? Dr. Swezey of the Arthritis and Back Pain Center points out that with new uses of the CAT-scan and other improved scanning procedures, doctors can often see degenerative changes in a body that the owner has yet to feel. "You can't just look at a guy with gray hair and know that there is disc deterioration," he says. "You can't just say he has got arthritis in the knees. With newer procedures, we are getting all sorts of new information unleashed because almost everyone in their late forties and fifties has some problems in their joints. All the pathology shows up."

The downside of this increased scanning capability is that there is a danger of encouraging unnecessary surgery in the absence of severe pain. Having completed a 250-page text for clinicians on arthritis, therapy, and rehabilitation, Swezey decided that patients themselves need to know more about arthritis. He is now writing a book on the subject for laymen, which will stress the importance of guided stretching exercises to prevent and treat osteoarthritis.

In the absence of quantum leaps in arthritis treatment, researchers and physicians have concentrated on the best available methods of coping with painful joints. There are those who favor pain-killing drugs, others who opt for body massage, rhythmic breathing, relaxation, or mind control. Still others propose rejuvenation treatments with a somewhat controversial compound called Gerovital, or GH-3. Developed in Romania by Dr. Ana Aslan, GH-3 is said to stave off painful effects of arthritis by helping the body unleash the natural, helpful neurotransmitters of the brain.

Nevertheless, the common thread running through the various coping strategies is activity. Even Dr. Kerlan, who has followed the careers of aching athletes for decades, thinks exercise of a sustained, regular nature is beneficial. Though toe touches by themselves are no guarantee of increased resistance to the effect of age on bones, muscles, and joints, years of steady workouts seem to provide an insurance policy for the body. It is a fact that a full range of movement in the joints can be restored or maintained with controlled, rhythmic exercise, regularly performed.

"Look at the Japanese," says Dr. Lane. "They blow a whistle in the morning, do more exercises, and work some more. It would be wonderful if the big insurance companies in the U.S. would blow a whistle and let everybody exercise." Perhaps in this age of international competition, Theory Z management, jogging with personal stereos, and Toyota-General Motors joint ventures, we can take another cue from our Oriental neighbors.

ON FUTURE MATTERS OF MUSCULATURE

In a graffiti-strewn, unfashionable section of the upper Upper West Side of Manhattan, Dr. Andrew Bassett, professor emeritus of orthopedic surgery at Columbia University's College of Physicians and Surgeons, has been working on a cure for one of the most common injuries among older people. Bassett heads a clinic in which electrical stimulation is used to repair serious hip fractures that in the past have required total hip replacement.

By treating "nonunion" fractures with electricity, Bassett has helped unfurl new thoughts on the matters of regenerating bone growth in humans. In a pilot program that started in December, 1980, Bassett has successfully treated 36 patients with 41 hip fractures, reports an associate in the department of orthopedic surgery at Columbia. Concurrent studies using electrical current are under way at Good Samaritan Hospital in Baltimore, Rush-Presbyterian Medical Center of Chicago, and elsewhere, all of which are searching for causes of lost circulation that in turn leads to faulty repair of the bones. There is room for optimism here, when one considers that slow-healing, fragile bones have seemed to be an unavoidable aspect of aging.

Outside of the Columbia clinic, Dr. Bassett is a partner in a Fairfield, N.J., firm called Electro Biology, Inc. The company provides bone stimulators to physicians on a leasing basis. If a doctor feels his patient is particularly suited to this type of therapy, and if the patient can afford the $2,600 leasing fee, Electro Biology makes available a bone-healing device. With it come specific instructions and warnings: The firm reminds users that the device must be prescribed by a physician, and that it has been approved by the FDA for treating fractures resistant to healing by more conventional therapies.

Bone stimulators are already used by doctors who work with the U.S. Olympic Ski Team, and it is likely that the treatment may be accepted by the orthopedic establishment. The middle-aged, concerned about future brittle bones, can hope for better mending in years to come.

MAINTENANCE: BONES AND MUSCLES

Creaky joints and muscle aches afflict everyone at one time or another. But these vague complaints get more pronounced in later years because bones, muscles, and connective tissue begin to wear out. Bones lose calcium, become more brittle and slower to heal. Cartilage in such joints as the knee and the elbow thins, and the discs in the back become compressed. So what can you do? The answer is, no matter how old you are, develop good habits of diet and exercise and stick with them.

- Exercise regularly. Over time this will increase your bone mass and forestall brittleness. Any aerobic exercise you choose, when done faithfully, will help your bones as well as your muscles maintain their health.
- Most of the problems of stiffened joints and stooped posture can be prevented by doing some simple mobility exercises. These exercises, repeated ten times each, take about three minutes a day, and will ensure a supple body frame:
    1. Stand straight, arms by your sides. Raise arms up and around past your ears, then back and down to your sides; then circle back the other way. Breathe in on the up movement, out on the return.
    2. Hands on hips, bend to one side and then the other, keeping the movement fluid.
    3. Lift one knee and bend over, trying to get your forehead to your knee, while bending the standing leg slightly. Hold onto a chair back for support. Repeat on the other side. Exhale as you bend, inhale as you straighten.
    4. Feet wide apart, reach your hands down one leg toward your ankle. Let the weight of your body pull you down. Breathe into the stretch. Repeat on the other side.
    5. With feet wide apart and holding your thighs and pelvis still, raise your arms straight out in front of your chest. Swing them at shoulder level to the right, letting your left arm bend at the elbow. Repeat on the other side.
- Even an older person who has been inactive can do modifications of the above exercises while sitting in a chair.
- Since most back pain is the result of muscular weakness, it is therefore preventable. Try to get your muscles strong and supple *before* trouble develops. Concentrate on strengthening and stretching the hamstrings and hip flexor muscles, as well as the muscles of the torso. Work on the abdominals by doing bent-leg sit-ups and other stomach strengtheners.
- Borrow from yoga to stretch out the spine: Do the Plough (lie on your back with arms at your sides and slowly lift your legs back over your head; relax, with knees bent near your ears) and the Cobra (lie face down, palms at shoulder level, and slowly lift head, shoulders, and chest; then arch back).
- Regular workouts of swimming, gymnastics, ballet, and yoga are good for those who wish to avoid back trouble, because these activities stretch as well as strengthen muscles. Running, while good aerobically, compresses the muscles of the back.

(continued)

- Learn how to lift correctly. Never bend from the waist. Always bend the knees and squat. As you lift, keep your back straight and your stomach muscles tensed.
- Stand rather than sit, if you have a choice. If you have to sit, do it right. Pick a chair where your feet can rest flat on the floor, with your knees at or above hip level, and that supports your lower back. Cross your legs and use the armrests. Get up, walk around, and stretch periodically.
- Sleep on a firm mattress.
- It's very important to stretch before a workout to get the muscles ready for movement and to prevent injury. The proper method is to ease gently into poses that put a mild tension in your muscles, without pain, and then hold them for about 30 seconds. Do not warm up with bouncing stretches, which are more likely to cause rather than prevent injury. Be sure to stretch after you exercise as well.
- After the age of 40, get plenty of vitamin D and calcium to help make up for the mineral loss in your bones. Milk, which many adults assume they don't need, is an excellent source of vitamin D and calcium, as well as protein. Green leafy vegetables and sardines are also rich in calcium.
- Remember: There is no reason physiologically that a healthy man in his 70s cannot walk tall and feel fit. If he's stooped over and feels weak, it is because of inactivity, not age.

Sexuality and
the Sex Organs

Soaring high over Los Angeles en route to New York, banking expert Ron Stern* finds time to mull over prospects in his personal and professional life. As a financial counselor who often helps companies merge, he is used to boarding the red-eye flights between coasts or taking off at a moment's notice for Denver, Houston, or Chicago. Over the years, Stern, 46 and single, has had occasion to meet women in several cities, and to strike up relationships with some of them. Though he has never married, Stern doesn't discount the possibility forever. But not just yet. He is used to the single life, used to making love from time to time with different partners in different cities, as his travel schedule allows. But all is not always blissful, as the dark-haired and handsome six-footer casually allows. He knows he is getting older, and he wonders how long he can keep up the pace, especially in view of the fact that while he may be ready to slow down some, his companions seem to be on different sexual schedules. Not to mention different time zones. Upon arrival in another major city, he wonders whether his libido might not be ready for departure.

And well he might wonder. Coming of age as he did in the late 1950s, Stern read more Hefner than he did Kinsey. Like many another middle-aged man who has an image of himself as a late-night, early a.m. multiorgasmic lover (as he was in his 20s), Stern finds sexual questions cropping up in his mind with increasing frequency. He keeps up with the popular literature— he knows that changes in his sexual organs are to be expected, but he's not sure how all the changes will add up. For instance, his scrotum, responding to the pull of gravity, hangs lower than it used to. He may not have noticed, but the angle of his erection began to decline in his 30s, and will continue to do so in his 40s, 50s, 60s, and 70s. Sperm production has also declined, imperceptibly. The force of his ejaculations is not as powerful as it was in his 20s. Stern *has* noticed that occasionally his erections don't last long enough for him to climax. He is not aware of an internal hormonal change, a drop in androgen levels, and in fact shrugs off a lessening desire for sex as the result of the pressures of business and travel.

To compensate for and acknowledge some of these changes, the stylishly dressed financial counselor takes care to stay in shape. He rides a

---

* not his real name

Organic Differences

While there is much variation in the degree of sexual activity among older men, several developments are to be expected. With age, the prostate gland enlarges. The scrotum hangs lower and the penis takes longer to become erect, longer to reach orgasm, longer to recover. The orgasm itself is shorter. If all goes well, however, the pleasure shouldn't subside.

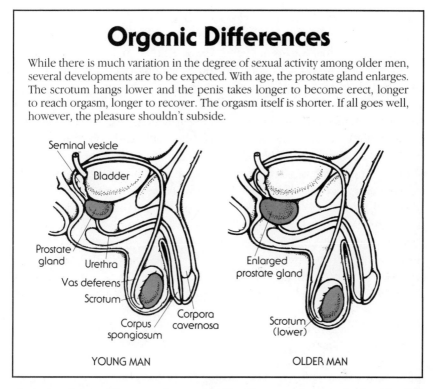

YOUNG MAN   OLDER MAN

stationary bike at home and uses the Nautilus machines at the health club. He *talks* more about sex with his partners these days. He experiments with positions and techniques and enjoys extended foreplay, where he once used to concentrate more on "lasting"—on what he thought meant good, manly sex. He allows that the mornings after mean more than they used to, and that the pleasure of intimacy are as important as the variety of his partners. At 35,000 feet, his eyes seem to fix less on flight attendants and more on annual reports than they did in decades past.

Yet as easily as Stern seems to take his sexual aging, he wonders, as so many men do, what the future will bring. He wonders what exactly is "normal" for a healthy man in mid-life or late life who values the many pleasures of sexual love and companionship. Not surprisingly, the normal is tough to nail down.

In recent years, it has become popular in guidebooks on sexuality to pose a seemingly simple question to curious readers: That is, what exactly is a man's most powerful sex organ? The answer is the brain. Another question follows: What, then, is a man's second most powerful sex organ? The answer is the skin. These questions are not devised to "trick" anyone so much as to challenge the conventional wisdom about sexual performance.

For the vast majority of men and women, the brain and skin are stable, healthy partners well past middle age, thus pointing to a continuing capacity for sexual pleasure no matter what physiological changes beset the other sex organs in later life. The "trick" comes in getting men to believe they are desirable, capable sex partners even as normal aging changes do affect the all-important erection. However, it should be stated early on that it is certainly possible for a man of 75 to have intercourse if he wants it, and it is not at all uncommon for the same man of 75 to be still producing sperm. What sexologists and gerontologists recently have come to learn about sex and aging is that the individual differences are great—and that those differences should be respected as normal. And while unquestionably there is decline in the frequency of intercourse in later life, that in no way means there is cessation of sexual activity. Or in no way does it imply that sex is less enjoyable for those who choose to engage in it in their 60s, 70s, and 80s. In recent years, the sexuality of those over 60 has worked its way out of the closet, steadily, with the door opening wider each decade.

Some 35 years ago, a remarkable body of work called *Sexual Behavior in the Human Male* was published by Alfred C. Kinsey, Wardell B. Pomeroy, and Clyde E. Martin. The pioneer study catalogued thousands of examples of sex in men's lives, from the commonplace to the then-extraordinary, based on 4,108 adult males whose experience was regarded by the researchers as "adequate" in scope. Documented were behavioral data such as number of orgasms per week; number of erections per week, night, and month; capacity for multiple orgasm; frequency of intercourse; levels of impotence and age of onset; and the like. For example, Kinsey and his partners, in contemplating statistics on orgasm, wrote: "Throughout the population it is customary for the male to reach a single orgasm and not to attempt to continue intercourse beyond that point. Exceptions are found chiefly among younger married males who are still in their teens. At that age, 15 percent of the population is capable of experiencing two or more ejaculations during a limited period of time during continuous erotic activity. The number of males who are capable of such multiple orgasm decreases with advancing age. . . ."[1]

Cited countless times in succeeding years, the data, though highly praised for its depth and breadth, has come to be viewed lately in a new light. Social scientists and sex researchers have expanded their perceptions of sexuality in general, and in particular they have revised their expectations of sexual behavior among the elderly. And although reliable data are still elusive (in the scientific scheme of things), better attempts are being made to chart how sexual beings actually age over time. The prospects are highly encouraging.

AROUSAL AND ORGASM

Before one can fully appreciate the changes that confront the penis and testicles in later years, it helps to renew one's acquaintance with a man's most private organs. Inside the outer sheath of elastic skin, the penis is composed of three parallel cylinders. Two of these, the corpora cavernosa, lie side by side, extending all the way down the shaft into the body to provide a foundation of sorts for the erection of the penis.[2] The third cylinder, the corpus spongiosum, runs beneath the other two and surrounds the urethra, the passageway through which the urine and semen both travel.

At the proper state of arousal in a healthy male's penis, millions of tiny blood vessels will have opened, allowing blood to surge into and through the corpora. Urologists say an erection is a reflex phenomenon over which a man has no voluntary control. It can be stimulated, of course, through thoughts about sex and through physical manipulation. It is the extraordinar-

---

Sex Changes

Just why a man's sex drive declines is unclear. Lower levels of sex hormones may be a factor, but psychological changes and a general loss of vitality in the body are probably more important. One thing is certain—variation is the rule when it comes to sexual activity among older men. Still, from data gathered by the National Institute on Aging, here are some averages gleaned from some 800 male respondents.

Frequency of orgasm
Age 20: 104 per year (49 solo)
Age 30: 121 per year (10 solo)
Age 40: 84 per year (8 solo)
Age 50: 52 per year (2 solo)
Age 60: 35 per year (4 solo)
Age 70: 22 per year (8 solo)

Frequency of awaking with erection
Age 20: 6 mornings per month
Age 30: 7 mornings per month
Age 50: 5 mornings per month
Age 70: 2 mornings per month

Angle of erection
Age 20: 10° above horizontal
Age 30: 20° above horizontal
Age 40: Slightly above horizontal
Age 50: Slightly below horizontal
Age 70: 25° below horizontal

ily rare man who can simply will an erection without either type of stimulation. This absence of conscious control is the reason most men do not realize
that their most powerful sex organ is the brain. But, indeed, it is the brain
that triggers both the erection and the orgasm. At the height of his arousal, a
man's brain sends a message down through the spinal cord to the sympa-
thetic nerves, which in turn stimulate the muscles at the base of the penis to
contract rhythmically, ejaculate, and provide the ecstatic sensation of orgasm.
Doctors who have studied the penis more carefully than even the most
tender lovers report that during ejaculation, the muscles surrounding the
base of the penis contract violently at .8-second intervals, sending semen out
of the urethra in a younger man with enough force to travel a distance of up
to two feet.[3]

Depending on how a man and his partner view their sexual activity,
some of the changes that occur with age can be thought of as negative or
positive. Noted urologist Dr. Sherman Silber catalogs seven basic changes
succinctly in his book, *The Male*. First, he says, it starts to take a little while
longer to obtain a good, firm erection upon arousal. The man who can recall
the frequent, seemingly instant responses of his teen-age years might initially
be wary of this newfound delay, but it can be viewed as an advantage rather
than a hindrance. The foreplay period will be lengthened—and hopefully
improved—for both partners. Second, while a 50-year-old man may take
longer to reach orgasm than a 25-year-old, as a benefit of this occurrence the
older man gains greater control over the timing of his ejaculation. Again the
change can be thought of as a blessing or a curse, or both. There is a good
chance the woman involved will welcome this physiological fact of aging.
Third, the orgasm becomes briefer each year. Concurrently, the fourth
change observed is that the force of ejaculation weakens over time. Fifth, the
associated volume of semen ejaculated drops steadily with age. Sixth, the
older man will find his penis returning rather more quickly to a flaccid state
after orgasm than it did in his younger days. Finally, Silber points out, the
refractory period lengthens as a man ages, meaning that it takes longer to
bring the penis back to an erect state after orgasm.[4] Masters and Johnson
have reported that an interval of 12 to 24 hours may be required before a
healthy, aging man can redevelop an erection. Too many men view this
change as a signal that they are becoming impotent, rather than simply
acknowledging its eventual expected occurrence. The normal, sexually active
man in his 40s, 50s, or 60s can function quite well between erections if he
creatively uses his prime sex organ, his brain. After all, a woman's capability
for reaching orgasm or multiple orgasm does not, fortunately, recede as the
man's refractory period grows. Furthermore, a regular pattern of sexual

activity (which may include self-stimulation) helps both sexes preserve sexual functioning.

It is also sometimes assumed that men cannot father children in their later years. This is not exactly correct. While sperm counts decline, sperm production can continue until a man dies.[5] If the sperm count is an issue, a man can have a relatively simple examination, in which his semen is tested microscopically.

THE STUDY OF SEX AND THE OLDER MAN

In their measurements, Kinsey and his partners found that the most potent men fell into the age range of 16 to 20, with a relatively gradual falloff in activity until the ages of 56 to 60. The newer breed of sex researchers point out the glaring gaps in their data concerning men over 60, as if they had no sex lives at all. In retrospect, it may be understandable why the older men were not studied, but not necessarily excusable. Increasingly today, men of 60 to 90 are being asked about their sex lives, and they and their partners are answering back with encouraging frankness.

In 1981, Bernard D. Starr, Ph.D., and Marcella Bakur Weiner, Ed.D., published results of a study in which 800 persons aged 60 and over completed open-ended surveys of 50 questions that asked them intimate details about their sex habits—including masturbation, frequency of intercourse, oral-genital sex, homosexuality, and impotence, among others. They set out to update some of the work of Masters and Johnson, especially among the graying set, and succeeded in reeling in 800 responses from senior centers nationwide. Where legendary studies on sex and aging left off, Starr and Weiner unabashedly dashed in. The results were surprising, even to these effervescent social scientists, especially in demonstrating the intensity of sexual feeling among older people. While other researchers in the field remain skeptical about the ground-breaking aspects claimed by the study, there is little doubt that it unearthed evidence of a sexier, more open, and more active group than had commonly been assumed.

Consider the response of a 69-year-old married man to the question, "What in the sex act is most important to you?" "When I have a chance to experience every possibility ultimately ending in orgasm," he wrote. When asked, "What can a couple do when the man is unable to have an erection?" a divorced 74-year-old man replied succinctly: "Touch, suck."[6] In answer to the same question, a 66-year-old divorced man replied: "The woman must find a response which causes the erection—helping penetration by hand, nude body, rhythmic contact."

Even with such frank responses from the ranks of the sexually active elderly, Starr and Weiner do not deny that there are real physiological problems the aged must contend with in their sex lives. Rather, in their study they chose to focus on the respondents' thoughts about sex, on what makes it enjoyable. They couched the questions for the most part in favorable terms. Their intent was not to sway responses, but instead merely to elicit reliable ones. Professional reaction to their work has been mixed, even as they have been received warmly on the television talk show circuit and on odd-hour radio programs. "Much to my dismay," says professor Bernard Starr, in his cramped first-floor office at Brooklyn College, "we may have sold [only] 10,000 hardback books. The study will make its mark eventually, though, I think, because it is unique. . . . But still there is a wall of prejudice to overcome, to get Americans to accept that people really do age and to accept that we are aging."

If the name Alex Comfort seems familiar, odds are it's not because he is a noted gerontologist. Comfort wrote the mega-best-seller *The Joy of Sex,* published in 1972, and followed it up with *More Joy of Sex* in 1975—but there is more to his story.

In the 1970s, when Gay Talese was researching his 1980 book, *Thy Neighbor's Wife,* his travels took him to a place called Sandstone, near Los Angeles, where experiments in open sexuality were the rage at the time. Wandering about the naked, coupling bodies, Talese spied Comfort, cigar in hand, watching various bodily couplings and minglings, and joining some himself. "He was a rarity in the medical profession, one who brought a bedside manner to an orgy," wrote Talese of Comfort. In a more illuminating profile of Comfort in *Harper's* magazine in December, 1982, writer P. J. Corkery described how this Britisher born in 1920 came to be an eminent political thinker, novelist, anarchist poet, gerontologist, and sex guru. As far back as the 1950s, Comfort was writing such journal articles as "The Biology of Senescence" and "Sexual Behavior in Society." He wrote an obscure novel, published in 1961, called *Come Out to Play,* in which an eccentric scientist is stranded in Paris without a job. He then sets up a sex clinic to give people "their first real experience of pleasure," as he wrote in the preface.

Years later, after scuttling an idea of writing a sex textbook for medical students, Comfort came to the conclusion that what society really needed was a sex book that would be read. "A sense of playfulness [about sex], I decided, was what people really needed. . . ."[7] And when the good doctor of aging delivered this message, millions responded. By 1973, *The Joy of Sex* had sold nearly 2 million copies. By 1975, the sequel, *More Joy of Sex,* was being snatched off of bookstacks at a furious rate.

"Mr. and Mrs. Sex, that's what we've become," he said to Corkery about himself and his wife, Jane. But Comfort has hardly rested on his sex-related fame. The sense of playfulness is still with him, as he turns toward what he feels are more important issues, such as the need for better health care systems for elderly people in the U.S. Appropriately, if the health care he seeks is to be truly improved, it will have to include updated thinking about sex in later life.

In this light, then, it is perhaps not surprising to find that one of this country's most eminent gerontologists, Dr. Robert N. Butler, the first head of the National Institute on Aging in Baltimore and now chairman of geriatric studies at Mount Sinai School of Medicine, has a strong interest in sexuality. A few years ago he coauthored with his wife, Myrna Lewis, a psychotherapist, an important work in this new field entitled *Sex After Sixty.*

On a crisp, bright Thursday in the spring of 1983, Clyde E. Martin, Ph.D., 65, arched his eyebrows, wheeled back in his desk chair at the National Institute on Aging's Gerontology Research Center, and invited a visitor in to talk about much of his life's work—sex through the ages. In his ten-plus years at the Institute, Martin has interviewed hundreds of men to find out exactly how their sex lives —along with their bodies—stand up to age. He was one of the authors of the Kinsey report, and his data are published regularly in scholarly journals and textbooks on sexology. For instance, in 1981 he found that a group of the "most active" normal, healthy men 60 and older reported having an average of 93.5 acts of coitus within the year—which translates to one act of intercourse every 3.9 days—while the "least active" group had coitus no more frequently than once every 60.8 days. More proof that variation is the one constant in data about sexual activity among the aging.

Martin likes to spice his comments with levity from time to time, and in this response to a question about government data on the angle of penile erection, he explained (in a letter about his research) the difficulty of measuring such an event with any scientific accuracy:

> The angle of the penile erection, when the male is standing, varies from being high enough to parallel the abdomen to some 45° below the horizontal, yet in the course of conducting nearly 800 interviews, no one has ever claimed that even at the extremes, angle of erection has interfered with coital activity.
> The question I use in the interview is, "When you are standing and have an erection, is the penis carried at the horizontal, above the horizon-

tal, or below the horizontal?" While asking the question I swing my left arm through an arc, hesitating briefly at each of six possible angles by way of illustration. A few individuals claim that they had never observed themselves in this regard. Others had no memory of events long past. Once the respondent had replied, he was then asked, "Has it always been carried at about this angle?" Of 60-to-79-year-old respondents, 30 percent indicated that a higher angle had been typical in the past.

Based on his interviews with subjects aged 20 to 39, 40 to 59, and 60 to 79, Martin found a full range of variation occurring throughout the life-span. He ascribed values to his subjects' erections, ranging from plus 20 degrees to "slightly above the horizontal" to minus 20 degrees to "slightly below the horizontal," and calculated that the average (median) angle of erection dropped some 15 degrees among middle-aged men, from 23 degrees to 17 degrees to 8 degrees above horizontal. Martin thus concluded that the changes occurring with age in this regard were considerably less dramatic than has been widely assumed.

IF ERECTION FAILS

Throughout their lives, men are bombarded with myths about sexual performance in general, and about the supposedly superior prowess of young men in particular. If they pay too close attention to these myths, and if they cling too resolutely to recollections of the erectile capabilities of their youth, men can run into difficulties in middle age. It is therefore particularly important for a man to understand exactly what impotence is, and what can be done to correct it. For as Dr. William A. Nolen noted in an article in the November, 1981, issue of *Esquire:* "There are few things in life more distressing to a man than impotence.... The man who cannot get an erection is a very sad man indeed."

In a sense, this includes all men, because all men are impotent from time to time because of fatigue, illness, tension, alcohol, drugs, or some combination of these factors. Usually potency returns by itself, but fear can readily wreak havoc in the normal functioning of a man's sex organs. When discussed clinically, impotence generally refers to the condition of men who cannot get a satisfactory erection more than once in four tries—a satisfactory erection being one that is firm enough and lasts long enough for a man to have intercourse and achieve orgasm. This also is the definition favored by Masters and Johnson. Excluded here are cases where semi-soft (or semi-hard, depending on one's perspective) erections still produce ejaculate, because it is possible for a man to have an orgasm and still be impotent.

Until the past few years, it was generally accepted that up to 90 percent of the reported cases of impotence had psychological causes. Yet this belief is now changing. Both Nolen in his *Esquire* article and, more recently, Myrna Lewis, point to many new research studies that reveal much higher percentages of physiologically based impotence. The reason this is viewed as good news to men is that with better detection of physiological causes of impotence, doctors can know which cases of impotence to treat medically or surgically and which to treat with psychotherapy. Long-term psychotherapy can properly be avoided in many cases in favor of drug therapy. Psychologically based impotence, meanwhile, can be more quickly treated with counseling rather than subjecting the patient to unnecessary tests or procedures.

Many of the scientific advances in this area have occurred in the sleep laboratories of ten medical schools and research centers around the country, where a useful diagnostic measurement known as "nocturnal penile tumescence" (NPT) is monitored. By checking to see how many erections men who report impotence have during sleep, and comparing those with results of "normal, healthy men," more accurate diagnoses of organic impotence can be discerned. It is generally accepted that most adult men have erections approximately every 90 minutes throughout the night during their dreaming (or REM, for rapid eye movement) stages of sleep, each of which lasts about 25 minutes. Whereas a pubescent boy will commonly average two and a half hours of erections each night, a healthy man at 65 will average about one and a half hours. By placing a gauge, or loop, around the shaft of a man's penis at a sleep lab, researchers can check not only the number of erections per night but also the precise circumference of each one (to check for possible blood flow impairment).

"Great," you might wonder, "but what if I have a problem? I am not about to pack my bags and spend the night at, say, the Sleep Research Center at Stanford's School of Medicine." This is fine. You might instead consider the "stamp test." As an alternative to the NPT test performed under ideal conditions, some doctors will simply tell a patient to wrap a strip of postage stamps snugly around the base of the penis before dropping off to sleep, with a tad of Scotch tape at each end to secure the postage. During the night, as the diameter of the penis increases during erection, it will be sufficient to break the stamp "collar" along one of the perforations. If you wake to find the stamps torn erratically, they probably have ripped during an uneven roll of the body or on rumpled sheets. If, on the other hand, you wake to find the stamps neatly torn along the perforated edges, you will be assured that you had at least one good erection while you slept. The natural psychotherapeutic benefit to this simple test is that it confirms the capabilities of the body. This knowledge can, in some cases, cure a psychological case of impotence absolutely, positively, overnight.

Part of Nolen's optimistic outlook on treating impotence today stemmed from a 1980 article in *The Journal of the American Medical Association* by Dr. Richard Spark et al. Spark had screened 105 patients with impotence and discovered by surprise that more than one-third of them, or 37, had previously unsuspected hormonal disorders. Spark did some more research, on up to 339 impotent men, and found that it supported his earlier findings of a much higher rate of physiologically based impotence. "We're obviously missing a lot of organic cases," Spark said of the medical profession in general.

His suspicion was confirmed three years later, when endocrinologist Dr. Michael Slag from the Minneapolis Veterans Administration Medical Center published an article in the same *Journal of the American Medical Association* that showed a dramatic increase in the percentage of organic causes among 1,180 men studied, 401 of whom were impotent.[8] In this study, a whopping 80 percent of the impotence cases were found to have physiological causes, with only 14 percent attributed to psychological or emotional causes (the rest defied diagnosis). It seems clearer today that Spark was certainly on the right trail in 1980, and that there is more to impotence than had heretofore been believed. "By virtue of our experience with this group of patients, it is clear that sexual impotence is a common problem in middle-aged and elderly men with associated medical problems," Slag wrote. And if it's organic in nature, then it can be treated, either medically or surgically.

TOWARD THE BIONIC MEMBER

With all this new information flowing into the mainstream of urological medicine, certain extraordinary treatments for impotence are no longer considered radical. Take, for instance, the penile prosthesis. For those men whose organic impotence has been unresponsive to medical treatment, a prosthesis can be implanted surgically to produce a rigid or semi-rigid constant erection that is big enough and firm enough for coitus. The operation itself is relatively simple. The corpora cavernosa are opened by incision and a long, narrow cylinder (or rod) is inserted into each corpus along the length of the penis; a few sutures are used to close the incisions. The problem, of course, is that many men do not care to bear a constant erection.

In his *Esquire* article, Nolen quoted one doctor who said: "One of my patients was a trombone player, and every time he stood up to play a solo, the bulge in his pants was very obvious. He came back and we replaced it with a pump-up prosthesis."

In this kind of device, the cylinders of the prosthesis are plastic and flaccid. They are connected by plastic tubing to a reservoir of fluid, which is itself inserted beneath abdominal wall muscles. From here, more tubing leads to a pressure-sensitive pump that is placed in the left or right side of the scrotum, where it resides like an extra testicle. Thus, when the occasion arises, the man can simply squeeze the pump a few times (or ask his partner to do the honors). Fluid flows from the reservoir into the cylinders at a steady rate until the penis magically becomes erect. When the mood subsides, the man or his partner presses a "release valve," also in the scrotum, which returns the penis to its flaccid state. This may seem a bit clumsy, but it has proven successful. Recent technology has improved the pump-up prosthesis so that sticking valves or loose connections—once a potential problem —occur less frequently. An even newer device, called the Jonas prosthesis, consists of two malleable cylinders composed of silicone that surrounds an inner core of braided silver wires. With this type of prosthesis, a man can virtually bend his organ into whatever angle or position he or his partner fancies.

The Jonas device itself costs less than $1,000, the rigid rod prosthesis about $500, and the inflatable device about $2,000. But when screening tests and doctors' and hospital costs are figured into the erectile equation, a penile prosthesis can cost anywhere from $2,000 to $5,000. For the record, insurance companies will normally pay for prosthesis insertion if it involves a case of "organic impotence." But most important is the fact that most follow-up tests on penile prostheses report satisfaction rates among couples in the 90 percent range, and often they are higher—which led Nolen to recommend to middle-aged and older men: "If your penis never gets firm or does so only once in every six or eight tries or always wilts before you've been able to use it satisfactorily, for heaven's sake, see a doctor. A bright one—one who knows enough not to say, 'What do you expect, you're almost sixty years old, aren't you?' and send you directly off to the mental health center. In 1981 an astute physician ought to be able to make a proper diagnosis and provide effective therapy—psychological, pharmacological, or medical—for almost all his impotent patients." This, of course, is even more true today.

Jack Haber is what one might call "an astute physician." He is bright, cheerful, bespectacled, and calls himself a political radical, among other things. He is also 74 years old and semiretired, after practicing as a general physician in Elmont, N.Y., for more than 40 years. Now he is more properly what one might call "a sex doctor." When he is not researching or writing on the study of sexuality and aging, he is often traveling to and from scientific conferences and classrooms, helping to spread the word that sex does not end at 60. On a chilly spring day in 1983, Haber sat at a desk looking out at his backyard, tinkering with a speech he was soon to present to the Society for the Scientific Study of Sex. If he wasn't in the best of moods at the time, he explained that possibly it was because he hadn't been to the pool that day, a regimen he follows four times each week. His interest in sex and aging all started with a particular problem he had a few years ago—in bed.

"I had an impotent erectile dysfunction," Haber says, "so I read a couple of chapters of Masters and Johnson [*Human Sexual Response* (1970)] on impotence. Luckily, I knew a little physiology and anatomy, and I used what they call the 'sensate focus method' because it seemed to fit my case to a T. It was just unbelievable to see that erection go up, with no pressures to perform!" (The sensate focus method Haber describes is popular in sex therapy circles as a technique to eliminate the pressures, or "musts," that so often burden the sexual act, especially as people get older. By concentrating on the pleasures of stimulation and sex *before* orgasm, sex can become freer, more enjoyable. And erections quite often rise out of the experience.)

PROSTATE EXPECTATIONS

With the help of a surgeon, Haber overcame another problem related to his sex life. Like many men his age, he started noticing some discomfort in and around his prostate. He went to a urologist, the chief of his department in a prestigious hospital in the New York area. "He was very knowledgeable and considerate" says Haber, "but when we discussed the scheduling of my prostate operation, and I asked him about how it might affect my sex life, he looked at me, questioning, and said, 'You're still sexual?' I said, 'Yes,'" Haber's prostate trouble dissipated after surgery, but not his frustration with the doctor's seemingly closed-minded question.

After age 50 or 60, men frequently experience an enlargement or inflammation of the prostate gland, which is normally about the size of a walnut and is located just below the bladder. It surrounds the outlet of the bladder like a doughnut; urination begins through this "doughnut hole." The prostate, as Dr. Sherman Silber has noted, is "one male organ which eventually goes wrong in all men."[9] The purpose of this gland is to contribute to the production of semen, which, when discharged into the urethra, transports sperm at the point of ejaculation.

In a man's preteen years, the prostate is smaller than a grape, but it grows larger during puberty, reaching its walnut size in early adulthood. Sometime after the age of 40 or so, the gland grows again, and can occasionally reach the size of a grapefruit by the time a man is in his 60s or 70s, according to Silber. This growth in later years seems to be a result of hormonal changes in the testicles over time. It is a normal physiological change called "benign prostatic hypertrophy," or enlargement, which, incidentally, does not occur in castrated men. Its primary warning signal is painful or more frequent urination (possibly awakening the man in the night), which is caused by the urethra being pinched smaller as the prostate swells. In 10 percent of all men over age 50, the prostate enlarges enough to interfere with the flow of urine. It is also said that about 10 percent of men already have some degree of enlargement at age 40, while at age 60 prostate enlargement is nearly universal.[10] Although this prostatism usually develops gradually, in an advanced stage it can cause a sudden and complete blockage of urine that requires emergency treatment. Fortunately, surgical techniques can safely remove excess portions of the gland. Unfortunately, though, the surgery often causes a condition known as "retrograde ejaculation," in which a man can still have intercourse but can no longer father children. This is because after the prostate is removed, semen is no longer ejaculated through the urethra. Instead, it travels backward along the path of least resistance into the bladder, where it is later expelled along with urine. After such surgery of the prostate, six weeks of healing time is generally required before a man can return to robust sexual activity.

If a man makes it through life without a bout of prostatitis, says *The Harvard Medical School Health Letter Book,* he can consider himself fortunate. This irregular inflammation of the prostate gland, different from enlargement, catches up with most men at one point or another in their lives, commonly before age 40. Signs of this condition are more frequent and difficult urination, along with irregular stabs of pain. Prostatitis can be acute or chronic, but it is rare that surgery is ever recommended. Tetracycline is a common cure.

Its cause baffles urologists to this day, but the typical prostatitis patient, curiously, is a man who has "sporadic bursts" of sexual activity between long episodes of abstinence.[11] Thus, it is one of life's few ailments for which doctors will prescribe "more sex" as preventive medicine.

Of all the troubles the prostate may cause, cancer of the prostate is not only the most frightening, but also the most common. Luckily, though, the vast majority of prostate cancer cases do not grow dangerously or cause death. This is because the cancer by and large is either extremely tiny compared with the rest of the gland or is relatively inert. Dr. Silber cites autopsy data of prostate gland specimens from patients who died of other causes. Traces of cancer were found in less than 10 percent of men under 50, as many as 30 percent of men between the ages of 60 and 69, and more than 80 percent of men over age 80.[12]

Cancer of the prostate is responsible for 17,000 to 20,000 deaths each year, which certainly is a cause for concern. Yet *most* cancers of the prostate, especially among older men, grow so slowly that they are not likely to spread or threaten life. The best advice experts can give in this area is that every man over age 50 should have an annual rectal examination as part of a regular physical exam. Because of the prostate's location just in front of the rectum, a doctor can feel cancerous growths of the prostate, leading to early detection and possible follow-up surgery. (Note, however, that unlike the surgery for prostate enlargement, radical removal of the prostate *does* cause men to become impotent.)

On a more positive note, a new ultrasonic machine has been installed at the Strang Clinic in New York City to help detect cancer of the prostate in its earliest stages. After hearing of the device at a medical meeting, doctors from the Clinic arranged for a demonstration in 1981 in Japan, where the device had already been used for mass screenings. In September, 1982, the Japanese sent a machine on loan, and doctors here eagerly await final results of the first year's "transrectal sonography" screenings. According to an article by New York *Daily News* science editor Ed Edelson, the machine resembles a large chair with a square hole through which an ultrasound probe protrudes. Once the probe is inserted into the rectum, doctors record ultrasound images of the prostate on film for later review and analysis. Of the first 750 men to be examined in the United States, the machine found four suspected cancers that the standard digital rectal exam had failed to detect.[13]

"We think that this technique can be for prostate cancer what mammography is for breast cancer," says Dr. Daniel Miller, medical director of the Strang Clinic, which is associated with Memorial Sloan-Kettering Cancer Center. Besides improving detection, doctors hope to see the ultrasound device eliminate many unnecessary operations that are performed in hopes of curing this type of cancer, second in incidence only to lung cancer in men over the age of 50.

LATE-LIFE RATIOS THAT FAVOR MEN

It should be clear by now that the workings of a man's sex organs are intricate and complex. With all that can possibly go wrong with the testes, prostate, penis, and scrotum—not to mention the brain—it is cause for celebration that sex over 60 not only occurs but indeed thrives among various aging couples. For a variety of reasons, not the least of which is demographics, it should continue to thrive through the end of the millennium and beyond. However, peering ahead, we see that there is also little doubt that older women will continue to face a nagging problem when it comes to sex in later life: a drastic shortage of available men. Because women typically outlive men an average of nearly eight years,[14] and because they usually marry men who are an average of three years older, women tend to end their lives as single persons. Myrna Lewis reports that most married women spend at least ten years alone in widowhood, and that over 60 percent of older women are without marital partners, compared with about 20 percent of older men.

In the early 1900s, the numbers of older men and women were fairly equal. By 1971, however, there were 13.9 million women 65 and over versus 9.5 million older men. Unless scientists can soon compress the disparity of life-spans between sexes, estimates for future female/male ratios will be even more lopsided. By the year 2035, Lewis says, there will be 34 million older women and only 23 million older men. Though these men will have ample chances for heterosexual activity in later life, other options may be embraced by the future female aged.

"There is kind of a perverse advantage," says Lewis, from her tenth-floor office at Mt. Sinai Medical Center overlooking New York's Central Park. "A man will have no problem finding a sex partner—even if he has grown up thinking of himself as unattractive—which may benefit someone who has been shy, or does not operate socially in a very positive way. In any institution, *any* man is in demand. But that is a terrible price to pay for losing the eight years of extra life—a terrific price. I would rather have those years."

Addressing this issue at the annual Gerontological Society of America's national convention in November, 1982, Betty Friedan finished a hurried cup of coffee and plastic-wrapped pastry and then told attendees at a Saturday morning panel that they will not see the nation's future elderly women being quite the same "caretakers" that they have been in so many decades past. She warned of "a new ball game," adding, "Don't expect women to be the martyrs." This last point related to one her copanelist Gunhild Hagestad, Ph.D., of Penn State University, amplified in an earlier discussion. The nation's future female elderly, Hagestad asserted, would increasingly be made up of women who have had multiple living patterns, including cohabitation, marriage, divorce, sharing a home with one or more women, and living singly. "One issue that I feel hasn't adequately been raised about women who have achieved high status despite the unbalanced sex ratio is: Will they have men? Will they need men? Nobody is talking about this," said Hagestad, "but I have noticed among my own students that they have started looking at younger men. In their case it means fourteen- and fifteen-year-olds, but I think it is interesting . . . I hope I will be around to watch it as it develops."

One of the practices that is more openly explored today is that of adult masturbation. Butler and Lewis, in *Sex After Sixty,* say that "when a partner is not available (as, for example, in widowhood) or circumstances do not permit contact with a partner, both men and women can protect much of their sexual capacity through regular masturbation, unless this is personally unacceptable." [15] Predictably, Starr and Weiner approached the subject in positive terms. In their 1981 study, they said that masturbation today is often recommended as a healthy sexual outlet for teen-agers and young adults, and then asked their older respondents how they felt about masturbation and whether they masturbated.

From an 83-year-old married man came the response: "It is necessary at times for a partner if he or she is rejected."

From a 69-year-old married man: "I think it's an excellent chance to use your imagination."

From a 65-year-old divorced woman: "Same as I did when younger. If you can't have a partner, it's a way to achieve climax—better than nothing."

And finally a single man of 72 answered: "People who say they don't are liars!" [16]

The results are indeed interesting when one considers, first, that these people were born early in the twentieth century, when Victorian attitudes about sex prevailed, and, secondly, that Kinsey had reported very little masturbatory activity in his landmark studies of older men and women in mid-century. Still, Myrna Lewis strikes a reasoned, cautionary tone when discussing masturbation and the aged. With over 20 years of professional training in gerontology and counseling, she is careful not to accept blindly the findings of a study she has not examined closely. "I have got to say I don't quite believe all the exuberence about masturbation [in *The Starr-Weiner Report*]," she says. "Masturbation is just not something that is totally accepted by the current generation of elders. It turns them off. Remember, the 1942 Boy Scout manual warned boys to 'save it.' " And she adds: "In *Sex After Sixty,* we were always careful to leave space where those people who were not interested in sex would be comfortable." On the other hand, Lewis does not deny that, on the whole, the younger generations of *future* elderly will be much more sexual, or at least more *flexible* in their sexuality. This again lends more credence to some sex experts' visions of a sexual renaissance among the elderly in the 2020s or 2030s. The signals, for older men and women, are slowly blinking with each new decade from red to yellow to green. And among the sexually active elderly, that is cause for celebration.

On the sex lecture circuit, the spry, graying, semiretired Dr. Jack Haber uses self-disclosure at age 74 to help loosen up his groups of students, be they college age or senior citizens. "I tell them there is such a thing as a second honeymoon," he says, "and I tell them it is better than the first. Without boasting, I tell them the honeymoon is in no way over just because you're older." Couples may very much enjoy penile-vaginal sex, he says, and yet not quite feel the full explosion they felt in prior decades. "Usually, in the forties, questions start to form, and I stress that what lies ahead is a physiological slowdown—*not* a pathological one." The real problem in sexuality and aging, he says, is a glaring lack of adult education, which he feels is responsible for much marital sexual dysfunction today. "In my forty-one years as a physician, I doubt whether I was consulted more than forty-one times about sexual problems," he says, only slightly exaggerating his point. In Haber's view, middle-aged and older couples should try to learn new things about sex with the same vigor with which they sign up for tennis lessons.

"We could teach them about what makes a body healthy, the various positions, oral-genital sex, how to have and exchange fantasies, and certain muscular exercises for both the male and female to increase their pleasure. We could teach techniques of masturbation, talk about vibrators, baths, and showers, and offer readings, counseling, and workshops to communicate learning about sex. To me, sex and aging is a geometric progression. It doesn't always have to mean a rock-hard penis in a vagina," he says. He inserts his raised right index finger into his clenched left fist for emphasis. "The wink of the eye, the joking, the gentle caress, reminiscing . . . all this enters into a sexual encounter. Since the brain and skin really don't deteriorate, in your fifties, sixties, and seventies, you have the basic ingredients so that sex need never end." Behind Haber, outside sliding glass doors, raucous birds are chirping in his backyard. "I am not enough of a poet," he says, "to describe not only the joy of sex, but also the physical affinity."

At the National Institute on Aging research facilities in Baltimore, Clyde E. Martin, Alfred Kinsey's longtime associate, does not claim to be a poet either. Yet he has tried to describe, through nearly 40 years of research, just what spurs the sexual response between men and women, and how it changes over time. His view is more restrained than Haber's. "You really are kind of faced with a situation in which a high proportion [of respondents] report they no longer have any sex at all," Martin says flatly. "Their sex lives are practically gone; yet these people approve of sex. I've talked to over eight hundred people now in this program [the Baltimore Longitudinal Study], and I am amazed at how well people get along in their sex lives."

To Martin, the proper question to raise about sexuality in the last third of life should not be how much is possible, but instead how much of a correspondence there is between what each partner desires from the other. "I feel it is equally permissible to give people permission *not* to have sex, rather than to lead them into an unreal world," he says. "If you are going to live comfortably with sex, you have got to deal with the disparity between what a person wants and what he gets—because you just can't will yourself a desire for sex."

Bernard Starr and Marcella Weiner, not surprisingly, feel that Martin is part of the old school, though they repeatedly give credit to the many landmark studies in which he and his colleagues were involved. "After their work, we could move in," says Weiner, speaking from a sofa in her Upper East Side New York office. "They opened the door for us, and we said we were going to go into the living room, dining room, and bedroom. We documented such things as oral sex, and we found that older people today *are* a part of society."

Bernard Starr, who at 47 looks more like 35, vividly recalls the obstacles he and Weiner surmounted as they tried to piece together the true sexual identities of so many older men and women in America. "We felt we knew what was really going on," he says, "but we had to ask them to 'cut the old act.' After that, it was like liberating a prisoner-of-war camp. Behind this old act, they were real people . . . who had been having sex three times a week all their lives. We had to think, why would they give it up, except where they had lost a mate?"

The Brooklyn College professor, who has wavy black hair and looks a bit like Dustin Hoffman, swirls his cup of coffee and collects his thoughts. Starr has read the scientific studies on sexuality. He has studied the psychological and psychoanalytic literature on the subject. He has taught the same. And he has crisscrossed the country in search of elderly people who would share their intimate feelings with him and his colleague. He has published the results to far less acclaim than he had hoped for. He is not, however, cynical. In his time outside the urban classroom, he is editor of the Springer Publishing Company's series on adulthood and aging, which he developed back in 1977. He thinks ahead to the year 2010 and says that, in his mind, sex will have to be radically different. By then, Bernard Starr will be a senior citizen. "Sex can mean many things aside from sexual intercourse," he says, "once people extricate themselves from the tyranny of the male erection." In their study of 800 men and women aged 60 and over, Starr and Weiner have, at the least, done that.

MAINTENANCE: SEXUALITY

How can one "maintain" a satisfying sex life? Obviously, no simple answer will do. It is not, for one thing, a matter for you alone but for your partner or partners, as well. You should be reassured by the fact that recent studies of aging lovers report a wide variation in the frequency and the kinds of sexual experience sought by older people. "Normal" appears to be everything from holding hands at midnight to going at it till dawn.

Perhaps the best general advice is to forget all the jokes you've ever heard about frustrated old men. Keep your head clear, your mind open, your senses alive, and you'll be able to make as much love as you want for years to come.

If you know that certain gradual changes will occur, you are less likely to worry. Remember that in older men:

- It takes longer to get an erection, and the penis may require direct stimulation before the erection occurs.
- Longer periods of stimulation are needed to reach orgasm.
- The period of "ejaculatory inevitability," or emission, becomes briefer and eventually disappears, thus reducing the two-stage aspect of a young man's orgasm to one shorter orgasmic period.
- The force and volume of the ejaculation diminishes.
- After ejaculation, the refractory period increases. A late middle-aged or older man may need from 12 to 24 hours before another erection is possible.

If a man is not ill and does not suffer from psychological blocks, his ability to have an erection will not be impaired by age. However, certain factors can cause a transitory loss of function. You should be aware of them:

- Therapeutic drugs: Medications such as tranquilizers, high blood-pressure drugs, and antidepressants can interfere with sexual function. Check your doctor to find out about side effects of any drug you are taking.
- Alcohol: Alcohol, being a depressant, can numb the senses and cause temporary impotence.
- The psychoactive drugs—marijuana, LSD, cocaine, and others that are sometimes taken to heighten sexual experience can interfere with erection in men and orgasm in both men and women.
- Mental stress: A man preoccupied with problems at work or problems in his relationships may lose both the desire for sex and the ability to attain an erection.
- Physical fatigue: Physical activity in a well-conditioned man does not interfere with sexual interest. However, unaccustomed physical activity for the out-of-condition older man can cause loss of sexual responsiveness for 24 to 48 hours.

A man's general vitality and continuing sexual activity in middle age seems to be the most important indicators of what his sex life will be like in later years. The man aged 40 to 60 who engages in sex on a regular basis is most likely to have a satisfying sex life after 60.

Encouraging
News About
the Heart

When Dr. Barney Clark took an unexpected turn for the worse and died in the wee hours of a March morning in 1983, it didn't take long for the news of his death in Salt Lake City to fan out across the country. As the first human ever to have his life extended by means of a permanent artificial heart implant, he had clearly made history. Later that same day, looking up from his desk strewn with papers at the National Institute on Aging's Gerontology Research Center in Baltimore, Dr. Edward Lakatta answered a visitor's questions about the artificial heart implant. "I think the whole thing was sensationalized," he said. "It was a great stride forward with milestone research, but all that coverage didn't really belong, in my mind." The point was not that Lakatta thought artificial heart research was wasteful. Rather, as an expert on aging and cardiovascular disease, he is trained to seek broad solutions to heart disease.

Lakatta feels that the Barney Clark-type operations will have a relatively small impact on society in general. Although he was inspired by the courage of the team treating Clark and by the patient's will to survive, Lakatta said, "It is like a soap opera. This type of procedure just may not be worth it. It puts a really big stress on the individual, and has a high risk. I could give you an answer of 'Gee, it's great,' but the cost is so high I'm wondering if the return is that high."

Like Lakatta, Dr. Lewis Thomas, the noted essayist and chancellor of the Memorial-Sloan Kettering Cancer Center in New York, is frank in his assessment of the state of cardiac research and treatment today. Before we march heedlessly into the world of artificial hearts, Thomas asserted in an article for *Discover* magazine, we, as a nation, "simply must invest more money in basic biomedical research." That—and not machinery—is what ultimately will lead researchers to understand more fully the changes in the cardiovascular system over time, according to Thomas. Discussing Barney Clark's heart disease, Thomas observed: "We do not really understand the underlying mechanism of cardiomyopathies [heart muscle disease] at all, and we are not much better at comprehending the biochemical events that disable the heart muscle or its valves in other, more common, illnesses."[1] So, while speculation continues that we may one day be able to trade in our 40-year-old hearts at the first sign of disease, basic research on underlying causes may yield more significant results.

118

Time and the Heart

A man's resting heartbeat stays about the same all his life, but his aged heart pumps less blood with each beat. The decline in blood flow is more marked during exercise, because his pulse can no longer rise as high as it used to.

The figures below represent data that is currently under revision. Studies done on healthy, fit aging individuals are changing gerontologists' views of cardiac decline. In fact, distance runners over the age of 45 have even *increased* their maximum heartbeat during exercise as they've gotten older. But, for the record, here are figures based on the classic cardiac decline studies conducted in the 1950s.

Blood pumped by the resting heart	*Maximum heartbeat during exercise*
Age 30: 3.6 quarts per minute	**Age 30:** 200 beats per minute
Age 40: 3.4 quarts per minute	**Age 40:** 182 beats per minute
Age 50: 3.2 quarts per minute	**Age 50:** 171 beats per minute
Age 60: 2.9 quarts per minute	**Age 60:** 159 beats per minute
Age 70: 2.6 quarts per minute	**Age 70:** 150 beats per minute

As one might expect, there is reason for both optimism and pessimism as researchers and cardiac specialists view the statistics of recent years. On the downside, coronary disease remains the number-one cause of death in the U.S. among those over 50 (and among men over 40). More than 1.25 million Americans suffer heart attacks each year. The annual cost associated with heart disease in this country easily exceeds $25 billion. And yet, these statistics, while grim, are balanced by certain positive trends. Much of what we're learning about heart disease indicates that changes in life-style can have an extraordinary effect on cutting down the risk. In addition, treatment has progressed to such a degree that it is estimated that some 200,000 Americans who would have died during 1982 are still alive because of the progress made over the past 15 years. And millions more who would have been disabled by severe pain or other cardiac symptoms are leading full, vigorous lives.[2]

THE HEART AT 40

By age 40, in the absence of prolonged, rigorous exercise programs, the normal heart will have started to weaken. It becomes less muscular, more fatty, and more full of useless connective tissue. Vulnerability to heart disease rises. Gradual changes unnoticeable to the owner become measurable during a cardiologist's examination or in an electrocardiogram (EKG).

Within the muscle fibers themselves an age pigment begins to accumulate at about age 20. By age 80 or so, this pigment, called lipofuscin—which is composed of protein and fat—has replaced as much as 5 to 10 percent of the muscle fiber.[3] The heartbeat weakens as the heart muscles wane, and consequently less blood is pumped with each beat. A kind of sluggishness sets in. And while this sluggishness may not be very noticeable as a man sits at his desk or goes about routine tasks, the decline in blood flow becomes marked during hard physical work or exercise. This is because the pulse simply doesn't rise as high as it used to.

The question that remains unanswered is how much of this decline is "natural," how much is disease. As the level of cholesterol in the blood increases with age, it tends to accumulate along artery walls, which are themselves thickening. The net effect is to clog the arteries, which increases the pressure of the blood against the arterial walls. This, in turn, forces the heart to work harder, provoking a pattern in which heart attacks and strokes become more likely.

The implantation of an artificial heart in the chest of Barney Clark, while historic, did not seem so astounding to those who already consider the human heart in mechanical terms. As it is often described, the heart is a pump, a hollow muscle that expands and contracts, receiving blood and then delivering it, under pressure, throughout the body. If the body is thought of as a machine, then the heart is its pulsing generator. Make a fist and you'll have an idea of the size of your heart. (A woman's is slightly smaller and lighter, weighing about eight ounces, compared with ten ounces in a man.) The heart is cone-shaped and lies beneath the breastbone, between the lungs. Because it slants slightly toward the left, people mistakenly believe the heart is off-center.

The heart, blood, and vessels together comprise the body's circulatory system. In normal operation, the heart sends blood surging through the pulmonary artery first to the lungs and then to every part of the body through arteries that keep subdividing into smaller vessels—arterioles and, finally, capillaries. There the blood begins its journey back to the heart, as the thinner-than-fiber capillaries join with slightly larger vessels that meet the systemic veins that then return the blood to the right auricle of the heart. This return trip through the veins is more placid than that through the arteries, where the effect of the heart's pumping action is more pronounced.[4]

On average, a man's heart beats slightly faster than one beat per second, which is slightly slower than a woman's and much slower than a dog's. More than a gallon of blood is pumped per minute, at an average pulse rate—for adults in general—of 72 beats per minute. (The range of at-rest pulse in adults is from about 35 to 110 beats per minute.) Elderly men and women and children have faster pulse rates than the average adult, while well-conditioned people have slower pulse rates than those in poor condition. Over an 80-year life-span, a healthy, well-functioning heart will beat about 3.2 *billion* times.

Pressures on the Heart

Heart disease is the most common cause of death in men over 40 and is responsible for more than half the deaths of men over 60. As the level of cholesterol in the blood increases with age, the cholesterol accumulates on the artery walls, which are themselves thickening—the net effect of which is to force the heart to work harder to pump blood. The figures below show the average cardiovascular decline among men who have taken no special measures to correct cholesterol build-up. More recent studies indicate that changes in life-style, diet, and exercise are having their effect in reducing dangerous levels of cholesterol.

Age 20: 180 milligrams cholesterol; 122/76 blood pressure
Age 30: 200; 125/76
Age 40: 220; 129/81
Age 50: 230; 134/83
Age 60: 230; 140/83
Age 70: 225; 148/81

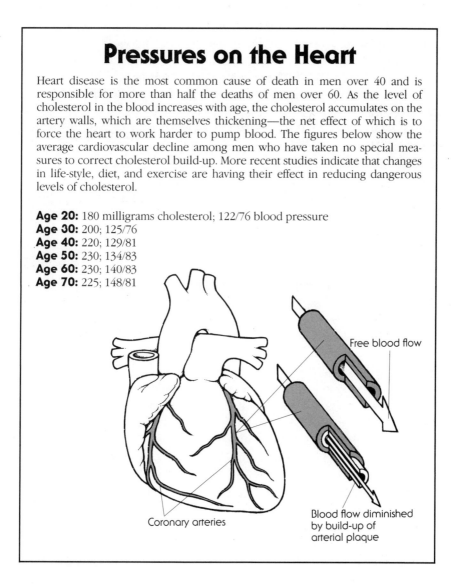

Free blood flow

Coronary arteries

Blood flow diminished
by build-up of
arterial plaque

THE MRFIT MYSTIQUE

Back in 1972, five years after Dr. Christiaan Barnard performed the first human heart transplant, the National Heart, Lung, and Blood Institute began a massive clinical trial in which thousands of American men participated to examine and demonstrate the value of special intervention to reduce the health risks from smoking, high blood pressure, and elevated cholesterol levels. A related question that was addressed was the extent to which such intervention could affect death rates from heart disease. The study was called the Multiple Risk Factor Intervention Trial, dubbed "Mr. Fit," or MRFIT.

Approximately 13,000 middle-aged males at high risk for heart disease became subjects in MRFIT. They were not by any means the most unhealthy physical specimens, nor were they singled out because of extreme obesity or prior heart trouble. Rather, they were a fairly typical group of middle-aged men who by virtue of age, diet, heredity, and stress level were considered to be in a high-risk category for heart trouble. It was up to the doctors and medical advisers associated with the study to try to reduce that susceptibility. Two types of intervention were intended—"special intervention" (meaning that intense efforts were made to reduce smoking, blood pressure, and cholesterol levels) and "usual care" (meaning that the men were advised to lose weight, get regular exercise, and reduce stress where possible).

In 1982, when results of the study were published, both groups had far fewer cardiovascular deaths than were expected; yet the differences between the "special intervention" and "usual care" groups were not statistically significant.[5] As had been predicted, special efforts to reduce smoking, high blood pressure, and cholesterol levels had a valuable—one could say, profound—effect on health. But the question not answered by the ten-year study was exactly how effective the "special intervention" was as opposed to the "usual care" treatment. One problem was that "usual care" had to be considered in the context of the overall move toward fitness made in the past ten or 15 years by normal, healthy Americans. Then, too, the very fact of selection for the study would have an immeasurable effect on the subjects. Michael Pollock, Ph.D., of Mount Sinai Medical Center in Milwaukee, thinks that MRFIT suffered from imprecise design, control, and measurement. "If you read the study," he says, "you'll see that what happened was that everybody made life-style changes once they realized they were in a high-risk category for heart disease."

However fuzzy the data from MRFIT, the overall implication of the study is clear and encouraging. If people are made aware of the risks they run and how life-style changes can affect that risk, they will do something about it. And whatever they do—whether it is to stop smoking, change their diet, or get more exercise—it seems to reduce their chances of succumbing to heart disease significantly.

For even more encouraging data on fitness and the aging heart, Michael Pollock is a good man to talk to. As director of the cardiac rehabilitation program at Mount Sinai, he guides people who have had heart attacks or histories of heart trouble back to better health. And as President of the American College of Sports Medicine, he knows a great deal about athletes and the effects of training. The question Pollock asks constantly about the heart's decline is: Is it aging or is it life-style?

In attempting to answer that question, Pollock has directed a compelling study of older distance runners to see how their bodies age and—just as important—how they don't (see chapter 12). After ten years of scrutiny, Pollock and his associates were able to show that a man's maximum heart rate does decrease with age, but that it does not necessarily fall in a straight-line, predictable path, as earlier researchers believed. Eventually even a champion runner experiences a drop-off in the power and efficiency of his heart, according to the evidence, but the study indicates that this aspect of aging can be controlled and modified with rigorous training.

"I think many of the athletes were expecting a decline," Pollock says in an interview in his Milwaukee office. "They could see it in their performances. But many were encouraged about what did finally show up."

CHALLENGING MYTHS ABOUT THE AGING HEART

Inside the darkened Sheraton Boston Hotel conference room, at the 1982 convention of the Gerontological Society of America, heads momentarily turned away from the podium toward the man who had just entered. Looking a bit like a football player dodging defenders on Astroturf, Dr. Edward Lakatta made his way through the crowded room to an empty chair alongside distinguished colleagues who had come to address this Sunday session about the aging heart. Apparently Lakatta was the only panel member to have been thrown for a loss by airport traffic that day. Yet, unruffled, he delivered his presentation flawlessly, telling of misinterpreted declines in cardiac output and of surprising new findings about higher "end-diastolic" volume of blood in aging hearts. Following a lively question-and-answer period, the moderator offered his praise: "Dr. Lakatta has given us much hope."

A few months later, seated at his desk in the Gerontology Research Center in Baltimore, Lakatta explained more about the message he felt he had rushed through at the Boston convention: There is little unavoidable decline in cardiac function due to age. It is time, he thinks, to update some of the classic studies on declining cardiac function that were conducted in the 1950s and reproduced scores of times since. The reasoning, in part, goes like this: When these earlier studies on the aging heart were made, many of the subjects were hospital patients, some of them very ill. One mission of gerontologists today has been to study changes in the physiology of the aging in the absence of disease. Lakatta thinks it is particularly important to examine the information scientists have gathered in each of three areas—true aging as separate from disease, physical deconditioning, and vascular disease. Based on this foundation, he feels, it may then be possible to state in general terms what we can expect of our hearts and blood vessels as we age.

One of the more important findings that follow, Lakatta says, citing study data, is that the process we know as arteriosclerosis is not simply a condition of the elderly or middle-aged. In fact, it has been "identified" in vessels from a substantial number of individuals in the 15-to-24 age range. In some Western populations, he adds, as many as 85 to 95 percent of all individuals have an early manifestation of arteriosclerosis. Even so, what seems like bad news can be good news: The fact that *young* people are known to have fibrous plaques already camping out in their bloodstream means that the condition cannot be thought of simply as a manifestation of age. And if it is not, then perhaps it can be treated—or at least prevented—by changes in life-style, diet, and exercise.

There are still many unknowns, however, in trying to explain how the heart and blood vessels age. For instance, the insides of the blood vessels (the intima) tend to narrow over time, but little is known about how this relates to the way the outer layers of the blood vessels (the media) promote blockage over time. People tend to concentrate on the accumulation of cholesterol on the artery walls without realizing that the vessels themselves lose some resiliency. In the walls of the arteries, elasticlike fibers called elastin become stiffer as collagen collects there. (Calcium also tends to accumulate inside these walls with age.) As Lakatta puts it, "Consider that the heart, pumping blood, 'forces' it through the vessels. With each heartbeat, the vessels expand somewhat to accommodate the blood. Stiffer vessels are less accommodating, and when the blood is pumped into them the pressure will be higher than in normal arteries. The heart will then have to do more work to pump out its blood into this higher-pressure system." In sum, all these changes should be studied together, Lakatta says, in order to gain a really clear understanding of arteriosclerosis.

Thanks to the rigid controls and able-bodied subjects of the Baltimore Longitudinal Study of Aging, Lakatta and other researchers at the Gerontology Research Center have been able to gain more accurate insight into the performance of the normal aging heart. For instance, contrary to past lines of thinking, the Baltimore researchers found that heart muscle thickens rather than thins as one ages. It is a kind of compensatory gesture that allows the heart to contract and empty itself normally in middle age and later, despite higher blood pressure.

Lakatta offers another age-related adaptation made by the heart. Cardiac output (volume of blood pumped per minute) is what you get when you multiply the stroke volume (the amount of blood pumped with each beat) by the heart rate (number of beats per minute). Since heart rates at maximum exercise levels decline with age, you might expect that cardiac output during vigorous exercise would also fall. Not so. Research now shows that, contrary to previous expectations, one's so-called end-diastolic filling volume increases as one ages. This means that during vigorous exercise the heart fills with more blood between beats, making more blood available to be pumped with the next beat. Again, this is a kind of compensatory gesture that the body seems to make to keep things running smoothly over time.

Summarizing the state of gerontological cardiac research, Lakatta emphasizes that (1) cardiac performance at rest is not affected by age as much as we previously had thought and (2) because of better-screened study populations and better diagnostic procedures, the notion that the aging cardiovascular system *necessarily* suffers a large decrease in functioning ability no longer holds true. In middle age and later years, symptoms such as breathlessness, sweating, or fatigue should not be attributed automatically to aging. And if such symptoms are related to cardiovascular function, they suggest the presence of cardiovascular disease or deconditioning—not aging *per se.*

This gives Lakatta pause for thought. He knows how long researchers and the general public have believed that a significant natural decline in cardiac function was expected; therefore he knows it will be a while before people accept some of the findings he and others have come up with regarding the aging heart. Instead of heaping praise on the artificial heart, and its various components, Lakatta feels the public should support researchers in their efforts to find a drug of some kind to take care of the plaque that clogs the arteries and leads to so many premature deaths. "The whole country is being lead around by the tail," he says, exaggerating only slightly, "when in fact we know less than one percent of what we need to know. It's the hard research to do when all the money is going to the Barney Clarks."

AS BLOOD PRESSURE RISES

During a blood pressure check, when the doctor or nurse wraps a black leather collar around your upper arm, what is being measured—with the aid of a sphygmomanometer and stethoscope—is the force of your blood against your arteries' walls. It is an important measure because high blood pressure is a well-known, age-related factor in presaging heart disease. The reading will be affected by when you last ate or exercised and by your emotional state—whether you are anxious, feeling under stress, or blissfully relaxed. Your blood pressure depends, too, on the volume of blood in circulation (typically eight to ten pints in adulthood) as well as the heart's ability to pump blood. Systolic pressure, the so-called upper bound of the reading, refers to the pressure during the rhythmic contraction of the heart, when blood is sent surging onward through the body. The lower bound, or diastolic, refers to the pressure measured when the heart chambers relax and fill with blood. A healthy man of 30 might have a blood pressure reading of 120/70, whereas an underexercised, overweight man of 60 might have one of 160/95 or higher. With a reading in this range, this man would be said to be suffering from hypertension.

In spite of its sound, the word hypertension does not mean an excessive amount of tension, but, rather, the existence of abnormally high systolic pressure. In men between 30 and 60, if the systolic pressure has risen and remained above 150, the likelihood of a heart attack doubles, while that of a stroke increases fourfold.[6] The National Heart, Lung, and Blood Institute estimates that 35 million adults in the U.S.—roughly 25 percent—have hypertension at a level where drug therapy is called for. As many as 25 million others have "borderline" high blood pressure that at least requires regular checkups.

Very simply, one's blood pressure rises if the heart pumps more (during exercise, physical strain, or stressful situations) or if the arteries are constricted, and it falls if the heart pumps less or if the arteries are dilated.

While high blood pressure is not in itself life-threatening, it is associated with life-threatening disorders such as heart attack, stroke, arteriosclerosis, kidney disease, and glandular problems. High blood pressure is sometimes brought on by these kinds of disorders, while at other times it may occur inexplicably in the absence of other disorders. Hypertension can set in as early as one's early 30s, or possibly sooner in some rare cases. Contrary to popular belief, high blood pressure is not caused by aging alone, although aging is a factor, along with heredity.

At least one way to reduce high blood pressure has to do with the salt shaker in your kitchen and on your dining-room table. It isn't a sure thing, but eating less salt may help prevent high blood pressure. The American Heart Association tells us: "Sodium is thought to aggravate high blood pressure in some people."[7] And because nearly everyone can get enough of the mineral sodium in fresh foods, there is no need to add more. More than half of the sodium in an average diet comes from the salt and other sodium compounds added by the manufacturers in processing food or by families at home. Considering that table salt is the biggest source of sodium in the diet, the AHA says, "The single most important thing you can do is to stop adding salt to food."

STRESS AND THE AGING HEART

Without stress, it is often said, life would be boring. Unfortunately for the aging man, with too much stress, life can be threatening. Stress and its effect on the individual are difficult to measure. But reducing stress has been a major focus of many cardiologists who want to help their hypertensive patients, including Dr. Herbert Benson, noted Boston cardiologist, associate professor at Harvard Medical School, and author of the compelling book, *The Relaxation Response*. Benson is not above using good ideas from other cultures, and has borrowed heavily from the theory and practice of transcendental meditation, extracting those principles that he feels can be best applied to stress-related disorders from anxiety to heart disease. As director of the division of behavioral medicine and the hypertension section at Boston's Beth Israel Hospital, he has worked out techniques that could be employed by healthy individuals as well as those suffering from hypertension.

For starters, Benson would like Americans to do away with one of their most entrenched daily rituals: the coffee break. In its place he would like to see people set aside time for "relaxation periods," in which they would train their bodies to relax and elicit healthful internal cures to combat overly stressful work environments. If the idea sounds trivial or unpractical, keep in mind that not too many years ago, the idea of corporate fitness centers or running teams sounded pretty far out too. "Not only may such an application prove beneficial to the individual, it may have further, broader benefits and ramifications for industry as a whole," Benson says. As for the hypertensive person, controlled studies of the technique have shown it can significantly lower blood pressure. But as a cautionary measure, proponents advise hypertensive patients considering its use to get their doctor's approval first.

With all the talk about stress circulating today, it is hard for many people to believe that a medical definition of stress is barely 30 years old. Before

The Relaxation Response

Training the body to relax may be one of the best things you can do for your heart. According to Herbert Benson, a Boston cardiologist and author of *The Relaxation Response,* this lessening of tension can be achieved in just 20 minutes of uninterrupted concentration. Those who have practiced meditation will recognize the technique. Here's what you do:

1. Find a quiet area, a comfortable chair, and sit down;
2. Close your eyes;
3. Relax your muscles, starting from your toes and working up to your neck and head;
4. Breathe through your nose and—becoming aware of your breathing—begin speaking the word "one" (or another simple, neutral word) as you exhale;
5. Continue the pattern for about 20 minutes. It is all right to open your eyes occasionally to check the time, although a timer shouldn't be used. After the 20-minute period has elapsed, you should stay seated, first with your eyes closed, then open for a few minutes, before carrying on with your daily routine.

that, it was primarily a word bandied about by engineers and physicists. The concept of stress and the individual has been highly popularized in recent years, largely because two California cardiologists noticed what they thought was a pattern among heart disease victims. After surveying more than a hundred internists about their patients, Drs. Meyer Friedman and Ray H. Rosenman were convinced they had discovered a correlation between aggressive, competitive personalities and heart trouble. They sat down and wrote *Type A Behavior and Your Heart.* Published in 1974, it became a bestseller.

Among the book's primary conclusions was that people who were harddriving and acutely time-conscious (the "Type-A" personalities) seemed to be more susceptible to heart attacks than were people who were more laidback and easygoing ("Type B's"). In a follow-up study testing the Type A-Type B personality hypothesis, researchers of the Framingham, Mass., heart study group found that over an eight-year period, Type A's were at least twice, almost three times as likely to develop a heart attack, angina, or coronary heart disease.[8] About the only good words to be said for the stress the Type A personality undergoes is that it is indeed modifiable. Benson's relaxation response seems to work, as does regular exercise. A change of jobs in some instances might help; streamlining the daily work routine might help more. So would cutting down on social "obligations." It seems that changes in life-style, then, are well worth the effort for Type A's interested in reducing stress.

HELPING HEARTS IN NEW WAYS

Victims say it's like having an elephant stand on your chest. Doctors describe it as a throbbing pressure beneath the breastbone, more like stress or discomfort than a stabbing pain.[9] However they are described, heart attacks continue to kill at a dizzying rate. More than 650,000 deaths each year in the U.S. result from heart attacks and coronary disease. In the best-known kind of heart attack, a coronary artery is typically obstructed, often causing a complete stoppage of crucial blood flow, or total coronary occlusion. As a result, a portion of the heart muscle begins to die, leaving an area of dead tissue, or infarct, from which comes the term myocardial infarction.[10] Other types of heart disease, such as angina, are less sudden or drastic, but can still be life-threatening. Angina describes the pain or discomfort that results from a temporary shortage of oxygen and blood in the heart muscle, when the supply does not meet demand. However, anginal episodes, despite the worrisome pain, are not heart attacks.

Fortunately, as medical researchers come closer to understanding heart disease more fully, treatments and therapies have increased manyfold along the way. As an aging nation, we have learned at least to control some of the high-risk factors that lead to heart disease. We have also benefited from new drugs such as beta blockers, which reduce the heart's need for oxygen by slowing the heartbeat and lowering blood pressure. Another new drug is streptokinase, a blood-clot-dissolving enzyme that has gotten high marks from the cardiac community. Streptokinase is squirted directly into a clot to try to stop a heart attack already in progress. Because of its revolutionary nature, and because timing is so critically important to effective use of the drug, this treatment is not expected to become widespread immediately. It will take some time to train and familiarize cardiac care staffs with the streptokinase procedure, which was first tried by Dr. Peter Renthrop in West Germany in 1979.

One experimental procedure now being tested as a possible replacement for some coronary bypass operations has been described as "squashing plaques with balloons."[11] It is designed to open clogged arteries, with the aid of a catheter that contains a balloonlike device. When the catheter is fed into the body and led to the obstructed artery, the balloon is temporarily filled with fluid to push the plaque away from the middle out into the arterial walls, thus opening the blood flow. The next variation on this theme (already being tested) is the use of carefully guided lasers to open blocked arteries.

Largely overlooked among the many high-technology advancements in heart care has been the gradual increase in hospital personnel trained to diagnose and treat heart ailments. Today most hospitals have special cardiac care units.

Advances continue to be made in replacement parts for damaged hearts. Pacemakers, those reliable regulators of unsteady heartbeats first used 25 years ago, are now almost invisible when they are implanted beneath the skin of the chest. As many as 500,000 people in the U.S. wear pacemakers today, many of which contain lithium batteries that can last as long as five years.[12] Also, until artificial hearts become a more practical surgical solution, surgeons are implanting artificial heart valves and "halves" of artificial hearts with some regularity and much success. The half-hearts are known as ventricular assist devices (VADs), and Thoratec Laboratories Corp. of Berkeley, Calif., the manufacturer, says its corporate goal is to make the new VADs available "on a mass basis." By early 1983, the firm had started shipping them to three medical centers. Meantime, Dr. Hossein Naraghipour, a Cleveland heart surgeon, says the prognosis for the devices appears bright. "At the present time they can save more lives than artificial hearts...."[13]

MAINTENANCE: THE HEART

Heart studies of large populations have identified a number of risks associated with heart disease and heart attack. One of these, the Framingham, Mass., study, examined thousands of adults over a 20-year period and concluded that the more risk factors one has, the greater likelihood of developing heart disease. You are considered to be "at risk" if you:

- lead a sedentary life
- are a cigarette smoker
- are obese
- have elevated blood fats (lipids)
- have high blood pressure
- have a personality designated "Type-A"

All of these risk factors are considered by specialists to be avoidable, controllable, or correctable (even personality—through behavior modification). What, specifically, can you do?

- You've heard it before, and you'll hear it again: If you smoke, *stop.* Don't be discouraged if you've tried to quit and failed. Many smokers have had to try several times before achieving a tobacco-free existence. For information on ways to stop smoking—both do-it-yourself and group support programs— see your local chapter of the American Heart Association, the American Lung Association, or the American Cancer Society.
- If you suspect you are at risk because of weight, hereditary factors, or lack of activity, be sure to have a thorough physical examination, especially before beginning a diet or exercise program. Any man over 30 who has not been exercising regularly should see a doctor before beginning a fitness program.
- Even if you think you're fit, see a doctor to find out your blood cholesterol level, and specifically the relationship of HDL (high-density lipoprotein), the "good" cholesterol, to LDL (low-density lipoprotein), the "bad" cholesterol. Your doctor may suggest a diet to reduce cholesterol. Aerobic exercise, in and of itself, has been shown to increase the levels of HDL, reducing the risk of heart attack.
- After you've been checked out by a doctor, begin (or maintain) a program of regular aerobic exercise. To ensure that you are getting a good aerobic workout, your pulse should be sustained at your target heart rate (see page 165) throughout 20 minutes of activity.
- Know how to measure your pulse. Check your pulse at the wrist for 15 seconds and multiply the number of beats by four. (If you check it at the carotid artery, there is some chance you will lower the pulse by pressing too hard.) When checking to see if you're at your target rate, take your pulse within 20 seconds after you stop exercising. A well-conditioned man, whose heart returns to a resting pulse more quickly, should add 10 percent to the measured pulse to get the actual heartbeat during exercise.
- Know your resting pulse rate, and look for improvement in it. One of the results of aerobic training is a lowered resting pulse, meaning that your heart

(continued)

is stronger and pumping more blood per beat; because of this improved efficiency, the beats per minute decrease.

- According to Kenneth Cooper, founder of the Aerobics Center in Dallas, the top five aerobic exercises are cross-country skiing, swimming, running, cycling, and walking. Remember that walking and swimming are a form of exercise most people can do at any age.

- Be flexible when it comes to exercise. Do more than one activity to get the most out of your body and the enjoyment that comes with greater variety.

- Build muscular strength and flexibility. Regular exercise of the major muscle groups increases the size of the muscle fiber and enables the muscles to pump more blood to the heart. Flexibility increases range of motion and reduces the risk of injury.

- If you are a few pounds overweight, you can probably successfully control your weight with exercise. However, it is still important to watch your intake of fats, particularly saturated fats. And if you're obese, you must work with your doctor to reduce both the amount of fat and the number of calories you consume.

- The feeling of inner stress, whatever its cause, can be alleviated by regular physical activity. You don't have to run a marathon to prove it to yourself. Just work gradually toward achievable goals. Your heart will appreciate it.

Resilient Lungs and Kidneys

After a baby emerges from the birth canal—sometimes only after a sharp slap is administered to its bottom—its lungs fill with air and expand, thrusting out toward a tiny rib cage. And with that first breath, a pattern is established that will last, literally, a lifetime.

As a man ages, although his full-grown lungs will shrink only slightly, his maximum breathing capacity declines measurably. This is because most aging individuals can't maintain as fast a rate of breathing as they could when they were 30. The body's maximum intake of oxygen during vigorous exercise—or "VO_2 max," in medical parlance—declines on average about one percent a year, usually beginning in a man's 30s. This means that the body is unable to extract as much oxygen from the blood. But although they can measure how much lung function declines, experts still do not fully understand *why* it happens.

One of the most appealing theories for why we age was offered in an eighteenth-century treatise entitled *Hermippus Redividicus, Or The Sage's Triumph over Old Age and the Grave, Wherein a Method Is Laid Down for Prolonging the Vigour of Man, Including a Commentary upon an Ancient Inscription, in Which this Great Secret Is Revealed, Supported by Numerous Authorities.* A man aged, according to the treatise, because he lost vital particles every time he exhaled. The Great Secret—how to find a new source of particles—was revealed by the discovery of a tomb whose occupant had reportedly lived to the age of 115. The fellow managed to live so long, according to the tomb's inscription, WITH THE AID OF THE BREATH OF YOUNG WOMEN. Today, physicians advise jogging.

And while today's gerontologists aren't looking for missing particles, they do regularly measure vital capacity (along with VO_2 max) to see how well the lungs are resisting the effects of age. Vital capacity is simply the amount of air that can be brought into the lungs in the deepest possible breath after exhaling. A handy measure, the average decline in vital capacity over the years looks like this:

Age 30: 6 quarts
Age 40: 5.4 quarts
Age 50: 4.5 quarts
Age 60: 3.6 quarts
Age 70: 3 quarts

According to the American Lung Association, a healthy man's lung function peaks when he's about 25 (a woman's normally peaks at around 20), then begins a gradual decline. "But it's not a decline that's noticeable," says the ALA. "Barring illness, a man's lungs will serve him well as long as he lives." Dr. Kenneth H. Cooper, who is often credited with starting the worldwide jogging craze through his books on aerobic exercise, agrees that vital capacity need not fall off with age. In his most recent manual, *The Aerobics Program for Total Well-Being,* Cooper reels off lists of beneficial physical effects from aerobic workouts including: "The capacity of the lungs increases, and some studies have associated this increase in 'vital capacity' with greater longevity."[1] This is good to know. Yet eventually the muscles that operate the lungs weaken as tissues in the chest cage stiffen. Neither regular running nor the aid of the breath of young women can keep lung function in its prime for too long. For in late adulthood, a general loss of joint mobility also reduces the elasticity of the rib cage, which, combined with the other changes mentioned above, helps make breathing more of a chore.

CHARTING BREATHING CHANGES

If you happen to hold your breath as you read this, you will temporarily disrupt the main task of your lungs, which is to supply necessary oxygen to the body and to remove from it carbon dioxide, a waste product formed from oxygen consumption. This gas exchange process takes place in microscopic air sacs called alveoli, which are bundled together deep inside the wing-shaped lungs themselves. The oxygen eventually makes its way throughout the body via the bloodstream, powered by the heart.

As the oxygen enters the body, it passes through two treelike bronchial tubes in the lungs. The main bronchi split into smaller bronchi, then into smaller bronchioles, then finally into alveoli, which have walls thinner than those of soap bubbles. There are more alveoli in *each* lung (300 million) than there are residents of the United States. Where the alveoli and capillaries from the pulmonary arteries meet is where the swap of oxygen for carbon dioxide takes place. Here is where the oxygen you breathe officially enters the body. Up to this point, the lungs have merely served as storage tanks.

The continual branching of the bronchial tubes inside the lungs increases their surface area immensely. And for this reason, the lungs in humans are not really sacs, as they are in many fish and reptiles, but rather intricate sponges. With all of their spongy branches, the lungs can boast of a total surface area of about 600 square feet.[2] So there is plenty of room for gas exchange. On average, adults inhale about 12 to 20 times a minute, with larger people tending toward the slower breathing rate, smaller people and children toward the faster. During vigorous exercise, the breathing rate can increase up to 40 breaths per minute. The act of filling one's lungs is both voluntary and involuntary, as someone who has just held his breath for a minute and a half might tell you. For when carbon dioxide builds up in excess in the lungs, the body seems almost to explode. The respiratory system must expel the waste carbon dioxide from the lungs in order to get the required oxygen.

Normal healthy lung tissue is elastic and is normally in a stretched state. With age, it has a tendency to contract, from age itself and from impurities gathered from the air, smoke, or other pollution. The lungs try—and mostly succeed—to cleanse and protect themselves from irritants with the help of nose hairs, bronchial cilia, mucus, and macrophages, which are fleet-footed cells in the alveoli that engulf bacteria and viruses. Among older people these natural lines of defense become somewhat weaker, which is why their susceptibility to lung diseases or disorders increases.

AGE AND RESPIRATORY DISORDERS

When it comes to unhealthy lungs it appears women have an advantage. Men have been and still are inclined to get lung diseases more frequently than women. "We think it's because they have more exposure to environmental and occupational hazards and because they have smoked more than . . . women," says Roberta Thumim, a spokesperson for the New York-based American Lung Association. In 1980, for instance, men suffered from emphysema at a rate of 17.5 per thousand. The rate for women was 5.6 per thousand, or less than a third of that for men. In 1980, 85,000 men had lung cancer, compared with 35,000 women who had the usually fatal disease. Reviewing comprehensive 1978 government health statistics, however, researchers have found that women suffered more cases of the less serious but more prevalent disorders of asthma, bronchitis, and hay fever than did men.

While most often afflicting children, asthma affects more than 6 million people in the U.S. today. In an asthma reaction, the bronchi or bronchioles are narrowed by tightened muscles, swollen tissues, or excess mucus, which temporarily make breathing a painful and scary event. Episodes can be mild or severe, and are set off by various substances that cause allergies or by exercise, infection, or even cold air. As sufferers age, their bronchial tubes sometimes grow less sensitive to offensive stimuli, effectively weakening the asthmatic episodes. Still, a fair number of older people who have had asthma in the past do find that their bronchial sensitivity can return unexpectedly.

AGING LUNGS

Emphysema hits men between the ages of 50 and 70 the hardest. Unlike the declining incidence of the bacterial diseases pneumonia and tuberculosis (in which modern antibiotics have played a critical part), the incidence of emphysema has risen markedly in the past few decades. Smoking, of course, is a primary causative factor, but air pollution and other environmental problems appear to have some murky, if elusive, effect. There is also a relationship between emphysema and chronic bronchitis, but it is not yet fully understood. We do know that in both disorders, irritated passageways in the lung bring on pain and loss of lung function.

A heavy, hacking cough and persistent winter colds may be the first warning signs of emphysema. Severe breathlessness is the mark of the disease. As emphysema progresses, the alveoli are obstructed or obliterated, a result of chronic irritation, and the lungs enlarge but become increasingly less efficient. The heart is then forced to work harder (as in the celebrated case of Dr. Barney Clark), and may enlarge or fail from the strain. There is no cure as yet for emphysema, but it can be treated. The best medicine is still preventive: Quit smoking and try to avoid air pollution, for starters.

Emphysema sufferers, in addition to their lung difficulties, may suffer sexual problems as well. Like heart attack patients, those with emphysema tend to have major fears about shortness of breath during sex. In an issue of the American Lung Association bulletin, Dr. James Kieran and Nan Pheatt tried to arrest those fears. "First," they wrote, "none of the commonly used medications for chronic lung disease . . . will inhibit sexual performance. This is not the case with some hypertension and heart disease medications. Second, in lung disease uncomplicated by heart disease, shortness of breath is uncomfortable but not life-threatening. It can be reduced during intercourse by using a bronchodilator to dilate the lung passages or by taking low-concentration oxygen during lovemaking. . . . Many counselors recommend the side-by-side position and resting at intervals. . . ." "The real solution," Kieran and Pheatt added, "is an improvement in communication. *Partners need to talk.*" [3] Shortness of breath, no matter how severe, shouldn't inhibit that kind of communication.

The kind of talk that ought to be inhibited, according to Dr. Michael Pollock, a prominent exercise physiologist, is that of the expected decline in lung function that until very recently prevailed throughout gerontology and cardiac rehabilitative medicine. This is the "one percent decline" in adults in VO_2 max per year, which is the standard predicted rate of decline in the body's ability to extract and use oxygen during vigorous exercise. Pollock and a cadre of other exercise physiologists have recently shown that some highly motivated, highly trained, and well-conditioned distance runners have staved off an expected decline in lung and heart function over at least a ten-year-span (see chapter 12). To take only one hopeful example from Pollock's study conducted at Mount Sinai Medical Center in Milwaukee: Hal Higdon, a "Masters" runner and author, had VO$_2$ max readings of 62.7, 69.4, and 63.2 at the ages of 41, 46, and 51, respectively, in 1971, 1976, and 1981. To even the most skeptical observer, those numbers do not indicate any kind of decline. Rather, they represent a gain in one aging man's capacity to extract and use oxygen in middle age. It is the kind of finding that should make fit, aging individuals everywhere breathe easier. A small step for a distance runner, perhaps, but a giant leap for the future outlook on aging and fitness.

CONSIDERING THE KIDNEYS

While there are many scientifically precise methods of studying kidney function, forget, for a moment, experimental laboratories. Think, instead, of your favorite neighborhood bar. To understand better how the kidneys work, it helps first to recap some barroom chatter. No doubt over the years you have probably heard the phrase "renting the stuff," referring to beer drinkers who run back and forth from the restroom all evening. But the reason beer seems to pass right through you, when you're drinking more than a couple, has little to do with its brewer or its taste. Rather, it has to do with a substance called antidiuretic hormone, or ADH, also known as vasopressin, which, in partnership with the kidneys, helps keep the body's internal chemistry in balance. Manufactured in the hypothalamus, ADH regulates urine production and thus affects the amount of water in the blood. When you are dehydrated, ADH tells the kidneys to stop producing urine in order to conserve water in the bloodstream at a safe level.[4] However, alcohol is one of the substances (caffeine is another) that inhibits the secretion of ADH—which means that when you drink beer (or any other alcoholic beverage) in quantity, the kidneys don't know any longer when they are supposed to stop producing urine. So they keep on doing their work, filtering and processing the blood and its contents and sending you rather regularly from the bar to the john. In addition, at the end of an extended mug-clinking session, there is a good chance you will arrive home dehydrated. As a result the water you drink before bed may turn out to be more important than the aspirin you might take to ward off a dreaded hangover.[5] Drinking too much beer—or any other alcoholic beverage for that matter—makes it tough for the kidneys to filter

MAINTENANCE: THE LUNGS

Keeping lungs healthy in an industrialized nation, where air pollution and cigarette smoking are significant hazards, is no easy task. A city dweller may feel helpless against the emissions from buses and automobiles, yet organized civic action has succeeded in reducing these pollutants. Far worse, from a health viewpoint, are the fumes smokers willingly suck into their lungs with every puff of a cigarette.

The best thing you can do for your lungs is to avoid cigarettes. If you smoke, gaining freedom from the habit should be your foremost health concern. The numbers are persuasive: The Surgeon General's office estimates that tobacco kills as many as 340,000 Americans each year. In a 25-state study conducted by the American Cancer Society, the following findings about smoking and longevity emerged:

- A 30-year-old nonsmoking man can expect to live, on average, another 43.9 years.
- A 30-year-old man who smokes from 1 to 9 cigarettes daily can expect to lose, on average, 4.6 years of his life; If he smokes 10 to 19 cigarettes daily, he can expect to lose 5.5 years; If he smokes 20 to 39 cigarettes daily, he can expect to lose 6.1 years; If he smokes 40 or more cigarettes daily, he can expect to lose 8.1 years.

On the positive side, stopping the habit at any age can dramatically reduce the risk of contracting heart disease, lung cancer, or emphysema.

- Damaged cilia within the lungs will regrow in about six months after all smoking has stopped. Studies have shown improvement in pulmonary function as early as three weeks after the last cigarette has been smoked.
- The physiological benefits are many. No longer will nicotine cause your heart to beat faster and your blood pressure to rise; no longer will it affect your automatic nervous system in other dangerous ways.
- No longer will you have to deal with a fuzzy mouth, lowered taste sensations, and yellow stains on your teeth.
- No longer will you suffer as many coughs and colds, or be as likely to get laryngitis and sinusitis.

Some people are able to stop smoking on their own, others need group support. Many groups exist to help. Contact your local chapter of the American Cancer Society or the American Lung Association, which distributes a do-it-yourself booklet called "Freedom from Smoking in 20 Days."

Breathing exercises are now frequently advised for both ex-smokers and nonsmokers to relieve tension and also to maintain healthy lungs throughout life. The American Lung Association recommends the following deep-breathing exercises to be done twice a day, or whenever stress seems to be getting the best of you:

1. Lie flat on your back with your mouth closed, hands folded on your stomach, and your knees flexed. Let your shoulders relax and inhale as deeply as you can—to the count of eight. Push your stomach out as you inhale.
2. Hold your breath to the count of four.
3. Exhale slowly to the count of eight.
4. Repeat this inhale-hold-exhale cycle five times.

blood and work efficiently. They inadvertently remain "switched on," making it seem as if your bladder is incessantly full.

As guardians of the body's internal chemistry, the kidneys have a lot more to do than manufacture urine. Their filtration function is essential for life, and their importance is underscored by the fact that at any one time as much as 25 percent of the body's total supply of blood may be passing through the kidneys' various microscopic tubes.

Contrary to popular misconception, the kidneys are not located in the lower back but above the waist, against the back wall of the abdomen, partially above the lowest ribs, and behind the stomach and liver. The kidneys are connected to the heart by short, thick renal arteries that constantly accept blood from the aorta. The tubules of the kidneys through which the blood passes are called nephrons, each about one to two inches long. An adult kidney is only four to five inches long, two to three inches wide, and one to two inches thick, but it contains about one million nephrons. If all the nephrons in a kidney were stretched end to end, they would reach some 40 miles—about the distance between the National Institute on Aging in Bethesda and the NIA's Gerontology Research Center in Baltimore, where ongoing studies of aging kidneys take place.

Enroute to and through the nephrons, the blood passes from the renal arteries to much smaller arterioles and then to capillaries, called glomerular tufts. These tiny branches of arteries and filters are so small there is plenty of time for the required blood drop-off, cleansing, and collection of water, ions, minerals, and wastes such as urea to occur. Once cleansed, the blood reabsorbs some of its temporarily lost water and nutrients along the length of the nephrons, and exits through the renal vein. In the meantime, urea, other waste materials, and water are shuttled out of the kidney through the ureter from the renal pelvis. The two ureters carry the urine to the bladder, from which it flows through the urethra and is excreted. Normally urine is 95 percent water, and the healthy adult body produces between two and four pints of urine in a day. If one is dehydrated, the kidneys will automatically reduce the amount of water lost through urine.[6]

AGE AND THE KIDNEY

In the absence of disease, the kidneys hold up pretty well through the years. They have tremendous reserve capacity, so while a man in his 40s apparently loses his ability to regenerate nephrons, the decline is not usually noticeable. In fact, he can lose thousands of nephrons each year and function normally.

Even if one kidney is removed, the remaining one, assuming it is healthy, can handle the job.

Another, more noticeable change with age is in bladder capacity. The maximum capacity of a male bladder is about 16 ounces, or a pint. In aged individuals, bladder capacity is reduced to at least a third, sometimes to a half of its former volume.

Discussing aging kidneys recently, Dr. Ira Greifer, medical director of the National Kidney Foundation and professor of pediatrics at Albert Einstein Medical Center in New York City, said, "In normal physical status, there is a decline relative to function, with age." This decline, added Greifer, is easily measured. First is the matter of size: The weight of the kidneys declines 20 to 30 percent between maturity and old age. In an average man of 30, each

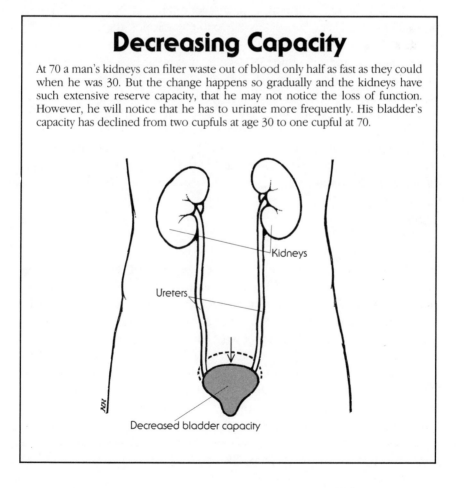

Decreasing Capacity

At 70 a man's kidneys can filter waste out of blood only half as fast as they could when he was 30. But the change happens so gradually and the kidneys have such extensive reserve capacity, that he may not notice the loss of function. However, he will notice that he has to urinate more frequently. His bladder's capacity has declined from two cupfuls at age 30 to one cupful at 70.

Kidneys

Ureters

Decreased bladder capacity

kidney weighs about 270 grams—slightly more than half a pound. By the age of 70, each is about 200 grams. At the Gerontology Research Center, an extensive longitudinal study of 884 subjects showed there is an accelerated rate of decline in what is called the "glomerular filtration rate," or the rate at which the kidneys filter waste from the blood.[7] "Between the age of 40 and 80, one can estimate the decline as one percent per year," writes Dr. Robert D. Lindeman, chief of staff at the Veterans Administration Medical Center in Louisville, Ky.[8]

So, in terms of function, a 70-year-old man's kidneys filter waste only half as fast as they could when he was 30. Yet, the fact that some kidney function will be lost over time ought not worry the average man in his 50s or 60s, says Greifer, who is 52. This is partly because the decline is so gradual, and partly because it tends to accelerate in the *oldest*—not merely aging—individuals. Researchers also frequently point out that individual variation in how kidneys age is enormous. Among 20-to-60-year-olds, there are normally 50 to 60 kidney-related deaths per million persons, according to Greifer. Among those in their 60s and 70s, though, that number rises, but not drastically, to 150 to 200 deaths per million. Although the kidneys' ability to regenerate and repair themselves falls off each decade, fortunately the overwhelming majority of elderly people are able to live relatively unaffected by these changes.[9] It is those who have extremely high blood pressure or various types of kidney disease, which come under the umbrella name "glomerulonephritis," who may suffer grave risk. But these are not conditions brought on necessarily by age.

KIDNEY ADVANCES

Despite the fact that kidney disease killed 80,000 people in the U.S. in 1982, more hopeful figures can be gleaned from the National Kidney Foundation files. In 1980, for example, some 52,364 people benefited from various forms of dialysis. In 1981, that number rose to 58,770, an increase of more than 12 percent. This increase may not seem particularly impressive at first, until you listen carefully to an explanation of what exactly dialysis means to a patient. Dr. Greifer, who has headed the National Kidney Foundation for the past 17 years, makes clear that dialysis is a matter of life and death.

"What we have had," Greifer says, "is an increase in 'immortality.' " The dialysis machine takes over completely the all-important blood-cleansing function for the body, without which the patient would die. (People tend to forget that Barney Clark's death was attributed in part to failed kidneys.) Greifer, who realizes that dialysis does not seem to generate the kind of excitement as, say, the artificial heart, sees dialysis as an incredible life-extending process.

One type of therapy that *has* generated excitement among families who have members able to use it is called "continuous ambulatory peritoneal dialysis" or CAPD. This treatment involves installing a permanent tube in the abdomen and pouring a dialysis solution into the peritoneum, the saclike tissue covering the intestines. Toxic and other wastes can be filtered in this added solution, which later flows into disposable bags attached to the skin. The treatment is continuous, while the bags are emptied up to five times a day. And as cumbersome as the "wearable" artificial kidney therapy sounds, Greifer says, it gives artificial kidney patients freedom and mobility that would not have seemed feasible even ten years ago.

In summarizing recent advances in dialytic therapy, Greifer mentions that one has to look carefully at the latest mortality figures. If you don't fully understand the impact of artificial kidney therapy, you might misread them. For instance, there are, today, numerous deaths attributed to cardiovascular causes that would have once been kidney-related. Now, with dialysis, people live long enough for their hearts to catch up with them. While dialysis techniques should continue to improve, and become more convenient, Greifer can say confidently that the state of the art is such that "the prolongation of life is a reality."

MAINTENANCE: THE KIDNEYS

The kidneys together weigh only about half a pound, yet their light weight belies their significance. If the kidneys were to shut down, and intensive medical care were unavailable, death would soon follow. Simply put, your kidneys' health is worth protecting.

To keep the excretory functions of the kidneys running smoothly, especially in middle age and beyond, make a habit of drinking water. Because approximately 50 percent of the body's water supply is gained from solid food and because the average person's caloric intake declines with age, it is particularly important for older people to drink plenty of fluids. Nutritionists recommend between six and eight glasses of liquids a day.

In addition, avoid excessive amounts of protein. The kidneys must rid the body of nitrogen from the protein it doesn't use, and this can overtax them, creating a potential for disease.

Finally, it is important to detect kidney disease early so that treatment may begin immediately. The six most prominent warning signs of kidney disease are:

1. A burning sensation while urinating or difficulty in urinating.
2. More frequent need to urinate, especially at night.
3. Excretion of blood-tinged urine.
4. Persistent pain in the small of the back just beneath the ribs.
5. Puffiness around the eyes or swelling of the hands and feet (particularly in children).
6. High blood pressure.

High blood pressure can mean trouble for the kidneys, and kidney problems can sometimes cause high blood pressure. The National Kidney Foundation reports that of all the people who suffer kidney failure, some 10 to 20 percent of cases are caused by high blood pressure. Your doctor can advise you on ways to reduce high blood pressure, and may prescribe diuretics, sympatholytics, vasodilators, beta blockers, or other medications. Preventive measures to keep blood pressure at a healthy level include:

• Weight control. If you are overweight, work out a reducing plan with your doctor.

• Reduction in salt intake. Most people eat much more salt than their bodies need, and diets high in salt have been linked to hypertension.

• Regular aerobic exercise.

Of Time,
Memory,
and the Brain

It was an honor, yes, but perhaps an honor Jerome H. Stone wishes he never had. It was, in the fall of 1982, a typical day in Washington, D.C., with tourist buses unloading in front of the Washington Monument every couple of hours, helicopters flying up and down the Potomac, and pockets of public officials streaming on and off shuttle flights at National Airport. On this day, Jerome Stone, a semiretired industrialist, had an appointment with the President. He met with Ronald Reagan in the White House, and afterward had his picture taken with him. Both men wore smiles. But while Reagan's wife was busy that day doing the sorts of chores required of our nation's First Lady, Stone's wife lay in bed in his home in suburban Chicago, virtually incapacitated, suffering from a progressive, severely debilitating brain disorder called Alzheimer's disease. As president of the Alzheimer's Disease and Related Disorders Association, Stone had flown to the nation's capital to help lobby for a Presidential declaration of an official National Alzheimer's Disease Week. And a couple of days later, he returned to O'Hare Airport with a signed declaration in hand, one that he knew would do a lot toward educating the masses about this feared disease. He also knew, however, that it was years too late for his stricken wife to read and comprehend the declaration and its meaning. For there is no cure, as yet, for senile dementia of the Alzheimer's type, one of the most serious age-related disorders of the brain, and possibly the most frightening.

"The President was very charming, very gracious," Stone said a few months later in his Chicago office. "He seemed very interested in and intrigued by talk about Alzheimer's, in part because he thought it was something his mother may have had. We spent seven or eight minutes talking about the various disorders . . . later we got into talk about the costs."

When Stone's wife was diagnosed as having Alzheimer's disease in 1970, he didn't have to worry about costs for treatment. As a top executive with the prosperous Stone Container Corp. of Chicago, he considered himself fortunate to be in the "upper one percent" of people in the U.S. in terms of financial status. Yet the most expensive medical care could not help her as her memory and then other parts of her mind slowly slipped away. "They called it 'presenile dementia' then," Stone recalled—*presenile* because his wife was then in her mid-50s. Stone's search took him to the neurology department of Northwestern University and then to Massachusetts General Hospital, where neurologist Dr. Raymond Adams, according to Stone, "was the first person to call it Alzheimer's disease." Unfortunately, Stone recalls, in the early 1970s there was barely enough neurological evidence to treat the disease at all, much less attempt an outright cure. Even now, after major scientific advances, treatment is temporary and weak at best.

"My wife was a guinea pig," Stone said in a soft, unhurried voice. He then cited Lewis Thomas's description of Alzheimer's: "It robs a patient's mind, but it breaks a family's heart." And he spoke again about his bed-ridden wife, whose faculties have progressively declined in the nearly 14 years since the diagnosis. "She knew French and German fluently, and some Yiddish. She played the violin and the piano, golf and tennis, and was a wonderful dancer. She is just a vegetable today," he said, as he opened his hands skyward.

Alzheimer's disease is not a normal part of aging, but a progressive, deteriorating neurological disease that was first described by a German psychiatrist and neuropathologist, Alois Alzheimer, in 1907. It usually strikes those in middle age and later, and its victims come from all ethnic, racial, and socioeconomic backgrounds. Experts in the field of neurological disease estimate that more than 1.5 million Americans suffer from Alzheimer's. They say it is also the fourth leading cause of death in this country, claiming more than 120,000 lives each year.[1]

Alzheimer's disease not only causes patients to suffer but strains the healthy members of affected families as well. As the disorder progresses, victims experience unusual personality and behavioral changes, and forget things like their last meal, their last job, how to dress correctly, or, more poignantly, a spouse's name—or even that they are married. It is the most common and important of the degenerative diseases of the brain.[2] Like other forms of dementia, its major symptom is a gradual development of forgetfulness, whereby small day-to-day happenings are not recalled.

Dr. Robert Butler, professor of geriatrics at Mount Sinai School of Medicine in New York, says as many as 8 million Americans may be affected by Alzheimer's disease in the next 30 years. With the foresight perhaps expected of the country's first director of the National Institute on Aging back in the 1970s, Butler anticipates that the "baby-boomers" of the 1950s will in the early 2000s be the "generation at risk."[3]

THE MID-LIFE TO LATE-LIFE BRAIN

Sitting on top of the spinal cord, not all that unlike the ball on top of a flagpole, the grayish-pink brain—a mushy mass of neurons, ridges, and grooves—make up man's control center, his most important coping tool.

After studying young neurosurgeons learning to operate on the brain at the Neurological Institute in New York, writer David Noonan offered *Esquire* readers this commentary in the December, 1982, issue: "Mysterious and intimidating to contemplate, the human brain is the most complex thing on earth. It is *the* wonder of the world, an electrochemical, metaphysical entity so elaborate and sophisticated that the most difficult task it can undertake is to understand itself—a goal it pursues with the distinct feeling that it may well be beyond its own comprehension. From the everyday miracles of sight and movement, speech and memory, to the dazzling glories of reason, emotion, and creativity, the functions of the human brain establish it as the dominant organ in existence. Without it, the human body is just an overdesigned eating machine."

This conglomeration of billions of interconnected cells grows to its full weight of three pounds in the first six years of life, as it rapidly accumulates and stores information as fast as it ever will. Its three main parts—the cerebrum, the cerebellum, and the brainstem—all contain neurons, or nerve cells, and glia, which are supporting cells. The largest portion, encased in the skull, is the cerebrum, which makes up about 85 percent of the brain's weight. A part of this is a roundish mass called the cerebral cortex, which is made up of extremely thin nerve cell bodies that help to relay orders from the brain to the rest of the body. The cerebrum is divided into hemispheres, left and right, which in turn are subdivided into four lobes each. And within these lobes the various tasks such as speech, hearing, and reading are categorized and, in a sense, put in their place. Recent theories of split brain function argue that the right hemisphere controls emotions and visual, spatial abilities, while the left is said to handle many logical and verbal skills.

Whether you are jogging in the park or shuffling along a snaking line outside a movie theater, the cerebellum of your brain is responsible for keeping your balance and posture erect, as well as for your overall coordination of movement. It is located squarely between the ears, just in front of the bony protrusion you can feel in the back of your skull. Containing densely packed bundles of nerve cells, the cerebellum also has a left and right hemisphere.

The brainstem, which connects the cerebrum with the spinal cord, is stalklike in composition and contains major nerve centers. In the bottom part of the brainstem, the medulla, reside the nerve cells governing the heartbeat, breathing, and other vital functions. As the major motor and senstory pathways pass through the medulla, they cross over, which is the reason why each hemisphere of the cerebrum controls the actions and sensations of the opposite side of the body.

The Shrinking Brain

As a man ages, his brain becomes smaller, lighter, and wetter, and it gradually pulls away from its sheath, the cortical mantle. This process, however, appears to have little effect on the brain's cognitive ability.

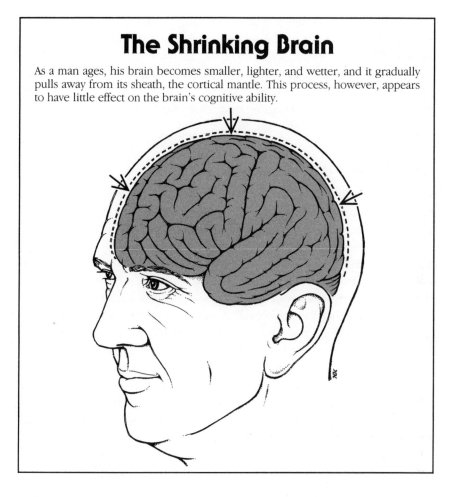

Over the years, the entire brain becomes smaller—and, as a consequence, lighter and wetter—than it was in one's teens. At the same time, the valleys (or gyri) that keep the brain sections compartmentalized grow deeper and wider, and the whole mass of brain pulls slowly away from its gray-matter cover, the cortical mantle. Billions of neurons are lost between adolescence and old age. In addition, some scientists have reported a distinct decline in dendrites, a network of branching, hairlike filaments that help transmit nerve impulses through the neurons.[4] Fortunately, man's brain contains from 10 billion to 100 billion neurons, and many more glia besides, to offset the losses and help the neurons keep moving messages along.

This loss of cells is peculiar in that it varies greatly with different parts of the brain—the region that controls head posture, for instance, doesn't seem to lose any, while the region that controls sleep stages is hit especially hard (which helps explain why aging men sleep up to two hours less than younger men).

Loss of brain function, however, is *not* an inevitable result of cell loss.[5] The tricky part of looking at aging brains, in fact, is differentiating the normal degeneration from the damaging kind. How much memory loss is to be "expected," for example, is anybody's guess.

AGING AND MEMORY

Imagine walking through your house on a well-traveled path, stopping along the way every couple of minutes, perhaps ten to 15 times in all, to pick up stray objects along the way. Say you snatch a pencil off the table in the front hallway, a portrait from the living-room wall, a wineglass in the kitchen, a videocassette in the den, and so on. By the end of your trip, you would not only have a hefty handful of household items, you would also have at your disposal an effective means of boosting memory. This way of remembering is especially suitable for the forgetful and the elderly. People who study mnemonics call this trick of remembering "method of loci." By linking something to be remembered to a familiar thing or location, you can effectively recall the new information learned. Such mnemonic devices can be thought of as exercises for the brain. They help your mind use what it has safely and irrevocably stored. And they help it store new information that might seem overwhelming at first, but when bolstered by the familiar and the commonplace, can be safely ingrained in your memory.

In the late 1970s, researchers at the National Institute on Aging tested a version of this "home association" method of recall on people as part of a study on how the mind ages. The goal was to track normal levels of memory function and then to try to improve that with so-called mnemonic devices and practice. It worked.

"In this procedure, the learners take a mental trip through their residences, stopping in order at 16 places," read the summary of an article in *Educational Gerontology*. "When they learn a list of words, they retrace the trip visualizing one of the items in association with each stopping place. This method was selected because it capitalizes on the familiarity of the stopping places and their natural order; these attributes provide strong retrieval cues that can be applied without adding to the information overload typically experienced by older learners."[6]

The experiment was found to be quite helpful to the test subjects, and repeated tests proved its validity as a tool for forgetful minds. Older people

Age and Memory

After about age 50, the slight loss of memory that typically afflicts a healthy man is more a matter of faulty retrieval than of lost information. If an old man and a young man each try to memorize a list of words and are then given clues to each of the words, the older man recalls them as well as the younger man. But without clues, the old man has a tougher time remembering what was on the list:

Age 20: 14 of 24 words recalled
Age 30: 13 words recalled
Age 40: 11 words recalled
Age 50: 10 words recalled
Age 60: 9 words recalled
Age 70: 7 words recalled

However, new tests show that older people can greatly improve their memory function when they are taught to use mnemonic devices.

tend not to use mnemonics on their own, it seems, but when these test subjects were asked to do so by the researchers during five sessions on five straight days, they not only embraced the procedure, they improved more than younger persons tested in similar fashion.[7] As the chances for recall were increased, chances for interference were decreased.

DEFEATING DEPRESSION

If your memory for historical-biographical detail is needle-sharp, you may recall that six score and seven years ago, or thereabouts, Abraham Lincoln suffered from depression. Like millions before and after him, Lincoln battled a condition that remains one of the most chronic and mysterious age-related disorders. A civil war of sorts can develop in the brain—altering moods and refusing to cede territory to more pleasant, positive thoughts.

As the mind ages, bouts of sadness, grief, or depression trip up even the healthiest people. These bouts may be expected or normal, but they needn't be chronic. In a recent article on new treatments for depression, Dr. Bruce J. Rounsaville of Yale University's medical school depression research unit said, "If you have depression, the news is good. The majority of patients— 80 percent—will get better with treatment."[8] Even as much remains unknown about the causes of depression, doctors do know a chemical imbalance or abnormality is present in many of the severe cases of the disorder among the aged. As a result, drug therapy can often alleviate the symptoms.

Dreaming for the Brain

When we sleep, our bodies rest. Our brains, though, use sleep for other purposes also. Strange as it may seem, more action takes place in our brain cells during dreaming sleep—and more blood flows to our brains—than during restful periods of wakefulness. Sleep comes in two varieties. The first is non-rapid eye movement (NREM) sleep, which can be divided further into two stages, light or deep; the second is "paradoxical," or rapid eye movement (REM), sleep. In deep NREM sleep the body and brain are thoroughly relaxed, but in REM sleep the brain is alert and the eyes move rapidly under the eyelids. It is during the periods of REM sleep that we dream.

With all the dozing that babies do, they spend up to half their days in REM sleep, but this falls to about 20 percent in adolescence, a level that remains fairly constant through adulthood. In old age, there is a further decline in REM sleep. In addition, as Dr. Elliot R. Phillips, medical director of the Sleep Disorders Center at Holy Cross Hospital in Mission Hills, Calif., explains, by age 50 for men and age 60 for women, most of the deeper stages of NREM sleep have vanished from the average person's sleep cycles. Doctors can't account for this difference any better than they can explain the difference in male and female life expectancy, although they allow there may be some connection between the two.

"Older people tend to have more pauses during sleep," said Phillips, while taking a lunch break during the annual American Psychiatric Association's convention held in New York in 1983. "And there is more drowsiness. But the problem with taking naps [in later years] is that it upsets the continuity. It's like taking a slice out of the pie of nighttime sleep."

Trying to explain the sleep problems older people have fairly frequently, Phillips said in his 1983 book, *Get a Good Night's Sleep,* that retirement can exact a price come bedtime. One's sleeping and waking rhythms, coached so often by a weekday alarm clock in the past, lose some valuable enforced structure. "The elderly destroy their circadian rhythm," wrote Phillips, "causing disruption of their sleep patterns." Thus, it is a good idea to maintain regular activity routines—even on weekends—to help the body's natural schedules stay on track. Sleep experts discourage the use of sleeping pills for more than a few weeks at a time (because of their questionable long-term value), while they encourage daily exercise to keep the body primed and to promote a healthy tiredness.

Regarding the types of sleep we undergo each night, it is believed that during REM sleep, new information is integrated into the brain. Also, REM sleep is said to reactivate the sleeping brain without waking its snoozing owner. Finally, while it's true that the quantity of REM sleep decreases with age, there is speculation that this may be a consequence of lowered mental stimulation rather than age itself.

However, not all older people can take antidepressant drugs. "A lot of patients can't take antidepressants because of possible heart or kidney problems," says Dr. David Burns, a psychotherapist at the University of Pennsylvania. Burns, who spends many of his days tackling cases of depression, uses

—often with encouraging results—a recently developed technique called "cognitive therapy." Developed in the late 1970s at the University of Pennsylvania by Aaron T. Beck and colleagues, cognitive therapy is used in place of or along with drugs to treat depression and other mental disorders. In his 1980 book, *Feeling Good,* Burns deplores the use of chemicals in cases where perhaps other techniques might aid a patient just as much—or more.

According to Burns, old age happens to be one of the most common reasons cited by patients to explain what they feel is a "realistic" depression. But psychiatrists like to point out that there is a difference between depression and sadness. Burns, for example, contends *there is no such thing* as "realistic" depression, because depression is caused by distorted thinking. He thinks (as do other kinds of therapists) that these distortions in thinking can be effectively treated and eliminated.

"When a genuinely negative event occurs, your emotions will be created by your thoughts and perceptions," Burns says. "Your feelings will result from the meaning you attach to what happens. A substantial portion of your suffering will be due to the *distortions* in your thoughts. When you eliminate these distortions, you will find that coping with the 'real problem' will become less painful." [9]

Of course, Burns, Beck, and their associates constantly face skeptics who wonder if cognitive therapy is little more than self-help pop psychology. "Actually," Burns answers, "cognitive therapy is the first form of psychotherapy, which has been proven to be more effective than antidepressant drug therapy through rigorous scientific research under the critical scrutiny of the academic community." [10] What's more, its proponents say, cognitive therapy is inherently practical to apply because it is based on common sense.

The first principle of cognitive therapy, according to Burns, is that *all* moods are created by cognitions, or thoughts. A cognition is a broad, sweeping view of the world. It includes perceptions, memory, judgment, and attitudes, and the way we interpret events and personalities. "You feel the way you do right now because of the thoughts you are thinking *at the moment,*" says Burns." [11]

If that sounds abstract, consider your own opinion about cognitive therapy right now. If you think it sounds reasonable and helpful in tackling depression, according to Burns, your reaction is caused not by these words but instead by how you are thinking as you read. By contrast, if cognitive therapy sounds to you like mere updated pop-psych pseudo-medicine, this too is a result of the thoughts you have been thinking—your opinion is not caused solely by the sentences written here.

People who feel depressed have thoughts that are dominated by incessant negativity. Everything appears clouded, dark, bleak, and gloomy. Cognitive therapists point out that the negative thoughts responsible for severe emotional turmoil almost *always* contain huge distortions. To depressed people the bleak views might appear valid, but the role of cognitive therapy is to show them these views are either irrational or wrong.

"I think depression can be triggered at any age by a loss of a personal relationship or a loss of career goals," Burns said in an interview from his Gladwyne, Pa., home. "They are both related to a loss of self-esteem—how well we do in our careers, and do we have those who love us, who care for us? If a man has been taught that worthwhileness [sic] is related to productivity, then if he no longer sees himself as productive, he tends to lose self-esteem and think, 'I'm not worthwhile.'" Burns frequently counsels patients with the words: "Your worth is not your work!"

For some men who have recently retired, this kind of counseling can be especially important. Sometimes their self-esteem drops drastically, or, as Burns bluntly says, "They begin to view themselves as worthless pieces of junk."

Like many other modern psychotherapists, Burns realizes cognitive therapy will have varying degrees of success with different people. Yet he feels it will be used more frequently in years to come among the aging because of the many drug-related side effects they typically encounter.

PIERCING THE BRAIN, PAINLESSLY

It is often no simple matter to identify a cause when an older person's brain goes awry. This is where the work of researchers like Alfred P. Wolf and his team come into play. Wolf is chairman of the chemistry department at the Brookhaven National Laboratories, and he directs a group of scientists who peer inside the human brain with the aid of a "second-generation" brain-scanning machine, the PETT VI. (PETT stands for positron emission transaxial tomography.) Allowing access to inner reaches of the brain that previously were unavailable except by surgery, the PETT scanner may now help them unlock unknowns about the brain's chemistry—particularly, in the case of the aging, the brain chemistry associated with depression, aphasia, or senile dementia. The PETT VI may even shed light on some elusive biological markers of how the brain ages.[12]

"At last we can interpret scientifically the differences between people who have neurological or psychiatric problems," Wolf told *The New York Times* in 1983. Later that year, he said in an interview for this book, "Because of the science itself, we are finding out more and more about the aging brain. He added that he himself has submitted to the PETT VI repeatedly as a test subject. "I hate to admit it, but my own ventricles are enlarging," Wolf said. "Thank God, there are no signs of senility. It is simply a fact that physical changes take place." He points out, like a proud father, that he and his Brookhaven colleagues were the first researchers to actually measure and witness glucose activity in the brain. This was an important research step because glucose is an essential form of fuel, or energy, for the brain.

The PETT VI, like CAT and PETT machines before it, scans the brain in slices and forms a three-dimensional picture with a computer's help. Whereas the PETT III could scan one brain "slice" in ten minutes, the PETT VI can scan seven slices of the brain in one minute and provide a picture in a few more. With a ring of flexible detectors that circle the head, the newest scanner can shoot and show any level of the brain.

Scientists at Brookhaven are now gathering information about such brain disorders as depression, senile dementia, Alzheimer's disease, and brain tumors. About five years ago, Brookhaven teamed with New York University Medical Center to study the brain's regional glucose metabolism in aging, dementia, and schizophrenia. "We now know that it's possible to study metabolic activity and make correlations to the aging process and senile dementia," said Wolf. Depression of glucose is noted in a number of regions of the brains of patients with senile dementia.[13]

REACTING TO THE BRAIN'S DECLINE

As debilitating as Alzheimer's disease appears, the bleak outlook for approaching a cure has slowly begun to brighten. To families who have members stricken with the disease, the experimental drugs now in use sometimes seem like hit-or-miss medications not much different from placebos. Yet, there are glimmers of hope. In March, 1983, for instance, *The New England Journal of Medicine* published an ordinary-looking letter signed by six staff members of the New York University Medical Center. It described a recent experiment in which naloxone appeared to improve cognitive function, at least as measured by clinical and "psychometric" tests. This preliminary report had not been confirmed, but NYU staffers noted: "In three of the patients, the clinical effects were of sufficient magnitude to be noted by family members."[14] Which, as families familiar with Alzheimer's disease could tell you, is no small feat.

Another type of medication that may help future senile dementia patients is physostigmine, which in past tests has been administered by injections and, more recently, orally. Dr. Kenneth L. Davis, associate professor of psychiatry at Mount Sinai Medical Center in New York, who headed a research team testing the drug at the Bronx Veterans Administration Medical Center, feels the drug could have short-term positive effects on Alzheimer's patients. Their study showed that several of 13 subjects tested improved their scores on tests of memory, but in only two cases were the gains considered "clinically meaningful." As limited as these tests are, one doctor, Joseph Cole of Johns Hopkins, told the *Los Angeles Times* that the results of studies testing naloxone and physostigmine "are the first glimmers of rational [therapy] for the disorder, which heretofore had no effective treatment."[15] Minute improvements in managing Alzheimer's disease patients won't have a significant effect on the quality of life of the patient or his family, but the fact that improvement is possible is something.

Another disorder of the brain is Parkinson's disease, in which patients suffer from involuntary shaking and stiffening of the head, arms, and legs—and sometimes eventual mental decline. Even though Parkinson's affects less than one percent of the population, it is well-known and feared among older people because some of the symptoms seem like those of senility. Fortunately, in the past decade, medical researchers have come up with a chemical solution to replace a deficiency in an important neurotransmitter called levodopa, which, in turn, produces the more active neurotransmitter dopamine in the brain. Using the drug L-dopa, many Parkinson's patients today lead relatively normal, symptom-free lives.[16] The question remains open whether L-dopa may turn out to help treat other forms of brain disease, including senile dementia.

PUTTING SENILITY IN ITS PLACE

In her book *The Myth of Senility,* medical journalist Robin Marantz Henig wrote of a pervasive self-fulfilling prophecy that affects aging brains. Many of the elderly slip into stages of forgetfulness, it seems, because of a lack of environmental stimuli and because the notion exists that old people are expected to forget things like names, places, or appointments. "The myth of senility is the stuff of our nightmares," Henig says. Adds Dr. Robert Butler of Mount Sinai in New York: "I believe people fear senility, fear growing old and losing their minds and being put away, more than they fear cancer."[17]

The problem is, all too often, that we are blind to the capacities of the aging brain, even with our X-ray and PETT scan machines. Doctors and families have been conditioned over the years to expect declines in motor performance among the aged, so they commonly go a step further and expect mental decline to follow. It is true that the brain shrinks and grows wetter with age, but it is also true that these changes do not seem to affect cognitive ability much at all. The point is not a simple one to make, even on impressionable medical students. Recently, Dr. Dennis Jahnigen of the V.A. Medical Center in Denver has instituted a program for the students at the geriatric unit he directs. He thinks it's important to confront young doctors with their prejudices. "If you think that everybody at eighty has lost their marbles, then how can you even pretend to provide good care?" he asks.

In what he calls his "professor-for-a-day" program, Jahnigen regularly invites certain Denver denizens to speak to his doctors-in-training to help rid a subset of the future physician population of that skewed mindset. These citizens talk about their lives, goals, medical experiences, and outlooks— from a vantage point of 90 years old or older.

"These people are interviewed by the students," Jahnigen says, "some of whom have never seen an active elderly person face-to-face outside of their families. They may assume all old people are wet, smelly, and confused." Staff members of the V.A. Medical Center attend the sessions although Jahnigen says they really don't need to be there to "lead" the questions between students and "professors." "You let an old person be his own spokesman and he'll do fine," says Jahnigen, 36, who was formerly an internist and has been a geriatric specialist for the past five years.

Trying to distinguish the difference between aging and diseased brains more clearly, neurologists are "seeing" more of the brain nowadays, partly due to technology and partly due to better understanding of the brain's messenger system. "One of the greatest strides that neuroscientists have made in the last few decades," says Dr. Carl Eisdorfer of Montefiore Hospital in the Bronx, N.Y., "is a change in their conception of the brain as an electrical system to the brain as a plumbing system."[18] According to Eisdorfer, a member of the medical advisory board of Jerome Stone's Alzheimer's Disease and Related Disorders Association, this concept fits better because the brain is more watery than most people realize. It does not send dry, electrical signal sparks from neuron to neuron in a flash, but instead it secretes a host of neurotransmitters that help the impulses cruise through the brain. Most of the current advances in biochemistry and the brain have been in the area of aiding the rusting "plumbing" system to work more efficiently in the face of constant use over time.

MAINTENANCE: THE BRAIN

On hearing that the brain shrinks and loses thousands of neurons over time, a man might well wonder about his mental capacity in the coming years. However, loss of brain mass does not mean a reduction in mental powers. You can continue to learn, to create, to reason, and to experience mental and psychological growth for the rest of your life. If ever you think your brain is "getting old," just remind yourself of the following:

- Recent studies with aged subjects indicate that the capacity to learn new information does not decline with age. It is not true that "you can't teach an old dog new tricks," but motivation is a key factor.

- The people who age most successfully are those who can shift their focus to mental pursuits, if various ills of the body cut down their physical activity.

- Like the body, the brain needs exercise. If you find your mind "running on automatic pilot" a lot of the time, seek stimulation or a challenge.

- It is never too late to take up a pursuit that interests you. Cultivate mental stimulation outside of your work. Learning and creativity, if fostered, will naturally continue into your later years.

- Senility is not an inevitable consequence of aging. Anyone who develops the symptoms of senility—marked mental deterioration, memory loss, disorientation—should be checked thoroughly by a physician. These symptoms can be caused by many factors, and may be treatable.

- Mild memory loss, common among older people, is often regained by some simple mental exercises. Researchers have shown that the mnemonic device called the "method of loci" can greatly boost one's memory power. The idea is to match information you wish to remember with familiar images or objects —household items, for instance. As you take a mental tour through your house, you will be able to retrieve the information.

- Cognitive psychologists and others have developed problem-solving strategies that can be learned at any age. Not only are we capable of learning more than we do, with training we can also use information more effectively.

- To minimize the effects of age-related slowdown in the central nervous system, research psychologists suggest continued practice of a skill, such as playing a musical instrument, that can serve to keep reaction time sharp.

- Some older people operate under the erroneous assumption that old age alone is cause for depression. While older people may suffer reverses and losses, they can also surmount them. Don't chalk up a depressed state to age. Get help.

Relative sleeplessness is a problem for some middle-aged and older people. Particularly if you've never had any trouble getting to sleep, bouts of insomnia can be upsetting. Here are pointers offered by the experts:

- Eat balanced meals and maintain a regular schedule of waking hours, eating, and exercise to keep the biological clock running smoothly.

- Take some time to relax before sleep by reading, or listening to music, or stretching, or performing some relaxation technique (see page 128), or tending to a hobby. This way you will put some distance between your daily concerns and your bedtime.

- If possible, don't use the bedroom for balancing the checkbook, paying bills, or watching an exciting movie on television. You want to associate your bedroom with the pleasures of sleep and sex, not with problems or anxiety.

With sufficient rest and stimulation, a man's brain should serve him well for the rest of his life. Psychologists have identified several stages of adult development beyond the "mid-life transition," which occurs around age 40. These distinctive and fulfilling periods of growth include what is termed late late adulthood, which begins around age 80. Many men have experienced tremendous bursts of creativity in this period—think of Bertrand Russell, Claude Monet, or George Bernard Shaw. Shaw, who lived to be 94, put it succinctly: "Your legs give in before your head does."

Stamina and Fitness Outlooks

Leonard Schwartz, 57, is an energetic Pittsburgh psychiatrist who likes to run with his hands. In doing so, he has given rise to a burgeoning cult of sorts, a cult of thousands of runners who carry hand weights while they run to maximize their exercise. And while it might seem a new form of fitness training, the principle behind the system actually goes back centuries, to the days when Scandinavian couriers crisscrossed the land on skis. By carrying one-to-ten-pound weights on the run, runners are able to simulate the stride-and-push movement of cross-country skiers, long hailed as among the best-conditioned athletes around. Schwartz claims that after three or four 30-minute sessions of "Heavyhands" training each week for five weeks, runners are able to improve their circulation enough to lower their pulse rate by as many as 25 beats per minute. Cruising through middle age, Schwartz watched his own resting pulse drop more than 50 percent in a six-year span. It went from 80 to 38 beats per minute—an impressive indication of improved circulation in his youthful, muscular body. "I can consume more oxygen than anyone I know," he says, "although from the neck up I don't look terribly young."

Below the neck, the doctor has much to be proud of. His muscles ripple in motion, from the shoulders to the upper torso and wrists and from the bulging quadricepses of the thighs on down. His training notions, set forth in the 1982 book *Heavyhands: The Ultimate Exercise System,* are built around the belief he developed in the 1970s that, while running is fine, it just doesn't do enough for complete body toning. Schwartz writes: "Using Heavyhands exercises, virtually anyone can exercise for 30 minutes without ever becoming anaerobic [reaching the state of oxygen debt.]" By spreading the work load over four limbs instead of two, and by varying weight loads and pace, even the unconditioned beginner, according to Schwartz, "can work out for 30 minutes without running out of gas."[1] In prescribing this improved aerobic exercise, Schwartz hopes to help improve the circulatory and muscular-skeletal systems that are prime targets in the aging process. In addition, over a five-year training span, Schwartz found that his grip strength and running times got better as his body fat percentage dropped from 16 percent to a lean 4 percent.

The question remains whether, at 57, Schwartz might be a physiological freak of nature. After some study, Dr. Robert D. Willix, Jr., director of cardiac rehabilitation and human performance in the North Broward Hospital District in Fort Lauderdale, Fla., says, "I don't think Schwartz is an unusual case. I think some of these [bodily] changes are predictable. Subjectively, I know the results. But objectively—scientifically—I wouldn't go on record yet on this point. The training has improved other people as well, but our findings are preliminary."

In striking a guarded yet optimistic tone about the benefits of this type of training, Dr. Willix, 42, barely masks his deep enthusiasm for Heavyhands. Formerly 30 pounds overweight, he has run marathons and is now in the grip of swim-bike-run triathlon fever. He has instituted Heavyhands training for his patients in cardiac rehabilitation after testing the regimen himself. Despite some doubts about the amount of improvement one could reasonably expect from the aerobic-weight training, Willix has no doubts that countless numbers of people can benefit from it. "I think Heavyhands is going to revolutionize cardiac rehabilitation," he says. "It has already changed our rehab program for the better. We're just beginning to find out how much it can do." The potential benefits go beyond cardiac rehabilitation patients, of course, to anyone interested in sustaining a sound level of fitness. More important, it confirms a key shift in American fitness programs toward more rounded approaches, and those that emphasize cross-training. Although Willix may seem shy about endorsing the concept "scientifically," he matter-of-factly mentions that Heavyhands-type training has replaced muscle-specific Nautilus and rowing machine workouts in the cardiac rehabilitation section at the Imperial Point Medical Center in Fort Lauderdale. "Everybody in our program uses it, regardless of age, sex, height, and weight," he says. "They do it because it makes them feel better." But will it help them to live longer? The guarded optimism returns. Doctors do not yet know.

Runners, however, think they know. Hal Higdon, marathon runner, Masters athlete, and author of *Fitness After Forty,* put it this way: "Ask any runner why he runs, and the answers that come back are: It is fun, it makes him feel better, he enjoys the easy camaraderie at races. But tucked away in the back of his mind is the fact /sic/ that running will make him live longer, that he can cheat Father Time."[2]

In *Maximum Life Span,* Dr. Roy Walford, a foremost authority on aging, stopped short of endorsing regular exercise as a way of extending life. He did, however, cite studies that showed marathon runners to have had unusually healthy coronary arteries, blood, and blood flow. Aerobic exercise including running, swimming, or cycling is what's effective, Walford says. Thomas Bassler, former president of the American Medical Joggers Association of North Hollywood, Calif., has gone so far as to claim that if a person trains for and finishes a full 26-mile, 385-yard marathon, and adopts a so-called "marathon life-style" consisting of a low-fat diet, lots of exercise, and no smoking, he will be immune from a heart attack.[3] Aerobic exercise helps the body to utilize oxygen more effectively at an increased rate, while the heart can pump more blood with each stroke. Both the resting pulse and pulse at various levels of activity are lowered, a healthy sign that the heart is working better than before.[4] Weighing the merits of exercise, David L. Costill, Ph.D., director of the Human Performance Laboratory at Ball State University in Muncie, Ind., has said, "There is no question in my mind that there is a benefit to cardiovascular health."[5]

As more and more people take up running and jogging, and as these runners and joggers mature, there is increased awareness that the true benefits of exercise go beyond powerful upper torsos or shrunken waistlines. Adult fitness has come to be viewed as having an overall effect on the entire body, on a massive scale, from the inside out. The beauty of a heart enlarged by exercise, pumping smoothly in an aerobically trained chest cavity, has begun to be appreciated well outside of exercise physiology circles.

In the wake of the fitness movement, there is now a widespread conviction among exercise physiologists that without at least 30 minutes a day of sustained exercise, men reach their physical peak at age 18 and start their decline at 26. The critical years in a man's exercise life are those that precede middle age, before his body has had much chance to decline. After testing more than 500 middle-aged men at Ball State, Costill found that one of every ten had oxygen deficiencies due to poor cardiovascular health. Among those over 65, Costill found that during maximum stress testing, inadequate oxygen supply to the heart muscles was a nearly universal event. He believes the greatest risk falls upon those who suddenly take up a vigorous sport in middle age without building up endurance.[6]

PUMPING HEALTH

If we agree with most aerobics experts, the key to good health through exercise is systematically building and developing the cardiovascular system. Whether it is called jogging, race walking, swimming, or bicycling, aerobic exercise consists of rhythmic activity using large muscle groups such as the arms or legs, performed at a level of intensity well below one's capacity for exercise. The relatively low intensity allows aerobic exercise to be continued for a long time, as a fairly constant, increased blood flow surges through the heart, lungs, and muscles. When all is going well during a lengthy run or swim, the energy requirements of the active muscles are met by the ability

Pulse Check

The best time to check for aerobic fitness on your own is immediately after a lengthy, steady workout of at least 20 to 30 minutes. If you are achieving proper aerobic benefits from the exercise, your pulse should be close to the target rate for your age. Keep in mind, however, that the better shape you are in, the quicker the pulse returns to normal. By taking your pulse after you stop exercising, you can only get an estimate. But it's a good indication. The following chart is adapted from *Running Healthy* by Sidney Alexander, M.D.; The Stephen Greene Press, Brattleboro, Vt.

Age	*Maximum expected heart rate adjusted to age*	*Target pulse rate*
20	200	140
25	195	137
30	190	133
35	185	130
40	180	126
45	175	123
50	170	119
55	165	116
60	160	112
65	155	109
70	150	105
80	145	98

of the lungs, heart, and blood vessels to bring the required oxygen to them. A 30-year-old who runs regularly will most likely have a better aerobic capacity than a 50-year-old who golfs sporadically and rides the fairways in an electric cart. In an exercise physiologist's laboratory, the 30-year-old will be able to run on a treadmill for a longer time than will the 50-year-old golfer, exhibiting a higher level of cardiovascular fitness. Likewise, in some cases, a 50-year-old runner could exhibit stronger heart, lung, and oxygen measurements than a fairly sedentary, stressful 30-year-old.

Cardiovascular fitness can be defined in terms of the amount of oxygen consumed by the body at peak exercise.[7] Besides the lungs and the heart, the arteries, veins, red blood cells, and active muscles are all part of the oxygen transport system. One of the benefits of exercise is that the arteries typically expand and contract more easily as the fitness level grows. In some cases, exercise may even help stimulate tiny new arteries to grow.[8] So, rather than merely accepting the so-called natural decline of the cardiovascular system attributed to aging, those who regularly perform aerobic exercise can experience the "training effect," whereby an individual's capacity can, up to a certain point, actually increase with age.

Unfortunately, the training effect and associated benefits don't come in a set or two of tennis over a weekend. To stave off the effects of aging, aerobic exercise must be done regularly—for at least 20 minutes per day, three to four times each week—according to the experts. Furthermore, it must be performed at a pace that increases the pulse rate to 70 percent of its maximum capacity. (To find out what that means to you, simply subtract your age from 220 and multiply the figure by .7.) An average 40-year-old should try to sustain his pulse rate at about 126—or slightly more than two beats per second—for 20 minutes of his workout for the most aerobic benefit. (That would be 220 minus 40, or 180, multiplied by .7, which equals 126.) For more accurate information about your body's capabilities, especially if you are over 30, you should delay any new fitness program until you've been examined by a doctor, who may subject you to an exercise stress test.

For those who are curious as to what activity provides the best aerobic workout, Dr. Kenneth Cooper, author of five books on aerobics and director of the Institute for Aerobics Research in Dallas, has ranked the top five activities in terms of their overall efficiency in the following order: cross-country skiing, swimming, running, cycling, and walking. It is interesting to note that Dr. Schwartz's Heavyhands system can be combined with three of these—running, walking, and stationary cycling—thereby increasing the aerobic benefits of those activities and ranking them close to the top-rated sport—cross-country skiing.

THE SEER THAT MADE MILWAUKEE FAMOUS

In Milwaukee, Wisc., at the Mount Sinai Medical Center, one of the most extensive studies on athletics and aging has been conducted since the early 1970s. Halfway across town from the fortresslike Pabst brewing factory that has stood its ground for 100 years, Dr. Michael Pollock flips a thick manila folder open and pulls out test results that have started to reverberate through the exercise physiology community.[9] Pollock, 46, a cardiac rehabilitation specialist and former researcher at Kenneth Cooper's Aerobics Institute, serves as director of the Center for Evaluation of Human Performance at Mount Sinai, and until recently was president of the American College of Sports Medicine. He directs a unique longitudinal study of a special group of 24 track athletes of championship caliber, many of them world record holders, ranging in age from 50 to 82.

At his Human Performance Center, where sports medicine and gerontology mingle, the offices look more like a transplanted health club than a standard hospital clinic. Rows of treadmills and stationary bicycles compete for space alongside exercise mats and various devices that gauge the status of bodies during exercise. In Pollock's own shelf-lined office, his leather athletic bag rests near the door, open, allowing the soiled sweatclothes inside to breathe. Above the bag, a coat rack displays two white knee-length lab coats, Pollock's other uniforms.

The athletes studied by Pollock and his associates have forced them to rethink the notion of predictable, inevitable decline in the body over decades. Some of what was thought to be inevitable, it turns out, is not. For instance, a man's maximum heart rate is commonly thought to decline at a fairly regular rate through adulthood, and his maximum oxygen uptake, or "VO_2 max" in sports medicine lingo, declines about one percent per year after he has reached athletic maturity. Yet some of Pollock's athlete subjects confirmed that training in mid-life and beyond can reduce the VO_2 max decline by half—to about 5 percent per decade. Some of these Masters (over 35) athletes have maintained virtually the same VO_2 max over the ten years of the study, while a few have even improved it.

Pollock strikes a predictable tone of scientific caution in making these findings public, but that is understandable given the weight he feels they will eventually carry. As he holds a couple of down-sloping charts at arm's length, he says, "I am not trying to say there is no aging curve. Rather, I think it is much less dramatic than has been assumed. It is curvilinear rather than linear." While that may not seem to be a ground-breaking prophecy, Pollock's work does support what has only been a vaguely optimistic notion: that high levels of physical training, continued over major portions of an athlete's life, can delay processes of decline, cardiovascular and otherwise, that are normally associated with aging.

However, no matter how many miles a Masters track star may log each week, his training is apparently not enough to postpone all important bodily changes. For instance, the aging athletes tested by Pollock showed a loss of muscle mass over time, even though their weight remained unchanged. Percentagewise, they are becoming fatter in their 60s and 70s. And despite continued, rigorous training, their maximum heart rates still decreased over the ten-year span, as do the maximum heart rates of normal, healthy individuals over time. But that doesn't mean aging runners should trade their Nikes and running regimen for bedroom slippers and increased dosages of TV. In the study, those runners who remained at a "competitive" level had a smaller decline in maximum heart rate than the runners in the "postcompetitive" group. Likewise, the runners who remained at a competitive level in late life

The Training Effect

A man who early on gets the habit of regular, vigorous exercise is likely at 60 to have much the same body shape as he had at 30. His shoulders will be narrower and he will have lost upper body mass, but he will have avoided that all-too-common result of age, overeating, and inactivity—the potbelly.

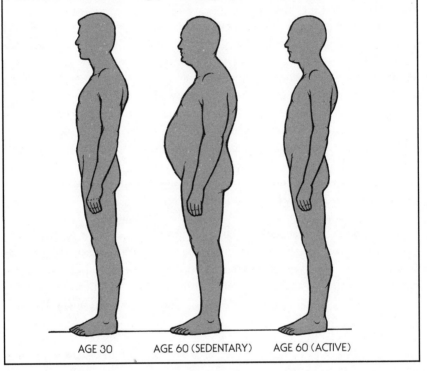

AGE 30   AGE 60 (SEDENTARY)   AGE 60 (ACTIVE)

showed and maintained higher readings in VO_2 max than did their less active counterparts.

How much, one wonders, does the information contained in Pollock's study apply to people who do not happen to run ten miles a day? In Pollock's view, plenty. "Take the best shape you have ever been in your life," he says, "and try to imagine keeping your body in that condition. A Masters athlete keeps his body closer to peak performance, so that if we can show changes associated with elite athletes, it should be easier to show improvement in bodies below that level."

Back at Ball State's Human Performance Laboratory, David Costill is conducting a study similar to Pollock's—with one major difference. Instead of competitive runners, Costill's subjects are mainly competitive swimmers.

Some are both. A former collegiate swimmer, and still active in Masters competition, Costill, 47, is curious about how the two sports stack up in the race against time. Though this swimming-aging study is barely under way, fitness experts will be surprised if the results don't substantiate at least some of the findings of the Mount Sinai study.

Pollock can cite aging athletes who actually look forward to getting older, so they can be "primed" for the next oldest age group of Masters runners. A 49-year-old miler, for example, may look forward to that 50th birthday if he knows he doesn't have a chance of setting any 45-to-49-year-old track records but may have a good shot at recording the best time among 50-to-54-year-old milers. That is a different sort of training effect—one that is as much psychological as it is physiological.

"You're talking about me," says Dr. William McChesney, 54, a Eugene, Ore., dentist who competes in the Masters runners events along with 100 other senior runners who represent the Eugene Track Club. "There's a definite impetus for me next year, because I turn fifty-five in two weeks. All last year I was fifty-four, and this is the year for me to do it, to go for the records in the fifty-five-to-fifty-nine-year-olds class. I'm putting in the work, and I'm looking forward to the national championships in Houston. I am turning a year older and looking forward to it." McChesney and his wife, Marcia, 52, along with their three speedy sons (a fourth, at 16, is just starting to compete in track events), were tagged "America's fastest family" by *The Runner* magazine in 1982, even before it was known that Marcia would clock a 6:17-mile world record time for women in her age group, and before it was known that their son Bill would be gunning for a spot on the 1984 U.S. Olympic team in the 20,000-meter (20-K) event.

In 1972, when McChesney went to see a doctor for an insurance-related physical exam, he stood five feet six inches and weighed 187 pounds. He flunked the physical. "I was determined to come back and pass," he recalls. "I was drinking too much beer, smoking too much, and I just didn't look in the mirror. Then, all of a sudden, you realize you're fat." McChesney started running and dieting and did pass the physical three months later. He now runs 50 to 60 miles each week, and tips the scales at nearly jockey weight, 118 pounds. "When I first started running, I was always draped around a telephone pole," he says. "Now I feel pretty good about things." And well he should. At the 1981 Boston Marathon, McChesney crossed the finish line in 2 hours, 46 minutes, an enviable time for a fit 25-year-old, much less a man of 52. "I'm not necessarily trying to live longer," he says. "I'm trying to live better. And I'm just having a ball."

The trouble is, despite even the strongest motivation and dedication to fitness, aging brings on concomitant changes in the body that displease everybody—athletes in particular. Even when bodies remain youthful through the 50s and 60s, the 70s seem to be particularly tough years for an athlete to pull through in top form. All the hours of aerobic exercise in a man's life may delay the decline in lung function and capacity, but eventually it will take place. Similarly, years of exercise will help strengthen the bones, but eventually they will lose minerals as their composition becomes more brittle. Overall flexibility, sadly, decreases as well.

Ingemar Johansson, the barrel-chested 1959–60 heavyweight boxing champion of the world, knows more than a bit about fitness. He has had his battles with weight, and while he left the boxing world nearly 25 years ago, he did not leave the world of conditioning. "I get up in the morning and I go for a run—that is part of my life. Everybody has something in their life that suits them," he was quoted in Bob Greene's American Beat column, *Esquire,* May, 1983. "If I can be in good shape and stay away from sickness, that's all I want. That's a lot."

FITNESS PICKS

Since how we spend our leisure time is increasingly being shown to affect how well we age, the census takers have gathered a wealth of information on the games people play. In assessing the nation's fitness habits, exercise physiologists look particularly at the sports people will play throughout life. There aren't too many opportunities for the former high school football, basketball, and baseball players in adulthood. Where do team sports players play in mid-life or beyond? In large part, they don't. They convert to the so-called "individual" sports, which has much to do with the running, aerobics, and exercise equipment boom we hear so much about. While team sports players play to win, athletes in individual sports tend to work more on self-improvement, health improvement, or achieving "personal bests." And if there is to be a lasting fitness movement in this country, it will occur because of increased participation in these individual sports.

One of the more interesting findings of the President's Council on Physical Fitness and Sports was the fact that some 50 million Americans say they *walk* for their exercise. "There are millions who are not counted in the sports surveys," says Verle Nicholson, a spokesman for the President's Council. "There are at least twice as many walkers as joggers." As an activity, walking is peculiar in another way as well. It is, according to the Council, the only exercise in which the participation rate increases with age. "The highest

What Do Men Do for Exercise?

When the President's Council on Physical Fitness and Sports looked at American fitness, it found mainly water and wheels. This is because three major surveys analyzed by the Council listed swimming and cycling as the most popular forms of sports and exercise for American men today. The results of the "top 10s" follow:

The Sporting Goods Dealer *Survey (1982)*	*Gallup Survey (1980)*
1. Swimming	1. Swimming
2. Bicycling	2. Bicyling
3. Fishing	3. Bowling
4. Exercises	4. Fishing
5. Camping	5. Hiking
6. Running or jogging	6. Camping
7. Bowling	7. Basketball
8. Weight training	8. Softball
9. Golfing	9. Tennis
10. Roller-skating	10. Volleyball

From *The Sporting Goods Dealer,* © 1983, The Sporting Goods News Publishing Co. Reprinted by permission of The Gallup Organization, Inc., 1980.

participation rate for walking is among men who are middle-aged and those who are sixty and above," says Nicholson. Walking for fitness, which has been sorely underrated, may gain new converts. Indeed, the most recent sports and fitness surveys begin to predict a decline in running in favor of walking, if only because of the demographics of age that will force many runners off the road. Results of a Gallup poll reported in the January 30, 1983, Chicago *Sun-Times* suggest an impending falloff in the number of runners nationwide, especially among more injury-prone runners in their 50s and 60s.

Michael Pollock of Milwaukee's Mount Sinai concedes that he has started talking on the lecture circuit about "the overuse syndrome." Too many adult runners suffer serious, nagging injuries of the foot, shin, knee, and back for the sport's own good. As healthy as running may be aerobically, a typical runner lands on each foot approximately 800 times each mile, with a force equal to at least three times his body weight. For the runner who logs 1.5 miles a day, that translates to more than 15,000 leg-absorbing shocks each week. So it should come as no surprise that pronation and supination (excessive ankle roll inward and outward) have become popular topics in running magazines. And in running-shoe companies worldwide, high technology continues its search for the ever softer run.

ONE STEP AT A TIME

In search of recruits for his sport, healthy-looking Howard Jacobson has taken to the streets. As president of the New York Walkers Club, former coach to Olympic race walkers, and former mid-distance runner, Jacobson knows the streets well. He had race walked them since he was 27 years old; now he is 53. These days the media refer to Jacobson as "the Pied Piper" of the sport of walking, in reference to the weekly walking clinics he heads up in New York and other cities across the land. A few years ago he wrote *Racewalk to Fitness: The Sensitive Alternative to Jogging and Running,* and he now supplements his race walking with fitness consulting for various enterprises, including Adidas, Metamucil, Mazola, and Club Med. "If I had named the book *Healthwalking,* it would have sold a million copies," Jacobson says in retrospect. Today he is in the midst of an unofficial movement to rename the sport healthwalking, in order to gain more devotees who may not be interested in racing.

A race walker actually burns more calories than a jogger, says Jacobson, when both keep a pace of five to seven miles per hour. In terms of health benefits, proponents say race walking does more for the body than running. With proper technique (that may look and feel awkward at first), race walking can shift weight from the midsection to the shoulders and chest, as well as improve aerobic capacity. These are precisely the gains an inactive 40- or 50-year-old might be seeking. Among race walkers, distance runners, and sprinters, race walkers have the best overall leg development and the lowest rate of injury, according to Jacobson.

The living room of Jacobson's apartment in a New York highrise looks a bit like an athletic club. More than 100 photographs, race numbers, ribbons, posters, and mementos of race walking and running events cover a wall lined with cork, off to the side of a bar one suspects is not often used. A ten-speed bicycle is parked next to the bar beneath a read-and-white sign that proclaims: "No Bicycles." Above that another sign reads: "No Smoking." Jacobson wears navy warm-up pants, beat-up boating shoes without socks, and a bright orange T-shirt with cartoon witch and ghost characters on the front, courtesy of the 1982 Halloween Night New York Road Runners Club Run. His six-foot-tall, 145-pound compact, trim body is its own advertisement for a sustained fitness regimen into middle age. When a friend converted him to race walking in the 1950s, "I took to it like a duck takes to water," he says. "I've never stopped training." When exercise physiologists at Columbia University subjected Jacobson to treadmill and other fitness tests a few years ago, they said his resting pulse, VO_2 max, and heart rate reminded them of a man in his 20s. "I hit my prime in race walking when I was thirty-nine," he says. "At age forty-eight I was walking faster times than I had done twenty years before."

Understandably, Jacobson believes that race walking is the "preventive medicine" we have all been looking for. In his book he lists its benefits as follows:

Racewalking may help prevent heart disease.
Racewalking will help to improve fitness and stamina.
Racewalking will help you lose pounds and inches.
Racewalking will help strengthen your muscles and tissues.
Racewalking will help to release tension and anxieties.
Racewalking will help develop more efficient blood circulation.
Racewalking will help your body to use oxygen more effectively.
Racewalking will help you to handle stress better.
Racewalking will help you to enjoy and perform better sexually.
Racewalking will help keep you alert and vital.
Racewalking will help strengthen your bones.
Racewalking will help give a woman a firmer and higher bustline.
Racewalking will help strengthen your skin.
Racewalking will help you to improve your posture.
Racewalking will help give you feelings of self-assurance.
Racewalking will virtually eliminate stress and overuse injuries.[10]

Apparently, many people are following the Pied Piper of walking. In Howard Jacobson's living room, bundles of letters from several states with questions about walking programs lie in ordered array, waiting to be answered. The magazine *American Health* recently entered the field by regularly reporting on fitness walks in various cities, sponsored by such organizations as Blue Cross-Blue Shield and the President's Council on Physical Fitness and Sports. "It means a lot to me," Jacobson says, "because I think our day is coming. I think we are more news than anybody realizes."

AGING AND CROSS-TRAINING

Walking may make even more news if Dr. Robert Willix of Fort Lauderdale, Fla., has his way. Willix has seen walkers and runners improve their health using hand weights, and now he regularly prescribes this exercise for his heart patients. One of these, Willix reports, was not happy about spending more than $17 for Heavyhands, so he took two plastic detergent containers, walked over to the beach, and filled them with sand. As far as Willix and the patient were concerned, these functioned just as well. Fitness is fitness.

In this more sophisticated era of exercise physiology, the idea of cross-training for cardiac rehabilitation may fall on newly receptive ears. It is also

Corporate Health

The Xerox Corporation runs a fitness program other companies would like to copy.

For instance, at the Xerox job-training center in the lush, rolling hills of Leesburg, Va., trainees can stay or get in shape at an impressive $3.5 million recreation complex. Xerox fitness stretches to eight other corporate recreation centers (including one overseas) and to 20 other locations with lesser facilities. The corporation's Health Management Program is run with the standards one expects of a firm in the top 40 of the *Fortune* 500, a firm that logs nearly $8.5 billion in sales each year and spends more than $60 million annually on insurance and medical programs. Fitness directors at Xerox do not claim to offer any new exercises, diets, gimmicks, or shortcuts to better health and longevity. Instead they promote the proven benefits of aerobic exercise and a common-sense life-style. They admit to "selling a concept," referring to fitness, and they hand out free orange "Day-Glo" shoelaces as inducements to employees to work out.

At the Leesburg site, about a two-hour drive from Washington, D.C., a visitor can hear the soft thud of rebounding racquetballs echoing throughout the ten-year-old building's spacious lobby, surrounded by acres of expansive, meticulous landscaping. Five "No Smoking" or "Thank You for Not Smoking" signs are clearly visible from the reception area, along with shelves full of shiny athletic trophies. The California-style recreation center has vaulted ceilings, earthy wooden beams, and skylights in its two separate gymnasiums, as well as two carpeted, pleasant-smelling locker rooms. Inside and outside there are facilities for running, swimming, bicycling, circuit training, racquetball, handball, squash, paddle tennis, tennis, volleyball, and basketball. Among the outdoor facilities is a putting green. About the only thing the complex seems to lack, on occasion, is its own exercising employees.

Programming has been expanded recently to include aerobic dancing, "jogging clinics," home health testing, and nutrition education. Xerox seems to have lived up to Kenneth R. Pelletier's assessment in his 1981 book, *Longevity: Fulfilling Our Biological Potential:* "As a model of future corporation-based health promotion organizations," he wrote, "the Xerox undertaking is an excellent prototype."

seen as the best way to prevent and treat injuries that can occur when you concentrate on only one sport. Since cardiac fitness and injury prevention are both major concerns of the middle aged, cross-training as the best way to maintain fitness might be seriously considered by those over 35.

Cross-training is not a specific technique or style, but a combination of different forms of exercise. For instance, runners would do well to supplement their miles on foot with regular cycling or swimming. And runners who have certain kinds of injuries might need to stop running altogether—at least for a while. Dr. Edward Colt, a New York endocrinologist who specializes in running injuries, was quoted in *Esquire*'s March, 1982, Sports Clinic column as saying: "The only treatment I have found that works for any knee injury is to stop running and do something else. I recommend bicycling and using toe clips to help strengthen the quadriceps and anterior tibial [shin] muscles. As you use the quadriceps, you tighten and strengthen the knee joint, and working on the shin muscles will help prevent shin splints. Cross-training effectively both prevents and treats running injuries." As other sports physiologists spread the word and, more important, as more amateur athletes heed the advice, cross-training may lead the fit to an even healthier later life. And for those who are belatedly getting in shape, cross-training could make their goals easier to achieve.

MAINTENANCE: FITNESS FOR THE ENTIRE BODY

What does it mean to be fit? How does this change over time? The answer at 80 is the same as it is at 30: Fitness means overall health of body and mind.

Three major inhibitors to fitness are smoking cigarettes, obesity, and inactivity; these factors happen also to be the major accelerators of the aging process.

- For smoking the prescription is simple: You should quit. (See Maintenance: The Lungs, page 139).
- For obesity: Establish with your doctor a wholesome reducing diet based on a variety of nutritious foods.
- For inactivity: Anything that works the muscles of the body (including the heart) is better than nothing, but the best program combines regular workouts of aerobic exercises with strengthening and stretching exercises. All three kinds of activity are possible at any age. Choose from among them, just as you would choose from the major food groups, to promote total fitness.

Aerobic Exercises: Any activity that pushes your heart to its target rate (see chart, page 165) for at least 20 minutes at a time, three or four times a week, will produce what is called "the training effect." There are several medically proven benefits of aerobic training.

1. The heart muscle grows stronger, and can pump more blood with each stroke.
2. Total blood volume increases, and the body is better equipped to transport oxygen.
3. Lung capacity increases. This increase in vital capacity has been linked to greater longevity.
4. High-density lipoprotein (HDL) increases, thereby changing the ratio of HDL to the "bad" cholesterol in the blood, and reducing the risk of arteriosclerosis.
5. Other important side effects of aerobic exercise are better sleep, better digestion, relief from stress without resort to alcohol or drugs, effective weight control, stronger bones, better muscle tone, higher levels of energy for longer periods of the day, and control of depression.

The top five aerobic activities, according to Dr. Kenneth Cooper of the Aerobics Center, are cross-country skiing, swimming, jogging or running, outdoor cycling, and walking. Jumping rope is becoming another popular route to aerobic fitness. Of the racquet sports, racquetball and squash give more aerobic benefits in a shorter time than tennis.

If you are over 30, and have not been exercising vigorously on a regular basis, be sure you are examined by a physician before you begin an aerobic program. Start slowly.

Strengthening Exercises: Working with free weights or with the many machines available and doing calisthenics are the chief ways to strengthen and maintain muscles in good condition. The goal of a strengthening program is to work all the muscle groups of the body.

Stretching Exercises: Stretching should be done both before and after strengthening or aerobic exercises, both as a warm-up for "cold muscles" and to promote flexibility. In addition, ballet, yoga, swimming, and fencing provide good stretches for the major muscle groups.

Motivation and time are two necessary ingredients for a good exercise program. Those who are well motivated tend to look at their exercise time as a necessity (even a reward) in a stress-ridden life. Others use lack of time as the excuse not to exercise. However, you can fit exercise into even the most crowded schedule. Here's how:

• Remember, anything that activates the heart and gets the muscles moving is good for you. And if done at the target heart rate for 20 minutes, it is the equivalent of a brisk jog. Dancing is one example, or climbing the stairs instead of taking the elevator; or walking to your next appointment instead of riding in a taxi. Work these into your office and social life.

• Instead of a coffee break, do the three-minute mobility exercise routine on page 93, or any series of stretches to relieve tension and improve flexibility.

• If you have time to watch TV, you have time to exercise. Combine stretching or weight-training or stationary bicycle riding with your favorite program.

Motivation is something that builds. The important thing is to choose an activity you like. If you thrive on competition, racquetball will offer more excitement than aerobic dancing. If you hate exercising alone, swimming may prove too isolating and running will be better enjoyed with a partner. Assess your social as well as your physical needs. And don't forget walking. It's in the top five, aerobically; it takes no special footgear; and it can be done anywhere, at any age.

Whatever sport or activity you choose, build gradually. Plan a program you can realistically fit into your schedule, and stick with it for at least six weeks. By then, your progress will feed your motivation. You should be able to reap the benefits of fitness for the rest of your life.

Nutrition and Weight Control

On December 7, 1973, Dr. Ronald L. Alkana ate 17 bananas in two minutes at the University of California, Irvine, thereby gorging his way into the *Guinness Book of World Records.* On May 3, 1975, Dave Barnes downed 424 littleneck clams in eight minutes at Port Townsend Bay, Wash., and gained similar notoriety. In a span of 15 days in March and April, 1977, Monsieur "Mangetout" (M. Lotito) ate a disassembled, pulverized, and stewed bicycle at a table in Every, France. And, in 1980, in Chicago, Jay Gwaltney, 19 years old, sat at a well-appointed table with flowers and munched on an 11-foot birch, branch by branch. It took him 89 hours to eat the tree, and one has to wonder whether his bite wasn't worse for the bark.

Not surprisingly, the world records for longevity are not found anywhere near the eating records section in *Guinness.* And, while the book tells us that Shigechiyo Izumi lived for more than 117 years in Japan, it fails to report what he ate. However, we do learn that one Robert Earl Hughes, who holds the world record for the heaviest precisely weighed man (1,069 pounds), died at the age of 32 in 1958.

If there is no precise correlation between eating foolishly and dying young, there may indeed be a subtle relationship between eating sensibly and living longer. The problem is that dieticians, doctors, nutritionists, and consumers can rarely agree on what exactly "eating sensibly" means. Some well-respected medical doctors believe that undernutrition may be a way to extend human life, based on more than 40 years of studies with underfed rats. Some other scientists, at the National Institute on Aging, have produced data suggesting that being about 15 pounds *overweight* might increase one's chances for living longer. Then there are people, like Arlyn Hackett, who strike a middle ground. Hackett, 38, is neither a physician nor a scientist. He works in a kitchen as a chef—the head chef, in fact—at the Pritikin Longevity Center in Santa Monica, Calif. He used to be obese at five feet ten inches and 220 pounds, but he is not fat anymore. While maintaining his weight at about 170 pounds, he prepares hundreds of meals each week for people who are often overweight and sometimes suffering from heart disease or battling other health problems. Fearing their lives might be cut short, they have enrolled in the rigid 26-day diet and exercise course known as the Pritikin program.

180

EATING RIGHT, LIVING LONGER

Nathan Pritikin, 68, used to be an inventor. Some 20 years ago he developed cardiac insufficiency and, like many others in the same predicament, was simply told to cut down on butter, eggs, and ice cream. Not satisfied with this meager advice, Pritikin began a long process of self-education and research in the fields of health and nutrition. In 1976 he founded the Longevity Center in Santa Monica, which has since spawned similar centers in Bal Harbour, Fla., and in Philadelphia. More than 10,000 people suffering from hypertension, heart trouble, adult-onset diabetes, and other degenerative diseases have come to the centers in search of rehabilitation. The Pritikin therapy, in brief, consists of an extremely low-fat diet and regular aerobic exercise.[1] The meals are prepared mostly with "natural" foods, and the exercise consists mainly of brisk walking. One doctor, a specialist in gerontology, in evaluating the Pritikin program, called it excellent and said it will "certainly increase life expectancy" for those who complete the nearly four-week stint and stick with it after they go home.[2]

In his daily routine, chef Arlyn Hackett tries to make the strict diet as inviting and interesting as he can. He talks about "designing" meals as much as he talks about cooking them. The Pritikin diet aims to prevent arteriosclerosis by providing the daily calorie intake as follows: 10 percent from protein, 10 percent from fat, and 80 percent from complex carbohydrates. (The average middle-aged American's diet contains closer to 20 percent protein, 40 percent fat, and 40 percent carbohydrates.) While it is true that cells can get necessary energy from fats, amino acids, and carbohydrates, the cleanest and most direct source is carbohydrates, according to Pritikin.[3]

As a result, Hackett designs a lot of raw vegetable salads, whole grain foods, soups, fish and poultry entrées, and occasional desserts along the lines of banana purée or pumpkin mousse pie. The meals are low in calories, of course, ranging from about 800 to 1,500 calories a day, with slight variation. The program prohibits alcohol, tobacco, table salt, and caffeine, as well as refined sugar, honey, and molasses. "A lot of people go into a kind of shock when they first eat here," Hackett says. "Probably one of the hardest things for people to give up is caffeine." Hackett, who once worked in a detoxification center, says the effects of caffeine withdrawal often resemble those he has seen among people addicted to other drugs.

Part of the success claimed for the Pritikin program rests on the premise that health-inducing eating habits, even when adopted in middle age or after, will lengthen one's life.[4] But before the diet can go to work on ailing bodies, it sometimes has ill effects. "Some people do actually vomit and have gas pains," Hacket says, "partly because their bodies aren't used to coping with that much good food." One of the major problems Hacket sees with the diets of mainstream America is an excessive reliance on oils for cooking, mixing, and flavoring. So, under the stern Pritikin guidelines, Hackett hunts for alternatives. Rather than broiling or frying food, for instance, he tends to do a lot of steaming, poaching, boiling, stewing, baking, and braising. "Most people don't realize that you can stir-fry vegetables with water," he observes. Another obstacle to healthy eating, according to Hackett, is America's love of butter. "I can remember in my 'traditional' restaurant days," he says, "when I don't think I ever set a vegetable out without butter. Here, when someone who is not used to it bites into a fresh ordinary green bean without butter, it can be the equivalent of having his first taste of wild game pheasant, compared with an ordinary supermarket chicken. I think men, in particular, are very heavy-handed with butter. They are not used to sprinkling spice on food instead."

The Pritikin meal plan resembles the American Heart Association's "Diet D," an extremely low-fat diet that is prescribed to at-risk heart patients under a doctor's care. In Diet D, as in Pritikin's plan, the primary goal is to reduce the fat and cholesterol content of the blood, thereby reducing risk factors for heart disease and premature death. Patients on Diet D are urged to:

1. Eat a balanced diet by eating more grains, grain products, fruits, vegetables, and legumes, and by using low-fat animal products, such as skim milk, egg whites, and rinsed cottage cheese.
2. Regulate the amount of fat in their diet by eating only three ounces of low-fat meat, fish, and poultry per day; using little or no foods that are predominately fat by nature, such as butter, margarine, shortening, oils, nuts, peanut butter, olives, and avocado; and by avoiding foods that are fatty because of the ways they are made, such as regular salad dressings, potato chips, fried foods, fancy breads, and rich desserts.
3. Restrict calories if overweight.[5]

Both diets share a belief that heart disease, arteriosclerosis, and other diseases are often preventable. If patients stay within the dietary guidelines, they can actually return to normal blood levels of cholesterol, glucose (sugar), and triglycerides (fats). There is some proof for such claims, culled from experiments conducted on monkeys, but a good deal of skepticism still prevails in medical circles.[6]

Both the Pritikin and American Heart Association plans stress exercise as a necessary component of their diets. "I know of no diet that works without an exercise program, especially this one," says Hackett. Going one

Maintaining an Ideal Weight

How much should you weigh? For years, Americans and their doctors thought they had a reliable source to help answer that question: the Metropolitan Life Insurance Company's Height and Weight Tables, derived primarily from data from the *Build and Blood Pressure Study*, 1959, Society of Actuaries. Then, in 1983, Metropolitan Life came out with revised figures—weights at ages 25 to 59 based on lowest mortality—which seemed to indicate that Americans could afford to be heavier without increased risk of death. For instance, in the 1959 table the weight range for men 5 feet 10 inches tall, medium frame, was 146 to 160 pounds; in the 1983 table, it had risen to 151 to 163 pounds. The publication of the new tables caused considerable controversy in medical circles. Reflecting the views of many physicians, Dr. W. Virgil Brown of Mt. Sinai School of Medicine in New York and chairman of the American Heart Association's nutrition committee recommended that Americans disregard the new figures. "When used as guidelines," he said, "the new tables will imply that for many Americans putting on weight may actually improve their health. Few health problems are improved by gaining weight. . . . In a population in which obesity and cardiovascular disease are major health problems, it does not seem prudent to raise the limits for recommended weight until more data are available." So, in the name of prudence, here's the 1959 version for men:

Metropolitan Life Insurance Company
Height and Weight Tables, 1959
According to Height and Frame, Ages 25 and Over

Height (in shoes with one-inch heels)	Weight in Pounds (in indoor clothing)		
	Small frame	*Medium frame*	*Large frame*
5' 2"	112–120	118–129	126–141
5' 3"	115–123	121–133	129–144
5' 4"	118–126	124–136	132–148
5' 5"	121–129	127–139	135–152
5' 6"	124–133	130–143	138–156
5' 7"	128–137	134–147	142–161
5' 8"	132–141	138–152	147–166
5' 9"	136–145	142–156	151–170
5'10"	140–150	146–160	155–174
5'11"	144–154	150–165	159–179
6' 0"	148–158	154–170	164–184
6' 1"	152–162	158–175	168–189
6' 2"	156–167	162–180	173–194
6' 3"	160–171	167–185	178–199
6' 4"	164–175	172–190	182–204

step further in their 1981 book, *Aerobic Nutrition,* Dr. Don Mannerberg and June Roth sent a message to the public that eating and exercise should be considered as almost one activity. Roth has written some 29 books on nutrition and cooking, while Mannerberg formerly served as director of medical services at the Pritikin Longevity Center in Santa Monica, and in a similar capacity at the Aerobics Center in Dallas. "Even Ken Cooper [founder of the Aerobics Center], who always said, 'Exercise, exercise, exercise,' is talking nutrition now," says Hackett. "Even he has recently put a couple of nutritionists on board."

KEEPING COUNT OF CHOLESTEROL

Since the 1960s, when cholesterol became a bad word, the nation has gradually turned from creamery-produced sticks of butter to plastic tubs of soft-spreading margarine. In the process, we forgot—if we ever had learned—that cholesterol in small amounts is actually essential to good health. It is a natural product that is, to some degree, in nearly every tissue of the body. It aids cellular metabolism, bile formation in the liver, and the production of steroid hormones.[7] Cholesterol is a lipid, or fat soluble substance, found in egg yolks, animal fats, and oils. We know from medical research that narrowed arteries result in part from excess cholesterol and other lipids in the bloodstream. With regard to age-related heart disease, there is a "bad" cholesterol, called low-density lipoprotein (LDL), and a "good" cholesterol, called high-density lipoprotein (HDL), both of which can affect the onset of arteriosclerosis. It is now believed that LDL is harmful because it causes changes in the coronary and cerebral arteries that can lead to narrowed arterial passages. Recently, the AHA nutrition committee surveyed the literature on heart disease and reported: "The most atherogenic of all the lipoproteins appears to be LDL."[8] On the other hand, HDL is believed to be beneficial because large amounts in the blood may help keep the arteries unobstructed. LDL has been described as a "delivery truck" for depositing cholesterol in cells throughout the body, while HDL has been termed a "garbage truck" that is helpful in collecting cholesterol throughout the body and carting it to the liver where it can be safely excreted.[9]

In a normal, healthy man of 45 who exercises on weekends, a typical cholesterol count would be about 210 milligrams. In a 45-year-old who is 30 pounds overweight, eats whatever, whenever, and exercises only occasionally, a typical cholesterol count would be about 260 milligrams. In the 1960s and again in the 1970s, the American Heart Association and its nutrition committee recommended that adults consume a diet that contains no more than 30 to 35 percent of calories as fat, and advised limiting cholesterol intake to less than 300 milligrams per day. By not eating large amounts of animal fats such as beef, pork, and rich dairy products, we can do our part to keep LDL levels down.

For people of normal weight, the American Heart Association recommends replacing saturated fats with unsaturated or polyunsaturated fats and complex carbohydrates. The disheartening thing for the health-conscious is that polyunsaturates—such as safflower oil or margarine—are not necessarily danger-free. Though it is too early to say for certain, some studies have suggested that excessive polyunsaturated fat in the bloodstream may inadvertently promote cancer. For this reason, the AHA concedes that "the consequences of prolonged ingestion of large quantities of these fats are not known. To be on the safe side, the AHA has not recommended very high intakes of polyunsaturated fats for the general population." So, until the food world comes up with suitable "safer" monounsaturated fats, it might even be prudent to go lightly with the knife in that shiny plastic tub of margarine.

DIETS TO DODGE CANCER

As the country's thoughts turned to Thanksgiving feasts, the article in the *Medical Tribune* of Nov. 22, 1978, could hardly have been better timed. In it, correspondent Jean McAnn filed a persuasive front page report on "what the experts do—unofficially—to dodge cancer." During an American Cancer Society conference, McAnn interviewed the convening scientists about what they personally ate, drank, or otherwise ingested to prevent cancer. Among those responding were Dr. Arthur C. Upton, then director of the National Cancer Institute; Dr. Ernst L. Wynder, president of the American Health Foundation in New York; and Roger J. Williams, a biochemist at the University of Texas in Austin (who discovered Vitamin B_3). Upton said: "I take vitamin C and a multiple preparation . . . I minimize my intake of animal fat. I also take a substantial amount of fiber, including a large amount of leafy green vegetables, and I eat bran for breakfast. And I try to control my weight. I guess you might say I try to hedge my bets!" Wynder said: "I think a high-fiber intake is important in preventing colon cancer. The evidence for carbohydrates is somewhat complicated, but we think fat—both saturated and unsaturated—is what's important."[10] In other words, eating too much fat, whether saturated or not, seems to increase the risk of developing certain kinds of cancer. Williams said: "I try to eat wholesome foods and avoid sugary things and too much alcohol. . . . I take vitamin supplementation. . . . I also exercise by walking about three miles daily." These were weighty votes in favor of vitamin supplements and fiber. In fact, it seemed particularly noteworthy that the president of the American Cancer Society doesn't merely eat his fiber, he "takes" it, in substantial daily amounts, as if it were prescribed medicine.

Nearly five years after McAnn's article appeared, *American Health* ran a similar article on the cancer experts' personal dietetic strategies. This time the votes for vitamins and fiber were, if anything, stronger. Over the past decade, evidence has mounted that a diet marked by low-fiber intake contributes to gastrointestinal diseases commonly associated with aging, such as gallbladder disease, (intestinal) diverticulitis, and cancer of the colon. There is, of course, disagreement over exactly how much fiber an average healthy man should consume to remain average and healthy, but there is little doubt that most people's daily intake could use a boost. Fiber cannot cure all age-related digestive ills, but it may help prevent some of the major ones.

Because fiber-laden foods retain water in the intestines, they provide bulk, which helps dilute toxins that might be present in the gut. The time it takes for food to pass through the alimentary canal is also a factor. Transit time for high-fat, low-carbohydrate foods is commonly 85 hours, while for foods high in natural carbohydrates it is from 20 to 40 hours.[11] Another important reason for bulking up the diet is that eating fiber replaces high-fat foods and therefore indirectly protects against cholesterol-clogged arteries. (Also, fiber actually lowers the cholesterol level in the body by making it harder for the small intestine to absorb cholesterol.)

As a sign that the public has become increasingly aware of fiber, the Kellogg Company of Battle Creek, Mich., recently added a special message on its boxes of sugar-laden Raisin Bran that reads: "Each serving contains 4 grams of dietary fiber." Underneath a smiling caricature of the sun on the front of the box, a bright yellow banner proclaims: FIBER-RICH!

DIGESTIVE CHANGES THAT COME WITH AGE

No matter how much fiber or cholesterol is consumed through the years, there are certain changes along the digestive tract that inevitably occur. Although it is not fully understood why, the stomach, the widest and most muscular portion of the alimentary canal, becomes sluggish. One reason is that the secretions from millions of tiny glands in the mucous membrane lining the stomach diminish as one ages. As a result, with less gastric juice present in the stomach, the body must work harder to absorb nutrients. Appetite decreases. Caloric intake dwindles. Without careful attention to diet, vitamin and iron deficiencies may occur.

Lower in the digestive canal, after the pancreas and liver have done their

The Human Digestive Plant

The reason man can consume a bewildering array of foods is that our bodies possess complex processing plants that can take everything from soup to nuts and break it down into absorbable products. With age, however, the processing plant slows down and careful attention to diet becomes even more essential.

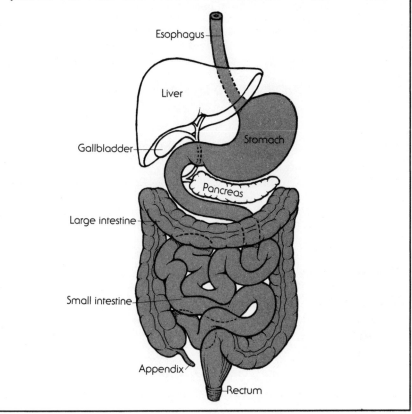

part to break down food further, the villi (small projections) of the small intestine set about the task of absorbing nutrients into the body. Traveling at the rate of about seven feet per minute, food normally makes its way through the 22 feet of small intestine in about three or four hours. When it reaches the five-to-six-foot-long large intestine, however, food being digested can remain there anywhere from five to 25 hours or more. It is here where the meals of today mix with those of yesterday or the day before, and where the general atrophy of the alimentary canal can lead to the problems of

Diets for a Longer Life?

Do we age as we eat? There can be only speculation at this point about how diet affects longevity. However, there is little doubt that some relationship exists between the percentage of fat in the diet and the incidence of heart disease and certain kinds of cancer. If we can avoid heart disease and cancer, we would certainly improve our chances of living to be 80. But that's not long enough, according to those involved in "life extension," who would have us reform our eating habits in order to live to be over 100.

Here are menu samples of two diets designed for improved health and/or longevity. The first, the Pritikin Diet, aims at balanced nutrition and weight loss. The second is from Dr. Roy L. Walford, a gerontologist who believes that undernutrition is one way to achieve what he calls "maximum lifespan."

THE PRITIKIN DIET—SAMPLE MENU

High carbohydrate, 1,200 calories, for weight loss (Italics indicate special recipes)

Breakfast
1 cup *hot oatmeal*
½ cup whole strawberries (fresh or unsweetened frozen, sliced)
½ cup nonfat milk, hot or cold
1 medium orange or ½ large grapefruit

Lunch
1½ cups *cream of mushroom soup*
Raw vegetable salad (¼ recipe)
¼ cup *yogurt-cheese dressing*
1 slice whole-wheat bread

Dinner
Salmon soufflé (¼ recipe)
⅓ cup *white sauce #2*
Cucumber-tomato salad (½ recipe)
Parslied potatoes (⅙ recipe) or *baked banana squash* (½ recipe)
Vegetable combination #1 (⅓ recipe)
¾ cup *carob-mint mousse* or 2 cups hot air-popped popcorn

Recipes mentioned in the menu above may be found in *The Pritikin Permanent Weight-loss Manual,* © 1981 by Nathan Pritikin. Menu reprinted by permission of Grosset & Dunlap, Inc.

THE WALFORD DIET—SAMPLE MENU

Optimal nutrition, 1,500 calories (Italics indicate special recipes)

Breakfast
1 T. brewer's yeast in low-sodium tomato juice
⅔ cup rye cereal
3 T. wheat germ
1 T. wheat bran
½ cup strawberries
1¼ cup skim milk

Lunch
2 sweet potatoes and 2 pears
2 cups spinach
½ cup buttermilk

Dinner
Computer chicken
Lima bean salad
Any remaining sweet potatoes and pears
1 cup green beans
1 cup grapefruit

Adapted from *Maximum Life Span* by Roy L. Walford, M.D., by permission of W. W. Norton & Co., Inc. Copyright © 1983 by Roy L. Walford.

constipation. At this point, for all practical purposes, the food has been digested, and the major task the body has left is to absorb the liquids, mostly water. Since the body has been generous with water in the various stages of digestion, it is only proper that the body get some of the fluid back. But when the wavelike, peristaltic action of the large intestine slows down or weakens, as is common among the elderly, there is an increased opportunity for water absorption. The feces then become harder and compacted, causing painful or difficult elimination.

This is one reason the folks from Kelloggs regularly advertise their All-Bran cereal in magazines such as *Modern Maturity*. It is quite possibly a reason why Kelloggs reports on the back of its All-Bran boxes: "No other cereal you can buy has more natural food fiber." What is not highly touted, however, is that one one-ounce serving of the product (without milk) provides five grams of sucrose and other sugars. That information is left to the careful reader of the fine print on the side of the box.

A related factor in digestive decline over time is in kidney or renal function. With age, the kidneys are not able to filter blood and produce urine as quickly or completely as in young adulthood, and the excretory capacity declines as well (see chapter 10). When one's metabolism is fine, the body transforms all complex carbohydrates and sugars into glucose. Unfortunately, as many people age, they consume more sugar and refined carbohydrates when they would be better off limiting their intake. A decreased ability to metabolize glucose can result. And research has shown that being overweight and consuming too much sugar can lead to "maturity-onset diabetes."

With this disease, which starts in the pancreas, insulin production is thrown out of kilter and sugar levels rise to a dangerous level after eating. But while healthy people can handle excess glucose by producing more insulin, diabetics cannot do the same. Their bodies react to excessive glucose by trying to remove it through the urine, and in so doing deplete their stores of necessary bodily fluids. That is why symptoms of diabetes include extreme thirst and near-exhaustion.

According to one estimate, the average American eats in one form or another some 128 pounds of sugar each year.[12] That is the equivalent of eating more than one pound of sugar every three days! About the only optimistic thing that can be said about the consumption of sugar in the American diet is that although it is frightfully high, it is also easily modifiable.

THE HEALTH FOOD PHENOMENON

"We go rather easy on sweets here," says Darwin Cook, 70, owner of Seattle First Natural, a 12-year-old health food shop and restaurant in the Pacific Northwest, "because you can't make a decent dessert without using brown sugar or honey." Instead of rich desserts, Cook offers his customers banana bread, blueberry muffins, and occasional cookies. Cook's rustic natural-foods establishment is decorated in various shades of wood tones intended to complement the greenery that fills up the well-stocked salad bar and the plates of as many as 90 customers at a time.

Located in a medical and dental building complex in Washington State's first city, Seattle First Natural draws, naturally, its share of doctors, dentists, other health professionals, and more than a few lawyers and businessmen. You can't get white bread in the place, Cook says, only "wheat with a handful of sunflower seeds thrown in." You can't smoke in the restaurant either, a policy that has been in effect long before California politicians proposed smoking bans in public places. For Cook, health foods have been a life-style rather than a fad picked up in the 1960s and 1970s. He got into health foods in the late 1940s, having learned the food business from his father. Cook's father suffered severe ulcers in his 60s and nearly was operated on. "Then, being an old produce salesman," Cook recalls, "he found out about a treatment using raw cabbage juice. He found a guy in Seattle who sold the juice and then he drank a quart a day for three weeks. When he went in for his final X rays, his ulcers had cleared up. I'll bet my dad cured three hundred guys that way." Cook's dad lived to the age of 93, ulcer-free for the last three decades of his life.

In the late 1950s, in the northern section of Seattle, Cook opened the All-Natural Eating Establishment, which became the first store in the area to start offering yogurt. In the 1960s, says Cook, his store was the first place around to sell alfalfa sprouts. Cook could very well take exception to John Naisbitt's claim, in the 1983 best-seller *Megatrends,* that "the whole granola ethic," as well as the vitamin and nutrition craze "leading to the invention of the salad bar,"[13] started in California.

Wherever the natural-foods movement started, it has burgeoned, which seems a good thing for Americans' future longevity. The number of health food stores in the U.S. rose from 1,200 in 1968 to more than 6,600 in 1978. Sales of health food sprouted from $170 million in 1970 to $1.6 billion in 1978. It is becoming increasingly difficult to even chart this growth, as supermarkets have started selling whole-grain products, fresh-squeezed juices, and the like. Americans are buying for health, and as a nation we have reduced our intake of certain kinds of fats. Butter consumption is down 28 percent, and milk and cream down 21 percent since 1965, says Naisbitt, despite population gains.[14]

AFFECTING ONE'S OWN SURVIVAL

It wasn't exactly a typical day in the fall of 1982, with overfilled cardboard boxes packed up and ready to be shipped to new offices, but Dr. Robert Butler, who is chairman of the nation's first full medical school geriatrics department, at Mount Sinai Medical Center in New York, had time to answer a few questions about nutrition and longevity. He clearly was not ruffled by a visitor asking about the striking new claims that two youthful California science writers, Durk Pearson and Sandy Shaw, had made in their book *Life Extension*. As regulars on the television talk show circuit, Pearson and Shaw were bringing their message to an eager public, who clearly wanted to know more about taking large doses of vitamins, nutrients, and chemicals to try to beat the odds of aging. Butler paused, but only momentarily. "There is a book coming out in a few months," he said, "by Roy Walford. It presents some of the same material, but in a more organized fashion. You'll want to read it."

Six months later, Dr. Walford's newly published *Maximum Life Span* was doing a brisk business in leading markets nationwide, although nowhere near the best-selling volume logged by *Life Extension*. Unlike Pearson and Shaw, who are not medical doctors, Walford of UCLA's school of medicine has spent 30 years in research on immunology and aging. He was new to the talk show circuit and only just beginning to stir interest in his work. His theory—which is not exactly conventional but cannot rightly be considered radical, either—has to do with undernutrition as a way to extend life-span. By eating less and supplementing the diet with antioxidants and nutrients over a five- to six-year span, Walford claims we can imitate the kind of life-span increase that has become almost commonplace in nutritional research with animals (see chapter 14). Scientists still don't know exactly why undernutrition seems to extend life in these animals, but it does. "Thus far," states a 1982 NIA special report on aging, "dietary restriction is the only intervention which repeatedly alters the rate of aging in experimental mammals. Other methods of intervention have been tested, including exercise and manipulations of the immune system."[15]

"With mice that are supposed to live fourteen months," says Dr. Kathleen Hall, an associate of Walford's at UCLA and a specialist in genetics and aging, "he's got some of them living four years." Walford is very careful in his claims in *Maximum Life Span,* probably because he would prefer to err on the conservative side, if indeed he errs at all. He cites as examples the classic studies made by Clive McKay at Cornell University in the 1930s that showed in some instances that the average and maximum life-spans of rats had doubled with undernutrition. "Undernutrition without malnutrition is the key concept in dietary modulation of the lifespan," writes Walford.

The good news here is that Walford and numerous others feel the undernutrition regimes could "almost certainly" be adopted for humans. Walford personally has adopted a strict regime, which he details in his book and which includes two days of fasting each week along with five other days of "supernutritional" low-calorie, low-fat foods. However, Dr. Leonard Hayflick of the University of Florida, an eminent gerontologist and a colleague of Walford's, is reluctant to endorse Walford's program. "In the forty years since we have known about undernutrition," he says, "no one has consciously chosen to do it, even the biologists, and even though it's widely known that it works and that it's not dangerous. Any method is unacceptable if it affects the enjoyment of life."[16] In an interview, Walford counters the criticism with the comment, "Hayflick may still think that way—but that's because he likes to eat." He insists that his regimen "is really designed to be no more difficult than becoming a vegetarian." Time will tell whether Walford himself ages his way, by virtue of undernutrition, into the *Guinness Book of World Records,* circa 2040.

MAINTENANCE: NUTRITION

Once upon a time, a typical well-fed American male ate bacon and eggs for breakfast, a hamburger for lunch, and steak and French fries for dinner. These dietary habits have changed, but Americans in general still eat too much red meat, too much fat, and too much sugar. This poorly balanced diet has been linked to cancer, heart disease, and other illnesses, so you would do well to take a good hard look at your nutritional input.

- For most men the time-honored advice is still the best: Eat a well-balanced diet. Well-balanced means choosing from a wide variety of foods in the four major food groups—milk (which include cheeses and yogurt), meat (which includes fish, poultry, legumes, cottage cheese, nuts, and seeds), grains (which include cereals, rice, bread, and pasta), and fruits and vegetables.
- Think of food consumption and physical exercise as one metabolic activity. If you work in an office and get only moderate exercise, don't eat as if you were chopping wood all day.
- Plan your meals around carbohydrates, (whole grains, dried peas and beans, and fruits and vegetables) instead of around meat. Nutritionists recommend that carbohydrates comprise the largest portion of the daily caloric intake.
- If you eat like most Americans, you need conscientiously to reduce your fat intake, not only from the obviously fatty foods like bacon or butter, but also from foods with hidden fats, such as roast beef, sesame seeds, avocados, and baked goods. Simply switching from butter to margarine is of little value unless you are cutting down on your entire fat intake.
- Eat poached, steamed, or broiled foods and avoid foods fried in fats.
- Become more aware of the fat/protein ratios of the foods you eat: 82 percent of a steak's caloric value is fat and only 17 percent protein, while 18 percent of white meat of chicken (without the skin) is fat, and 76 percent protein.
- Many men eat almost twice as much protein as they actually need. The Food and Nutrition Board of the National Academy of Sciences recommends for a healthy 160-pound man a daily intake of 57.6 grams of protein. This is the amount found in four ounces of roast turkey, a baked potato, two glasses of milk, two ounces of baked beans, and two ounces of spinach.
- Eat plenty of starch. Complex carbohydrates (whole-grain breads and cereals, rice, pasta, legumes, and potatoes) provide essential energy and are low-fat sources of protein.
- Whether or not you are on a weight-reducing diet, you should avoid the "empty" calories of heavily sweetened desserts, and reduce your intake of processed foods, which tend to be sugar-laden even when they aren't sweet. Physiologically, we have no need for sweets. The body converts starches to sucrose and also gets plenty of sugar from fruits and vegetables.
- Some men, as they grow older, need to alter their diet considerably in order to correct a specific health problem (obesity, cholesterol buildup, hypertension, et cetera). If you are thinking of radically changing your diet, always consult a physician first. Avoid fad diets. Try to establish a program with your doctor that will lead to a lifetime of better eating habits. Understand what you are changing and why, and take advantage of the many tasty recipes developed in recent years for special low-fat or low-sodium diets.

(*continued*)

- A healthy man of 35 may consume as much as 2,600 calories a day, but by the time he's 65 his caloric needs will be much reduced. However, his nutritional needs are if anything even more urgent, in order to keep aging body cells in good repair. An older person eating 1,500 calories a day has to be very careful to eat a well-balanced diet and not consume empty calories.

New Thoughts on Longevity

At the age of 81, Groucho Marx was in no mood to talk about eating less to live longer. He was hungry. It was a Tuesday afternoon in 1972 at Le Bistro, a fashionable restaurant in Beverly Hills, and there, helping to delay his meal, were two companions: one, a fine-looking, dark-haired woman some 50 years his junior—"his secretary," Erin Fleming called herself ("A likely story," Groucho answered); the other, Roger Ebert, a young writer and film critic who was there to chronicle the man and the moves for *Esquire.*

After steak tartare, cheesecake, and Sanka, Groucho was ready to talk about life as an octogenarian. "I try to exercise a little every day," Groucho said. "I like to take a walk. And I do try to sing a little every day. The throat is a muscle, and if you don't use it, like any other muscle it goes to hell."

Back at Le Bistro 11 days later, at a pre-Academy Awards party, Marx approached a starlet wearing a floor-length white gown that was, as Ebert reported, ". . . you couldn't be sure . . . from certain angles . . . see-through."

> "Wanna dance?" he asked, softly.
> "Aren't you Groucho Marx, the living legend?" the starlet breathed, running a finger under his chin.
> "It's not my fault all the others are dead," Groucho said. . . .
> A waitress approached Groucho with a tray of pineapple slices. He took one with his fingers.
> "You want a fork?" she said.
> "Your place or mine?" Groucho said.

The irrepressible comedian lived five more years before succumbing ultimately to pneumonia in 1977. He had lost much of his hearing; his famous voice was feeble. He had entered the hospital earlier that year for surgery to repair a damaged hip joint—an injury that turned increasingly severe—then for a respiratory ailment. Even so, Marx made sure he got in the last word. His epitaph, which he wrote in advance, spoke for itself: "I hope they buried me near a straight man." [1]

If he were alive today, Groucho Marx surely would have a few words for scientists who claim they are "fast approaching" a reliable means to slow the aging process. (On his television quiz show, he asked a contestant her age, and when she said she was "approaching forty," Marx replied: "From which direction?")

"Cures" for aging today are coming from many directions. Some approaches are cautious and already offer good reasons for optimism. Others are more radical and will take time to confirm.

We have long suspected that part of aging is simply the result of wear and tear, as examples in the previous chapters have indicated. Gravity pulls down the skin. Eyes blur; hearing and taste fade. Joints become more sensitive. Bones weaken in the absence of vigorous exercise, and even a man's sex organs seem weighted down by time. Yet life goes on vigorously, as we have also seen. But what governs the body's waning capacity to grow and repair itself? Why do organs that once had enormous reserve capacity finally fail to perform? Is there an underlying key, or mechanism, that explains aging at the cellular level? And what can be done to arrest the process?

THE FREE-RADICAL THEORY

In search of an extended life with vigor, some scientists and health-conscious Americans are finding themselves in health food stores. Alongside wooden shelves full of banana nut bread, soy products, aromatic herbs, and alphabetized vitamins, scores of nutrient products called "antioxidants" have recently grabbed a good bit of display space.

According to some gerontologists, antioxidants—ingested together in precise amounts—may help the body protect itself from aging-related damage. These antioxidants include vitamins A, C, and E, the element selenium, the food additive BHT (or bis-hydroxytoluene), and the amino acids cycteine and methionine, and in experiments with animals, at least, they have contributed to longer life-spans when regularly taken in carefully controlled amounts. It's not certain that antioxidants can extend human life—yet key leading researchers in aging such as Dr. Roy Walford of UCLA and Dr. Richard Cutler of the National Institute on Aging feel that antioxidants offer tangible hope today as anti-aging elements.[2] Walford, for one, recommends a combination of undernutrition, antioxidants, and exercise as the best practical, available means for man to try to extend his life-span.

The use of antioxidants is a response to something known in aging circles as the "free-radical theory." Put simply, free radicals are highly reactive chemicals that lug around an extra electron like a weapon. They cause irreversible reactions to take place inside the body, sometimes attacking DNA, proteins, and other molecules, sometimes causing unwanted chain reactions. Free radicals oxidize and slowly damage body tissues, particularly cell membranes. Walford calls them "great white sharks in the biochemical sea."

It's not that free radicals are the only cause of aging, but rather that they seem to be a major cause. The free-radical theory was first introduced to the gerontological community by Dr. Denham Harman, working from experiments at the University of Nebraska School of Medicine in the late 1950s and 1960s. Since then, the idea of using antioxidants to neutralize the free radicals has been the subject of countless research studies. Science writers Durk Pearson and Sandy Shaw dedicated their best-seller of 1982–83, *Life Extension,* to Harman. Walford included Harman's free-radical aging theory in his chapter in *Maximum Life Span* on "Theories of Aging I Love Best." Kenneth R. Pelletier, Ph.D., in his 1981 book, *Longevity,* calls the free-radical theory "one of the major theories" in the area of age-related biochemical processes.

Proponents of this popular theory say that by taking extra antioxidants (which can cost about $1 a day), people can arm their insides with ammunition to keep their bodies from breaking down at their expected rates. Pearson has said that he swallows the food preservative (and antioxidant) BHT regularly because "the body is like a piece of steak, and some of the same aging mechanisms apply."[3] It's not all that different from imagining a Pac-Man video game creature chasing and swallowing speedy colorful discs on a screen, for in a sense the antioxidants gobble up the free radicals. And in so doing, the exposure of the cells to the chemical reactions caused by the free radicals is reduced. Dr. Harman says that his tests with mice and antioxidants have results that would be the equivalent of raising human life expectancy from 73 to 95 years. And Dr. Walford is not shy about predicting life extension to well beyond 100 years—under a regimen of antioxidants, undernutrition, and exercise working in tandem over time.

OF CELLULAR CLOCKS AND DNA REPAIR

Around the same time that Denham Harman began his experiments at the University of Nebraska, Dr. Leonard Hayflick developed his own theory of aging at the Wistar Institute in Philadelphia. The theory became known in the early 1960s as "the Hayflick limit," in reference to Hayflick's discovery that pieces of lung tissue seemed to die out after the cells had divided a certain number of times (roughly 50). Even when Hayflick froze cell cultures after, say, 25 divisions, and then thawed them, they would somehow "recall" they had only 25 doublings left. Near the end of their life cycles, the cells would appear "old," and increasingly they would sport age pigment, or lipofuscin, the same substance found in aged hearts and brain cells.

Scientists still don't know why cells die out after what seems to be a preset limit, but because of the Hayflick limit, some scientists adhere to theories about aging "clocks." These state that internally our own cells have timekeepers of sorts that prevent immortality (in the form of repeated cell divisions) from occurring indefinitely. Some proponents of cellular clock theories say the secret to aging someday will be found within the cells' nuclei, our regulators of energy and growth. (Others say the hypothalamus of the brain may contain the aging clock.)

Still other theories rely on DNA as the controlling force in the aging process. The reasoning is that since DNA contains our genetic blueprints, then it makes sense that DNA also controls how well our bodies hold up over time. While there are not many who will argue for the existence of a "senescence gene," there is a growing group of researchers who believe the real reason for aging will be found somewhere within the double-helix-shaped strands of DNA. As Drs. James Fries and Lawrence Crapo put it in their book, *Vitality and Aging:* "Probably, aging just happens, as the result of cumulative, random, and inevitable errors in translation of DNA into protein. The errors may even be a crucial part of a process that allows variation among individuals and thus allows natural selection."[4]

As these mistakes in cell division accumulate, they take their toll. It becomes increasingly difficult for the masters of our biochemical makeup to shrug off the damage. And it has been shown that plenty of cell damage does accrue over a lifetime. Viruses, free radicals, radiation, and chemicals all combine to alter healthy, regenerating DNA, until one's means of repair become deficient.

In the laboratory, scientists have shown that those organisms or animals that have better DNA repair mechanisms tend to live longer than those that don't. At UCLA Dr. Roy Walford and his associate, Dr. Kathleen Hall, believe they have located and identified collections of genes that contain aging "controls" or instructions. Perhaps eight to ten genes or gene groupings control life-span—or possibly more. Yet at least one of them, according to Walford, resides in a gene region called the "major histocompatibility complex," or MHC. Using mice that were bred to resemble identical twin pairs, Hall and Walford showed that differences in life-span were in large part related to differences in MHC.

"Our demonstration of these differences provided the first direct evidence that the MHC is an important regulator of the rate of aging," says Walford confidently. "Dr. Ed Yunis at Harvard University quite elegantly confirmed our findings."[5] Walford predicts that within five to ten years, newly developed genetic engineering techniques will be used to transplant MHC of the genes in a number of key experiments.

To appreciate fully the potential for this line of thinking, it helps to know a little something about a laboratory creature called the white-footed deer mouse. This is no ordinary mouse, for while many types of laboratory mice live on average about three years, the white-footed rodent lives on average up to seven years. The UCLA researchers are readying themselves to perform gene splicing of MHC between the white-footed mouse and the shorter-living strains of mice. They can't yet be certain that the MHC contains *the* crucial system associated with aging. Yet they do feel that the genetic swap will have to at least include MHC to be effective—especially in light of the knowledge that MHC helps cells to repair themselves and fight diseases.

If it happens that an MHC-gene swap between lab mice results in longer-living strains of "ordinary" lab mice, the question comes up as to whether some form of MHC might not be synthetically produced, then spliced into human DNA. "The ability to control DNA will be more significant than the discovery of fire or the printing press," says Donald Coffey, professor of urology, oncology, and pharmacology at Johns Hopkins University School of Medicine. "Then we can control heritage and biological events." [6] Getting a handle on the MHC of DNA may be one reason why Walford, in his book and in interviews, is glib in predicting that in the next 50 years, people who are 70 will look as 35-year-olds do today, and people who are 100 will only appear to be 50.

HORMONES AND HAPPENSTANCE

Through the 1970s and beyond, Dr. W. Donner Denckla got to know the workings of the pituitary gland better than many scientists would have once imagined possible. In lab work at the National Institutes of Health, Harvard, and the National Institute of Alcoholism and Alcohol Abuse, he discovered the hormone called DECO (for decreasing consumption of oxygen) that is now referred to some in aging-research circles as the "death hormone." After removing the pituitary gland from the brains of rats, then injecting the animals with thyroid, growth, and other hormones, Denckla observed that the organ systems of the rats in the absence of DECO appeared much younger than normal. Old rats' hearts and lungs seemed to be rejuvenated. When rats were injected with DECO, however, their organs aged at an accelerated pace.

As potentially rich as Denckla's discovery seems, DECO by itself can't tell the whole story about aging—nor is it the only hormone involved in aging. Other scientists, including Dr. Allan Goldstein of George Washington University Medical School, have their own related theories. Goldstein's revolves around thymosin, a thyroid hormone that helps the immune system stay strong. As people age, their thymosin level drops, and their susceptibility to disease seems to rise. Similarly, with high levels of a naturally occurring hormone in the blood known as DHEA (for dehydrepiandrosterone), experimental animals and humans alike were shown to have higher correlations with longevity than those of the same species with lower levels of DHEA. DHEA is a curious hormone, relatively unknown and relatively scarce by late life. Oddly, it is in ample abundance in the teen years and among vegetarians, for reasons not yet understood. On the whole, while perhaps trickier to decipher than wear-and-tear theories of how a man ages, hormonal theories should be fruitful areas of biochemical research both in regard to aging and to other physiological changes. Still, at the moment, trying to understand hormonal triggers to aging is a bit like entering a darkened room knowing how to turn on a light, but not being able to find the light switch.

THE REPLACEABLE MAN

While the tricky, intertwined causes of aging are being unraveled, the area of artificial organs and organ transplants offers an increasingly bright outlook for prolonging life. It appears that decades of research have started to pay off. Over the past five years, the number of transplants in the U.S. has soared, thanks to better surgical procedures, better drugs such as cyclosporine that effectively suppress the body's immune system, and better means of matching potential donor partners. Charts showing the recent incidence of transplants in this country resemble in shape the number of personal computers sold in the same years since 1976. Graph lines point toward the heavens. They may point even higher with the advent of even more advanced genetic engineering methods. Dr. Willem J. Kolff, who heads the University of Utah's artificial-organ program, has predicted, "If there aren't too many impediments, there will be five thousand people with artificial hearts in the next five to eight years."[7]

Other areas of artificial organ development that are particularly appealing include replacements of skin, blood vessels, inner ear, pancreas, and joints such as the hips, fingers, and knees. Even today, doctors can pick and choose from a variety of artificial joints. A spokesperson at Rush-Presbyterian St. Luke's Medical Center in Chicago, speaks of her facility's "bone bank" as if it were a five-and-dime. "We have some two hundred different knees to choose from," she says matter-of-factly.

In the case of cornea transplants, which ophthalmologists have performed more than 125,000 times in the U.S., the success rate for improved vision now stands at an impressive 90 percent.[8] As of this writing, more than 41 percent of the heart transplants Dr. Norman E. Shumway and colleagues

Toward the Bionic Man

In the twenty-first century, if you need a spare body part, chances are you'll be able to get it. Already, dramatic improvements in technology and in methods of suppressing the body's immune system have made possible these tissue transplants and artificial prostheses.

TISSUE TRANSPLANTS

PROSTHESES

Hair (transplant)
Hair (hairpiece)
Vitreous
Cornea
Lens
Eye (lens)
Bones of ear
Teeth
Eye (vitreous, cornea)
Artificial larynx
Lung
Shoulder
Ventricular assist device
Heart
Pacemaker
Heart valves
Heart valves
Liver
Elbow
Pancreas
Kidney
Blood vessels
Blood vessels
Artificial arm
Hip
Testicle
Penile prosthesis
Bone marrow
Artificial leg
Skin
Knee
Bone implant
Bone plate

NH

at Stanford University have performed since 1968 can be termed "hugely successful." For most of the 114 of 275 patients who received transplanted hearts, the alternative would have been imminent death. One of those patients has survived 13 years.[9]

Dr. Barney Clark, speaking with his doctor on videotape from the hospital in which his own life was extended for 120 days, was asked three months after his historic operation whether his artificial plastic heart had been uncomfortable. "Not at all," he responded. "It's comfortable. It's a thing you get used to."[10] Whether the rest of us get used to the idea of replaceable organs is becoming almost a moot point.

In addition to whole body parts, body regulators are now routinely implanted. In 1982, surgeons put in place approximately 130,000 pacemakers in heart patients. Some of these are now regulated by means of a computer chip that stores and relays the doctor's orders. Ventricular assist devices (see chapter 9) continue to offer other heart patients the added blood-pumping power their bodies require, without the shock or bulk of a complete artificial heart implant. Seemingly overnight, companies have sprouted up to make and market this device to all medical centers. Meanwhile, quiet but concerned debate continues about all areas of life extension—be it free-radical theories or wearable artificial kidneys. The results might indeed "work," but are they safe and are they natural?

COUNTERING AGING "UNNATURALLY"

In his rather optimistic book and in forthright interviews, Roy Walford makes an effort to temper the new developments in gerontology with appropriate scientific skepticism. He cautions people not to follow his strict personal dietary and antioxidant program without the approval and careful supervision of a physician. Everybody is different, he says, and no one should be popping vitamins or chemicals indiscriminately. He points out that the antioxidant selenium, for instance, can be toxic if taken in excess. No matter how careful he is, however, Walford and others who proffer theories of life extension repeatedly face the question of whether it is proper, or "natural," to undernourish oneself and take megadoses of vitamins to prolong life.

"No, it is not natural," says Walford without hesitation. "But I don't care if it is natural, unnatural, or *super*natural! That is not the question to ask. The question is whether a technique extends the life-span. You have to look at the experiments, not the concepts of 'natural' or 'artificial.' " In short, Walford says, "My answer is, it works." The curious twist here is that the very stores that were the first to market health foods and "natural" items in the late

1960s are now among the leading vendors of antioxidants that include the preservatives BHT and BHA—two of the "least natural" ingredients to be found in any health food outlet around.

Another charge the life extenders face is one of commercialism. Dr. Walford's book lists three sources from which one can buy antioxidants by mail: Gerontix Biological Research Products of Torrance, Calif., Life Extension Products of Hollywood, Fla., and Health Maintenance Programs of Valhalla, N.Y. All of these entities got into the business of selling life-extension substances within the past five years. One of them, Gerontix, has an indirect link to Walford's goals and ideas. Early in 1983, Dr. Kathleen Hall of UCLA set up Gerontix with her husband and a few others to make and sell life-extension nutrients and products. However, by company charter, they are designating a percentage of the profits for life-extension research in the UCLA labs and elsewhere. They also wanted to provide a reliable outlet for consumers to buy antioxidants and related products that typical health food stores don't always carry. Walford serves as adviser to the fledgling firm, but he says he has no direct financial stake in Gerontix, save one: He gets his ample supply of antioxidants—vitamins A and E, selenium, and the like—free from the company.

AGING GROUPS MAKE AGING NEWS

Long before Senator Alan Cranston of California announced his candidacy in the 1984 Presidential race, he had entered the race against time. Cranston, in his late 60s, has been well-known for years as a tough competitor and world record holder for the 100-yard dash in the Masters running circuit. He also has been well-known as a somewhat liberal legislator, though not so well-known as a leading light in the politics of aging. Rep. Claude Pepper of Florida (Dem.) has always seemed to snatch that spotlight. But back in 1979, Cranston shepherded a band of scientists together in his Los Angeles office to explore the formation of a life-extension support organization. Eventually they combined their energies to form FIBER, which stands for Fund for Integrative Biomedical Research.

The group got started because, in the view of those on the aging frontier, the government was doing little to provide a network for information and funding in the field of life extension. Its scientific director is Dr. William Regelson, professor of medicine and microbiology at the Medical College of Virginia in Richmond, who regularly shuttles about the country in search of funds for the Fund. On a recent trip to New York, his briefcase was well-worn and bulging; his manner was perhaps more blunt than one might expect of a scientific director. In a brief introduction to FIBER's goals, Regelson said, "We are looking out for our own asses. The big problem of disability is what we are all scared of. . . . In short, we have to be concerned about our own fate." Regelson, 58, with bushy, unkempt hair and sturdy glasses, rolled up his sleeves and continued his progress report.

"I think the pendulum is beginning to swing in our favor," he said, "with all the talk these days about aerobics and cardiac rehabilitation." The fact that hundreds of thousands of runners practice a limited form of life-extension therapy by running daily regimens of at least a few miles is not lost on Regelson, who has a tough job soliciting funds nationwide. His task is to convince philanthropically minded individuals and organizations to devote large sums of money to research that may not produce concrete results (in extending the life-span) in the next decade, or even the next generation. It is a gamble that Regelson and his group must make sound enticing—especially when one considers that in the event of success, say 20 to 30 years from now, society will already be feeling the strains of larger numbers of elderly people in its midst. For, even without drastic life extension of any kind, more than one out of every five persons will be 65 or older—more than 20 percent, according to conservative government estimates. Medicare and other health care administrators have been duly warned.

FIBER is counting on the sports medicine community to help bridge the gap between pure research and applied science. Thankfully, Regelson says sports medicine is already viewed by the general public as an "acceptable" forum for new health ideas. It is not such a long leap from investing energy in oneself by training one's body and mind to actively promoting a "live longer" life-style or, as FIBER likes to put it, to "intervening" in the aging process. But before FIBER or any group can effectively intervene in the human aging process, certain biological and physical changes—well beyond graying hair—known as biomarkers, must be precisely identified. Here is where much research remains to be done. Only then can scientists set out to prevent or reverse these changes with some degree of sophistication.

The American Longevity Association in Torrance, Calif., outside Los Angeles, is another group concerned with life extension. Born in 1982, the national nonprofit group boasts its own impressive list of supporters and advisers, including ten Nobel Laureates for medicine; Armand Hammer, M.D., chairman of Occidental Petroleum; Jerry Buss, Ph.D., owner of the Los Angeles Lakers; Dr. Christiaan Barnard; Nathan W. Shock, Ph.D., formerly of the National Institute on Aging; and, with Groucho Marx no longer living, it seems fitting that its chairman is Milton Berle. Besides sponsoring aging and medical conferences for gerontologists, the ALA is committed to educating the public in new research areas of life extension as well.

"The media sometimes confuses the public more than anything," says Dr. Robert Morin, professor of pathology at Harbor-UCLA Medical Center and director of the Longevity Association. "We want to give people the scientific data straight, and let them make their own decisions. If we are to obtain support for public funding or for the belief that more needs to be done in this area, they need to be informed."

Toward that end, at its annual symposium, the American Longevity Association devotes one of three days—usually the final day—to matters of interest to laymen. At its October, 1982, meeting, for example, paying particular attention to arteriosclerosis and heart disease and showing good foresight, the association scheduled Dr. Robert Jarvik to speak on organ replacement. On the same day, Dr. Robert Butler addressed conferees on "The Science and Art of Living Long and Well," while Dr. Leonard Hayflick talked about cellular theories of aging. Morin, 48, closed the day's session with a talk on "The Essence of the Latest, Most Reliable Knowledge for Prevention of Heart Disease, Cancer, Diabetes, and Aging."

"My concern has always been how to prevent life-threatening disease," says Morin, in a reference to aging and the rectangular curve (see chapter 1). "And with government cutbacks in research, it seemed to me there was going to be a tremendous waste of scientific talent in this country." So while FIBER gained momentum in Washington, Morin decided to set up the ALA in Torrance. He, too, like Regelson, found it rough going raising money for longevity. The 1982 budget barely reached $100,000, according to Morin. "There is some reluctance on the part of the general public," he says, "but there are others who say, 'It's about time an organization like yours came around.'"

People in the various disciplines that comprise the field of gerontology are feeling today more than ever before that they are on the cutting edge of a movement—one that will be comprised of waves of citizens as they age in the decades to follow. They would do well to remember the story former director of the National Institute on Aging Robert Butler often tells of his friend Morris Rocklin. When Rocklin was 101 years old, he went to see his doctor one day complaining of a pain in his left leg. "Morris, for Pete's sake, what do you expect at one hundred and one?" his doctor said. "Look, my right leg is also one hundred and one," Morris snapped back, "but it doesn't hurt a bit. Now explain that!"

Now, we can finally see answers to Rocklin's query starting to appear—if hazily—on the horizon. And as the experts ponder the implications of lab experiments and research studies, the rest of us are waking up to a brand new idea of what it means to get older.

"The forty-five, fifty-five, or sixty-five-year-old today is a different animal," reports Carole B. Allan, a Washington-based psychologist who was an adviser to the White House Conference on Aging in 1981. "These people are much healthier than were people their age in previous generations." Not only healthier, but also fitter, more active, and perceived to be sexier. Recently a New York advertising account executive saw reason to comment on an ad placed in the "Fashions of the Times" section of *The New York Times*. It was, he said, probably "the first time a woman in her fifties has ever been shown in such a romantic, evocative pose." [11]

Recently, too, we have acknowledged the fact that men and women do not cease to grow and change once they reach 65, 70, or 75. Which is why psychiatric experts such as Dr. Lionell Corbett of Rush-Presbyterian St. Luke's Medical Center in Chicago are recommending more programs for and developmental studies about the growing numbers of active elderly, from 65 to 85: "You have to acknowledge the pursuit of wisdom," he says. "People who age well get wiser."

At the very least, advances in medicine and gerontological research will allow countless numbers of people to have the chance to grow wiser. The gains of the mind and spirit that can occur in later life have no limit. They go well beyond the measurable gains demonstrated by the Masters runners who have increased their cardiovascular capacity despite their advancing years. Sometimes, as these athletes have shown us and as we've heard from the experts in this book, "expected" declines don't arrive on schedule. Already, there are hopeful signs that the quality of our later years will get better and better. And the longevity game has not even begun to hit its stride.

Notes and Sources

CHAPTER 1

1. *The New York Times,* Apr. 3, 1982, p. 8; Apr. 5, 1982, p. B5.
2. Robert N. Butler, *Why Survive? Being Old in America* (New York: Harper & Row, 1975), p. 17.
3. "How People Will Live to Be 100 or More," *U.S. News & World Report* (July 4, 1983), p. 74.
4. James F. Fries and Lawrence M. Crapo, *Vitality and Aging* (San Francisco: W. H. Freeman and Co., 1981), pp. 28–30, *passim;* U.S. Department of Commerce Bureau of the Census, *Current Population Reports: Population Estimates and Projections,* Series P-25, No. 922 (Washington, D.C.: U.S. Government Printing Office, 1982), pp. 1–15; Stephen Wermiel, "Sex-Discrimination Suit May Force Big Changes in Retirement Benefits," *The Wall Street Journal,* Jan. 10, 1983, sec. 2, p. 1; "Elderly May Outstrip Census Projection," *AARP News Bulletin,* American Association of Retired Persons, Vol. 24, No. 7 (Long Beach, Calif.: 1983), p. 2.
5. Fries and Crapo, *ibid.,* p. 60.
6. *Ibid.,* p. 65.
7. U.S. Department of Commerce Bureau of the Census, *Current Population Reports, op. cit.,* p. 1.
8. Edith Gilson, "We're All Getting Older," *Madison Avenue* (October, 1982), p. 77.
9. Roy L. Walford, *Maximum Life Span* (New York: W. W. Norton & Co., Inc., 1983), p. 2.

CHAPTER 2

1. The Diagram Group, *Man's Body: An Owner's Manual* (New York: Grosset & Dunlap, 1976), p. D-01.
2. Isaac Asimov, *The Human Body: Its Structure and Operation* (New York: New American Library/Signet, 1963), p. 261.
3. Arnold W. Klein, James H. Sternberg, and Paul Bernstein, *The Skin Book: Looking and Feeling Your Best Through Proper Skin Care* (New York: Macmillan/Collier Books, 1980), p. 32.
4. Gail Sheehy, *Passages: Predictable Crises of Adult Life* (New York: Bantam Books Inc., 1977), pp. 400–403.
5. *Los Angeles Sunday Herald Examiner,* Dec. 19, 1982.
6. *Ibid.*

CHAPTER 3

1. Linda Allen Schoen, ed., *The AMA Book of Skin and Hair Care* (New York: Avon Books, 1978), p. 128.
2. Norman Orentreich and Nancy P. Durr, *Clinics in Plastic Surgery,* Vol. 9, No. 2 (April, 1982), p. 197.
3. *Ibid.,* p. 198.
4. Durk Pearson and Sandy Shaw, *Life Extension* (New York: Warner Books Inc., 1982), p. 217.
5. James J. Reardon and Judi McMahon, *Plastic Surgery for Men* (New York: Everest House, 1981), p. 71.
6. *Ibid.,* p. 80.
7. *The New York Times,* Nov. 9, 1980, p. 43; Feb. 21, 1981, p. 13.

CHAPTER 4

1. U.S. Department of Health and Human Services, *Monocular Visual Acuity of Persons 4–74 Years, 1971–1972* (Washington, D.C.: 1972).

2. Jack Botwinick, *Aging and Behavior: A Comprehensive Integration of Research Findings* (New York: Springer Publishing Co., 1978), p. 143.

3. Richard S. Kavner and Lorraine Dusky, *Total Vision* (New York: A & W Visual Library, 1978), p. 59.

4. "National Ambulatory Medical Care Survey (1976)," of the National Center for Health Statistics, Rockville, Md., reprinted in *Medical Care for Eye Disorders,* the American Academy of Ophthalmology (San Francisco, Calif.: 1976), table 4.2 (p. 35).

5. Kavner and Dusky, *op. cit.,* pp. 40–41.

6. *Ibid.,* p. 41.

7. *Ibid.,* p. 143.

8. *Ibid.,* p. 153.

CHAPTER 5

1. Based on interviews with ground crew and ramp personnel and corporate communication departments at Trans World Airlines, New York City, and at American Airlines, Dallas, Texas.

2. *The New York Times,* Jan. 14, 1981, p. 12.

3. Jack Botwinick, *Aging and Behavior: A Comprehensive Integration of Research Findings* (New York: Springer Publishing Co., 1978), pp. 146–149.

4. Sue V. Saxon and Mary Jean Etten, *Physical Change and Aging: A Guide for the Helping Professions* (New York: The Tiresias Press, 1978), p. 64.

5. Botwinick, *op. cit.,* p. 147.

6. *Ibid.,* p. 148.

7. *The New York Times,* Mar. 24, 1981, p. C2.

8. Saul Kent, *The Life Extension Revolution: The Source Book for Optimum Health and Maximum Life-span* (New York: Quill, 1980), pp. 224–225.

9. *The New York Times,* June 23, 1981, sec. 3, p. 1.

10. *San Francisco Examiner-Chronicle,* Jan. 2, 1983, Scene sec., p. 6.

CHAPTER 6

1. *The New York Times,* Dec. 27, 1955, p. 31.

2. *The New York Times,* May 23, 1983, p. C3.

3. The Siesel Company, "Gum Disease—Almost as Common as the Common Cold" (A report for the American Academy of Periodontology in Chicago, 1983).

4. David Owen, "The Secret Lives of Dentists," *Harper's* (March, 1982), p. 85.

5. "Does Your Dentist Use the Keyes Method?" *American Health* (January-February, 1983), pp. 27–30.

6. William Killoy, et al., "Is Antimicrobial Therapy Reducing Our Need for Periodontal Surgery?" American Academy of Periodontology *News* (February/March, 1983,) pp. 5–11.

7. Vincent M. Cali, *The New, Lower-Cost Way to End Gum Trouble Without Surgery* (New York: Warner Books Inc., 1982), p. 15.

8. Killoy, et al., *op. cit.,* p. 5.

9. Jack Botwinick, *Aging and Behavior: A Comprehensive Integration of Research Findings* (New York: Springer Publishing Co., 1978), pp. 146–148; U.S. Department of Health, Education, and Welfare, *Vital Health Statistics: Basic Data on Hearing Levels of Adults 25–74 Years, U.S., 1971–75,* Series 11, No. 215 (Washington D.C.: U.S. Government Printing Office, 1980), pp. 1–49.

CHAPTER 7

1. Isaac Asimov, *The Human Body: Its Structure and Operation* (New York: New American Library/Signet, 1963), p. 82.

2. Caleb E. Finch and Leonard Hayflick, eds., *Handbook of Aging,* Vol. I: *The Biology of Aging* (New York: Van Nostrand Reinhold Co., 1977), p. 470.

3. Jean L. Marx, "Osteoporosis: New Hope for Thinning Bones," *Science* (Feb. 8, 1980), p. 629.

4. Anastasia Toufexis, "That Aching Back!" *Time* (July 14, 1980), p. 38.

5. *The Wall Street Journal,* Oct. 21, 1982, p. 32.

6. Henry Gray, *Gray's Anatomy, Descriptive and Surgical,* 1901 edition (Philadelphia: Running Press, 1974), p. 1112.

7. Toufexis, *op. cit.,* p. 31.

8. "Standing Tall at the Top," *Time* (Nov. 8, 1982), p. 62.

9. "New Hope for Bad Backs," *Newsweek* (May 2, 1983), p. 85.

10. Toufexis, *op. cit.,* p. 34.

11. Darrell C. Crain, *The Arthritis Handbook: A Patient's Manual on Arthritis, Rheumatism and Gout* (Smithtown, N.Y.: Exposition Press, 1972), pp. 22, 24.

CHAPTER 8

1. Kinsey, et al., *Sexual Behavior in the Human Male* (Philadelphia: W. B. Saunders Co., 1948), p. 579.

2. Sherman J. Silber, *The Male: From Infancy to Old Age* (New York: Charles Scribner's Sons, 1981), pp. 3–7.

3. *Ibid.,* p. 7.

4. *Ibid.,* pp. 68–69.

5. Robert N. Butler and Myrna I. Lewis, *Sex After Sixty: A Guide for Men and Women for Their Later Years* (New York: Harper & Row, 1976), p. 23.

6. Bernard D. Starr and Marcella Bakur Weiner, *The Starr-Weiner Report on Sex and Sexuality in the Mature Years* (New York: McGraw-Hill, 1982), pp. 92–93, 152–153.

7. P. J. Corkery, "Tidings of Comfort & Joy," *Harper's* (December, 1982), p. 43.

8. *Chicago Tribune,* Apr. 1, 1983, sec. 1, p. 6.

9. Silber, *op. cit.,* p. 101.

10. *Ibid.,* pp. 105–107.

11. *Ibid.,* p. 104.

12. *Ibid.,* p. 107.

13. New York *Daily News,* Jan. 17, 1983, p. 27.

14. U.S. Department of Commerce Bureau of the Census, *Current Population Reports: Population Estimates and Projections,* Series P-25, No. 922 (Washington, D.C.: U.S. Government Printing Office, 1982), p. 1.

15. Butler and Lewis, *op. cit.,* p. 37.

16. *Ibid.,* pp. 58–61.

CHAPTER 9

1. Lewis Thomas, "Who Will Be Saved? Who Will Pay the Cost?" *Discover* (February, 1983), pp. 30–31.

2. Harry Schwartz, "Toward the Conquest of Heart Disease," *The New York Times Magazine* (Mar. 27, 1983), p. 42.

3. Isaac Asimov, *The Human Body: Its Structure and Operation* (New York: New American Library/Signet, 1963), p. 156; Durk Pearson and Sandy Shaw, *Life Extension* (New York: Warner Books, 1982), pp. 121–122.

4. Asimov, *op. cit.,* p. 160.

5. Statement made by Edward N. Brandt, Assistant Secretary of Health, upon release of findings from the Multiple Risk Factor Intervention Trial (MRFIT), September 16, 1982.

6. The Diagram Group, *Man's Body: An Owner's Manual* (New York: Grosset & Dunlap, 1976), pp. B-28, B–30.

7. The American Heart Association, *Salt, Sodium and Blood Pressure: What's It All About?* (Dallas: 1982).

8. The American Medical Association, *The AMA Book of HeartCare* (New York: Random House, 1982), pp. 66–67.

9. *Crain's Chicago Business,* Aug. 16, 1982, p. 31.

10. The American Medical Association, *op. cit.,* p. 106.

11. *Ibid.,* p. 60.

12. Schwartz, *op. cit.,* p. 50.

13. "Half a Heart," *Fortune* (Dec. 27, 1982), p. 14.

CHAPTER 10

1. Kenneth H. Cooper, *The Aerobics Program for Total Well-Being* (New York: Bantam Books, 1983), p. 113.

2. Isaac Asimov, *The Human Body: Its Structure and Operation* (New York: New American Library/Signet, 1963), p. 145.

3. James Kieran with Nan Pheatt, "No End to Love," The American Lung Association *Bulletin* (December, 1981).

4. Tad Tuleja, *Fabulous Fallacies* (New York: The Stonesong Press, Inc., 1982), p. 176.

5. *Ibid.,* p. 177.

6. Jane E. Brody, *Jane Brody's* The New York Times *Guide to Personal Health* (New York: Times Books, 1982), p. 64.

7. D. Danon, N. W. Shock, and M. Marois, eds., *Aging: A Challenge to Science and Society,* Vol. 1 (New York: Oxford University Press, 1981), p. 227.

8. *Ibid.*

9. *Ibid.,* pp. 230–233.

CHAPTER 11

1. "What is Alzheimer's Disease?" The Alzheimer's Disease and Related Disorders Association news release, Chicago.

2. Raymond D. Adams and Maurice Victor, *Principles of Neurology* (New York: McGraw-Hill, 1981), p. 799.

3. *The New York Times,* Oct. 3, 1982, p. 58.

4. Robin Marantz Henig, *The Myth of Senility* (New York: Anchor Press/Doubleday, 1981), p. 26.

5. *Ibid.,* pp. 30–34.

6. David Arenberg, Carol P. Hausman, and Elizabeth A. Robertson-Tchabo, "A Classical Mnemonic for Older Learners: A Trip That Works!" *Educational Gerontology,* Vol. 1 (New York: Hemisphere Publishing Corp., 1976), pp. 215–226; also reprinted by National Institute on Aging's Gerontology Research Center, Baltimore, Md.

7. *Ibid.*

8. Abigail Trafford, *U.S. News & World Report* (Jan. 24, 1983), p. 39.

9. David D. Burns, *Feeling Good: The New Mood Therapy* (New York: New American Library/Signet, 1981), pp. 208–209.

10. *Ibid.,* p. 11.

11. *Ibid.,* pp. 11–12.

12. *The New York Times,* July 10, 1983, sec. 21, p. 17.

13. *Ibid.*

14. "Effects of Naloxone in Senile Dementia: A Double-Blind Trial," *The New England Journal of Medicine* (Mar. 24, 1983), Vol. 308, No. 12, pp. 721–722.

15. *Los Angeles Times,* Mar. 24, 1983, p. 16.

16. Saul Kent, *The Life Extension Revolution, The Source Book for Optimum Health and Maximum Life-span* (New York: Quill, 1980), p. 155.

17. Henig, *op. cit.,* p. 197; also The Alzheimer's Disease and Related Disorders Association *Newsletter,* Vol. 2, No. 3 (Fall, 1982), p. 6.

18. Henig, *ibid.,* p. 27.

CHAPTER 12

1. Leonard Schwartz, *Heavyhands: The Ultimate Exercise System* (Boston: Little, Brown & Co., 1982), p. 185.

2. Hal Higdon, *Fitness After Forty* (Mountain View, Calif.: World Publications, 1977), p. 105.

3. *Ibid.,* p. 105; also American Medical Joggers Association, North Hollywood, Calif. (1983).

4. Roy L. Walford, *Maximum Life Span* (New York: W. W. Norton and Co., Inc., 1983), pp. 150–151.

5. Higdon, *op. cit.,* p. 235.

6. *Ibid.,* p. 112; also David Costill, Ball State University, Muncie, Ind. (1983).

7. Sidney Alexander, *Running Healthy: A Guide to Cardiovascular Fitness* (Brattleboro, Vt.: Stephen Greene Press, 1980), p. 12.

8. *Ibid.,* pp. 15–16.

9. John Jerome, "Don't Pity the Aging Runner," *Running* (July/August, 1982), pp. 26–33; also "Results of Exercise on Elderly Athletes to Be Reported," *Annual Scientific Session News,* American College of Cardiology Department of Communications, Bethesda, Md. (March 20–24, 1983), p. 2.

10. Howard Jacobson, *Racewalk to Fitness: The Sensible Alternative to Jogging and Running* (New York: Simon and Schuster, 1980), p. 39.

CHAPTER 13

1. Pritikin Longevity Center brochure, Pritikin Longevity Center (Santa Monica, Calif.: 1983), pp. 1–16; Nathan Pritikin, *The Pritikin Permanent Weight-Loss Manual* (New York: Grosset & Dunlap, 1981).

2. Roy L. Walford, *Maximum Life Span* (New York: W. W. Norton & Co., Inc., 1983), p. 108.

3. Jack L. Hofer, Jon N. Leonard, and Nathan Pritikin, *Live Longer Now: The First One Hundred Years of Your Life: The 2100 Program* (New York: Grosset & Dunlap, 1974), pp. 88–90.

4. Kenneth R. Pelletier, *Longevity: Fulfilling Our Biological Potential* (New York: Delacorte Press, 1981), p. 215.

5. *A Maximal Approach to the Dietary Treatment of the Hyperlipidemias: A Manual of Dietary Modifications and Instructions for Patients with Hyperlipidemia as a Prescription from Their Physicians; Diet D: The Extremely Low-Fat Diet,* Subcommittee on Diet and Hyperlipidemia, Council on Arteriosclerosis, American Heart Association (Dallas: 1978), p. 4.

6. Walford, *op. cit.,* p. 109.

7. Saul Kent, *The Life Extension Revolution: The Source Book for Optimum Health and Maximum Life-span* (New York: Quill, 1983), p. 74.

8. *AHA Committee Report: Rationale of the Diet-Heart Statement of the American Heart Association,* Report of the Nutrition Committee, Circ. 65, No. 4 (Dallas: 1982).

9. W. I. Bennett, "High-Density Lipoprotein and Heart Disease," *Harvard Medical School Health Letter,* Vol. 5, No. 1 (November, 1979), pp. 3–4.

10. Jean McAnn, "What the Experts Do—Unofficially—to Dodge Cancer," *Medical Tribune* (Nov. 22, 1978), p. 1.

11. Pritikin, *op. cit.,* pp. 42–43.

12. Pelletier, *op. cit.,* p. 227.

13. John Naisbitt, *Megatrends: Ten New Directions Transforming Our Lives* (New York: Warner Books Inc., 1982), p. 6.

14. *Ibid.,* pp. 134–135.

15. *NIA Special Report on Aging,* U.S. Department of Health and Human Services (Washington, D.C.: 1982), p. 12.

16. Walford, *op. cit.,* p. 99.

CHAPTER 14

1. *The New York Times,* Aug. 20, 1977, pp. 1, 7.

2. Roy L. Walford, *Maximum Life Span* (New York: W. W. Norton and Co., Inc., 1983), p. 87.

3. K. G. Jackovich, "Two Fitness Faddists Have a No. 1 Best-Seller, But Are They Stretching Life Spans or Truth?" *People* (Oct. 4, 1982), pp. 40–42.

4. James F. Fries and Lawrence M. Crapo, *Vitality and Aging* (San Francisco: W. H. Freeman & Co., 1981), p. 40.

5. Walford, *op. cit.,* p. 94.

6. "Medicine Dares to Dream of the Impossible," *U.S. News & World Report* (May 9, 1983), p. A6.

7. *Ibid.*

8. "The New Era of Transplants," *Newsweek* (Aug. 29, 1983), p. 40.

9. *Ibid.,* p. 42.

10. *The New York Times,* Mar. 3, 1983, p. A1.

11. "One Who Broke the Age Barrier," *Advertising Age* (Aug. 29, 1983), p. M-11.

Bibliography

Aegerter, Ernest. *Save Your Heart*. New York: Van Nostrand Reinhold Co., 1981.

Alexander, Sidney. *Running Healthy: A Guide to Cardiovascular Fitness*. Brattleboro, Vt.: The Stephen Greene Press, 1980.

American Academy of Dermatology. *Program to the 41st Annual Meeting of AAD*. Evanston, Ill.: National Education Center for AAD, 1982.

American Heart Association. *The AMA Book of Skin and Hair Care*. Ed. Linda Allen Schoen. New York: Avon Books, 1978.

American Heart Association, Subcommittee on Diet and Hyperlipidemia, Council on Arteriosclerosis. *A Maximal Approach to the Dietary Treatment of the Hyperlipidemias: A Manual of Dietary Modifications and Instructions for Patients with Hyperlipidemia as a Prescription from Their Physicians; Diet D: The Extremely Low-Fat Diet*. Dallas: 1978.

American Medical Association. *The AMA Book of HeartCare*. New York: Random House Inc., 1982.

Asimov, Isaac. *The Human Body: Its Structure and Operation*. New York: New American Library/Signet, 1963.

Barnard, Christiaan, consulting ed. *The Body Machine: Your Health in Perspective*. New York: Crown Publishers Inc., 1981.

Blanding, Forrest H. *The Pulse Point Plan*. New York: Random House Inc., 1982.

Botwinick, Jack. *Aging and Behavior: A Comprehensive Integration of Research Findings*. New York: Springer Publishing Co., 1978.

Braverman, Jordan. *The Consumer's Book of Health: How to Stretch Your Health Care Dollars*. Philadelphia: Saunders Press, 1982.

Brody, Jane E. *Jane Brody's* The New York Times *Guide to Personal Health*. New York: Times Books, 1982.

Bronstein, Arthur J., and Beatrice F. Jacoby. *Your Speech and Voice*. New York: Random House Inc., 1967.

Burger, Sarah G., and Martha D'Erasmo. *Living in a Nursing Home: A Complete Guide for Residents, Their Families and Friends*. New York: Ballantine Books Inc., 1979.

Burns, David D. *Feeling Good: The New Mood Therapy*. New York: New American Library/Signet, 1980.

Butler, Robert N. *Why Survive? Being Old in America*. New York: Harper & Row, Publishers, Inc., 1975.

Butler, Robert N., and Myrna I. Lewis. *Sex After Sixty: A Guide for Men and Women for Their Later Years*. New York: Harper & Row, Publishers, Inc., 1976.

Cali, Vincent M. *The New, Lower-Cost Way to End Gum Trouble Without Surgery*. New York: Warner Books Inc., 1982.

Cooper, Kenneth H. *The Aerobics Program for Total Well-Being*. New York, Bantam Books, 1983.

Crain, Darrell C. *The Arthritis Handbook: A Patient's Manual on Arthritis, Rheumatism and Gout*. Smithtown, N.Y.: Exposition Press, 1972.

Danon, D., N. W. Shock, and M. Marois, eds. *Aging: A Challenge to Science and Society*, Vol. I. New York: Oxford University Press, 1981.

Diagram Group, The. *Man's Body: An Owner's Manual*. New York: Grosset & Dunlap, 1976.

Eyton, Audrey. *The F-Plan Diet*. New York: Crown Publishers Inc., 1983.

Finch, Caleb E., and Leonard Hayflick, eds. *Handbook of Aging*, Vol. I: *The Biology of Aging*.

New York: Van Nostrand Reinhold Co., 1977.

Fries, James F., and Lawrence M. Crapo. *Vitality and Aging: Implications of the Rectangular Curve.* San Francisco: W. H. Freeman and Co., 1981.

Gray, Henry. *Gray's Anatomy, Descriptive and Surgical,* 1901 edition. Eds. T. P. Pick and R. Howden. Philadelphia: Running Press, 1974.

Gross, Leonard. *How Much Is Too Much? The Effects of Social Drinking.* New York: Random House Inc., 1983.

Henig, Robin M. *The Myth of Senility: Misconceptions About the Brain and Aging.* New York: Anchor Press/Doubleday, 1981.

Higdon, Hal. *Fitness After Forty.* Mountain View, Calif.: World Publications, 1977.

Hofer, Jack L., Jon N. Leonard, and Nathan Pritikin. *Live Longer Now: The First One Hundred Years of Your Life: The 2100 Program.* New York: Grosset & Dunlap, 1974.

Jacobson, Howard. *Racewalk to Fitness: The Sensible Alternative to Jogging and Running.* New York: Simon & Schuster, 1980.

Jerome, John. *The Sweet Spot in Time.* New York: Avon Books, 1980.

Kavner, Richard S., and Lorraine Dusky. *Total Vision.* New York: A & W Visual Library, 1978.

Kent, Saul. *The Life Extension Revolution: The Source Book for Optimum Health and Maximum Life-span.* New York: Quill, 1980.

Kinsey, Alfred C., Wardell B. Pomeroy, and Clyde E. Martin. *Sexual Behavior in the Human Male.* Philadelphia: W. B. Saunders Co., 1948.

Klein, Arnold W., James H. Sternberg, and Paul Bernstein. *The Skin Book: Looking and Feeling Your Best Through Proper Skin Care.* New York: Macmillan/Collier Books, 1980.

Mylander, Maureen. *The Great American Stomach Book.* New York: Ticknor & Fields, 1982.

Naisbitt, John. *Megatrends: Ten New Directions Transforming Our Lives.* New York: Warner Books Inc., 1982.

Neugarten, Bernice L., ed. *Middle Age and Aging.* Chicago: University of Chicago Press, 1968.

Orentreich Foundation for the Advancement of Science, Inc. *1982 Report.* New York: 1982.

Orentreich Foundation for the Advancement of Science, Inc. *Report of the Director, 1981.* Ed. Nancy P. Durr. New York: 1981.

Orentreich, Norman, Nancy P. Durr, and Ronald J. Trancik. "Physical Methods for Altering Surface Texture of the Skin." In *Principles of Cosmetics for the Dermatologist.* Eds. Philip Frost and Steven Horowitz. St. Louis, Mo.: C. V. Mosby Co., 1982.

Pearson, Durk, and Sandy Shaw. *Life Extension.* New York: Warner Books Inc., 1982.

Pelletier, Kenneth R. *Longevity: Fulfilling Our Biological Potential.* New York: Delacorte Press, 1981.

Phillips, Elliot R. *Get a Good Night's Sleep.* Englewood Cliffs, N.J.: Prentice Hall/Spectrum Books, 1983.

Pritikin, Nathan. *The Pritikin Permanent Weight-Loss Manual.* New York: Grosset & Dunlap, 1981.

Reardon, James J., and Judi McMahon. *Plastic Surgery for Men.* New York: Everest House, 1981.

Saxon, Sue V., and Mary Jean Etten. *Physical Change and Aging: A Guide for the Helping Professions.* New York: The Tiresias Press, 1978.

Schmeck, Harold M. *The Semi-Artificial Man: A Dawning Revolution in Medicine.* New York: Walker & Co., 1965.

Sheehy, Gail. *Passages: Predictable Crises of Adult Life.* New York: Bantam Books Inc., 1977.

Silber, Sherman J. *The Male: From Infancy to Old Age.* New York: Charles Scribner's Sons, 1981.

Silverstein, Alvin, and Virginia B. Silverstein. *So You're Getting Braces: A Guide to Orthodontics.* New York: J. B. Lippincott Co., 1978.

Starr, Bernard D., and Marcella B. Weiner. *The Starr-Weiner Report on Sex and Sexuality in the Mature Years.* New York: McGraw-Hill Inc., 1982.

Tresidder, Jack, ed. *Living Well: The People Maintenance Manual.* London: Mitchell Beazley Publishers, 1977.

U.S. Department of Commerce Bureau of the Census. *Current Population Reports: Population Estimates and Projections,* Series P-25, No. 922. Washington, D.C.: 1982.

U.S. Department of Health, Education, and Welfare. *Epidemiology of Aging: Summary Report and Selected Papers from Research Conference on Epidemiology and Aging.* Eds. Adrian M. Ostfeld and Don C. Gibson. Bethesda, Md.: U.S. Department of HEW, 1972.

U.S. Department of Health, Education, and Welfare, National Institute on Aging. *Nutrition and Aging,* Science Writer Seminar Series, NIH Pub. No. 79-104.

U.S. Department of Health, Education, and Welfare. *Vital Health Statistics: Basic Data on Hearing Levels of Adults 25–74 Years: United States, 1971–75,* Series 11, No. 215. Washington, D.C.: 1980.

U.S. Department of Health, Education, and Welfare. *Vital Health Statistics: Serum Cholesterol Levels of Persons 4–74 Years of Age by Socioeconomic Characteristics, United States, 1971–74,* Series 11, No. 217.

U.S. Department of Health and Human Services. *Monocular Visual Acuity of Persons 4–74 Years, 1971–1972,* Doc. No. HE20.6209: 11/201.

U.S. Department of Health and Human Services, National Institute on Aging. *Perspectives on Geriatric Medicine,* NIH Publication No. 81-1924. Washington, D.C.: 1980.

U.S. Department of Health and Human Services, National Institute on Aging. *Special Report on Aging, 1981,* NIH Publication No. 81-2328. Washington, D.C.: 1981.

U.S. Department of Health and Human Services, National Institute on Aging. *Special Report on Aging, 1982,* NIH Publication No. 82-2464. Washington, D.C.: 1982.

Walford, Roy L. *Maximum Life Span.* New York: W. W. Norton & Co., Inc., 1983.

Yalof, Ina L. *Open Heart Surgery: A Guidebook for Patients and Families.* New York: Random House Inc., 1983.

Index